THE TIGH

THE TIGERS

6th, 7th, 8th & 9th (Service) Battalions of the Leicestershire Regiment

Matthew Richardson

Pen & Sword Books Limited, Barnsley
LEO COOPER

First published in Great Britain in 2000 by Leo Cooper
an imprint of Pen & Sword Books Limited
47 Church Street, Barnsley, South Yorkshire S70 2AS

For up-to date information on other titles produced under the Pen & Sword imprint, please telephone or write to:
Pen & Sword Books Limited
FREEPOST
47 Church Street
Barnsley
South Yorkshire
S70 2BR

Telephone (24 hours): 01226 734555

ISBN 0-85052-719-8 Cased Edition
ISBN 0-85052-740-6 Paperback Edition

British Library Cataloguing in Publication Data

Printed by Redwood Books Ltd
Trowbridge, Wiltshire

Contents

Foreword

In 1951 at Glen Parva Barracks I was extremely fortunate to receive my initial instruction on the history of the Regiment from Regimental Sergeant Major John Meredith DCM. This excellent introduction to the splendid history of the Regiment was to prove invaluable to me in my service. In 1981, I left the Army and took up the appointment of Regimental Secretary of the Regiment. I soon realised that my job would require a more detailed knowledge of Regimental history. The initial instruction I had received some 30 years before was a good basis on which to start and I was lucky enough to be able to call upon many retired members of the Regiment for help and advice.

On examining the written histories I found that there was some excellent material. The general history was very well covered by Richard Cannon's Historical Record of the 17th Foot (1688 to 1848), Lieutenant Colonel E A H Webb's revision and continuation of Cannon's work in his History of the Services of the 17th (Leicestershire) Regiment (1688 to 1912) and Brigadier W E Underhill's history of the Regiment from 1928 to 1956. This latter work includes a very informative account of each Battalion in the Second World War. The period from 1912 to 1928 is covered by a number of publications, including The 1st and 2nd Battalions The Leicestershire Regiment in the Great War (Wylly), Footprints of the 1/4th Leicestershire Regiment 1914 to1918 (Milne) and The Fifth Leicestershire 1914 to 1919 (Hills). There was one obvious omission, an account of the Service Battalions from 1914 to 1919.

In a brochure titled *'Come on Tigers'*, which was printed in 1955 I found the following paragraphs relating to the Service Battalions:

> *'The 110th (Leicestershire) Infantry Brigade of the 37th Division was composed of the 6th, 7th, 8th and 9th Service Battalions of the Regiment and they did credit to the name they bore. They won great glory by their brilliant attack on the BAZENTIN-Le PETIT village and wood in the battle of the Somme in July 1916.'*

> *'The sterling courage of the 110th Brigade in the defence of EPEHY was a fine example of British grit. Exposed to the full blast of constant attacks delivered by three fresh German divisions, the stubborn soldiers of Leicestershire refused to budge, but met each attack with such devastating rifle and machine gun fire that, when night fell the front of their position was marked by heaps of German dead. Only at one point did the enemy succeed in piercing the line-at VAUCELLETTE FARM, defended by a party of Leicester men who held it.'*

From these extracts I realised that an account of the Leicestershire Brigade needed to be written if the history of the Regiment was to be complete. Matthew Richardson has done this by writing his book. He has carried out detailed research and by using extracts from published material, unpublished personal accounts, letters, newspaper cuttings, war diaries and other sources has produced a moving account of Leicestershire men who answered the call to arms in the Great War and did so with such gallantry and indomitable courage.

J L Wilson *Lt Col (Retd), Leicester, July 1999.*

Acknowledgements

It is often said that no book is the work of just one person, and that was never truer than in this particular case. Throughout the preparation work I have been repeatedly moved by the kindness, willingness to help in whatever way, and the generosity to lend treasured photographs or documents, which countless people, many of them previously strangers, have shown to me.

Firstly, I would like to thank my girlfriend Natalia. Without her expertise in constructing a database of 110th Brigade members, the nominal roll which accompanies this book, would not have been drawn up. Natalia also made possible the copying of many of the photographs which appear on the following pages, and was full of new ideas and new directions for research. I would like to thank my parents, who also made extensive treks to collect photographs or to have photographs copied, all in the name of the cause. I hope that they feel the end product was worth the effort.

I am deeply indebted to Colonel Wilson, of the Royal Tigers Association, for kindly providing the foreword to this volume, which I consider a great honour. The Royal Tigers Association, in particular in the person of Colonel Swallow, secretary of the association, offered me much support and encouragement during the preparation of this book, and it gives me great pride to have this seal of approval.

It was Peter Liddle, my friend and former colleague at the Liddle Collection, University of Leeds, who perhaps first encouraged me to begin this project. In addition to convincing me that I could make this idea work, he gave me considerable practical help by allowing me to use whatever material from the Liddle Collection I felt would be appropriate. Not far behind Peter was Chester Read, who had just deposited his father Dick Read's extensive collection of papers, photographs and artwork in the Liddle Collection. Copyright of the Read material is held by Chester's grandson, and I am grateful to the Read family for permission to reproduce it. It is no exaggeration to say that, if Chester had not been so willing from the outset for me to use both Dick Read's text and photographs, then this book would probably have advanced no further than the discussion stage.

At Leicestershire Record Office in Wigston, Mr Carl Harrison, Mr Robin Jenkins, and Mr Aubrey Stevenson offered a great deal of support and I am grateful to them for this and for permission to use the many LRO illustrations which follow. Jean B.Sleath was kind enough to allow me to use the photographs of her father, George Griffin Ward Sleath, which are held at the Leicestershire Record Office. Jean also offered me many insights into her father's army service and later life, which I greatly appreciate.

At every stage after this, I was met with co-operation and enthusiasm. The *Leicester Mercury, Coalville Times, Ashby Echo* and a host of other newspapers published my appeals for information, and I am grateful to their editors. An army of people then came forward with photographs. I would like to thank each and every one of these people for permission to use their photographs, their names here given in no particular order: Mr Peter Abney-Hastings, Mr Graham Jones, Mrs S.Kendrick, Mr Michael Kendrick, Peter & Sue Sturman, Jim Briggs, Peter Greenhill & John Hurst, Mrs Mary Bentley, Paul Reed, Mr W.J.Newman, Mrs M.Preston, Mrs Janet M.Davis, Mrs J.Partridge, Mrs Betty Potter, Mr Shane Beaver, Mr J.Gimson, Mr W.Chambers, Mrs Jean Ogle, Mrs Ruth A.Pearson, Mrs Dorothy Parry, Mrs Eileen Springthorpe, Mrs Clare Hawkins, Mrs J.Moreton, Mr Walter Malkin, Mr Neville A.Easingwood, Mr Norman Hastings, Mr Ken Holt, Mrs Yvonne White, Mrs Cynthia Buckingham, Mr Sid Smith, Mrs Mary Snart, Mrs D.M. Tidmas, Mrs K.Best, Mrs G.Cook, Mrs P.Packwood, Mrs S.Chatham, Mrs Freda Nicholson, Mr John Storey, Mr Sonny Monk, Mr R.J.Cattell, Ruth Broadhurst, Beryl & Stuart Blythe, Stuart Farmer, Katrina Dobson, Joan Poultney, Peter Voss, Cameron Coxon-Smith, Alan Petcher, the Durrant family (in particular Fergus Durrant) and Simon Jervis of the Jervis Photographic Archive, who kindly allowed me to reproduce photographs from his collection.

I am most grateful to Squire de Lisle of Quenby Hall for the information which he was able to provide concerning his uncle, Lieutenant Alexander de Lisle. Margaret Nobbs, a kind and generous friend for many years, excelled herself in finding her grandfather's superb photographs, and allowing me to use them. Rose Holyoak, whose father appears on the cover of this book, also deserves special mention, not least for providing me with a photograph of my 'long lost' great great uncle, Harry Holyoak. Annie Damiens of Berles-au-Bois helped me with a number of illustrations of her village during the First World War, and I would also like to thank Yolanda Courtney and the staff of Leicester Museums Service for providing a photograph of Arthur Newberry Choyce.

In Wigston, Duncan Lucas allowed me freedom of access to his archives, which contained a number of photographs of Glen Parva barracks. Likewise, Fergus Read of NWMS, and Steve Law of Great War Medals allowed me access to material in their private collections. Steve deserves special mention here, for it was he who selflessly gave me access both to data which he had gathered from the Public Record Office, and to the products of his own research into the Leicestershire Regiment over a number of years. Eric Kellaway and John Taylor, two Leicestershire Regiment collectors of many years standing, were exceedingly generous in allowing me access to their collections and in allowing me to use anything which I felt might be useful. I would like to express my deep gratitude to them both.

Barry Summers in Market Harborough provided me with information and photographs relating to a number of soldiers from that town. His research into the history of Market Harborough and its soldiers, and his efforts in presenting this information via a web site, are worthy of great respect. Likewise, Greg Drozdz has been unstinting in his willingness to share his information on Hinckley soldiers - I am particularly grateful to him for the material on Togo Bolesworth which appears herein.

Three people provided me with photographs of locations as they appear today, Sarah Saunders-Davies, Richard Lane and Roger Lewis. To each I extend my thanks. Diane Merryweather was kind enough to carry my appeal for information in the Leicestershire & Rutland Family History Society Journal.

The family of David Kelly, the author of '39 Months With the Tigers' proved impossible to locate, as did that of R.H.Kiernan. However if any surviving descendants of these two gentlemen happen to be reading this text, I would like to express my appreciation of their distinguished forebears, and of their foresight in recording their memoirs for posterity. Colonel Terry Cave kindly allowed me to quote from the diary of his father, RQMS Arthur Cave, and provided the photographs of his father which appear in this book. I would also like to thank the family of Jack Horner who, many years ago now it seems, entrusted to me his private papers in connection with his war service, including his memoir. Patrick Gariepy, of Eugene, Oregon, helped me with much research on Major Wallace McCutcheon in the United States. In all cases I have tried to contact copyright holders, but any errors of omission or commission are my own.

Julian Putkowski provided information on the case of Private James Nisbet. Martin Middlebrook allowed me to quote from his book, *The Kaiser's Battle*, and Bill Mitchinson helped with both advice and photographs. One person whom I would like to thank for his direct help with the production of this book is Bill Hartley, who read through the draft and offered many improvements upon my use of grammar in particular.

Finally, my thanks and admiration go to Pen & Sword Books Ltd, for turning my idea into reality. I am especially grateful to Charles Hewitt and Henry Wilson for supporting my project, and to Paul Wilkinson, for his outstanding work in turning a manuscript and a set of photographs into a book.

THE LEICESTERSHIRE REGIMENT,
17th Foot.

9

Introduction

'The Tigers' is very much the book that I always wanted to read, but in the end had to write myself. The Leicesters were always 'my' regiment. Other people had football teams, but I followed the Tigers. Growing up in Wigston it seemed that evidence of their presence was all around me – a Great-Grandfather served with them in the Boer War; other relatives had served at different times. Friends at school also had grandfathers who had served in the regiment. Hunting around junk shops and flea markets, we looked for photos and badges connected with it. Yet it gave me a strange feeling to think that the regiment had now gone, absorbed into the Royal Anglians before I was born. Stopping to look at memorials from the Great War in the county, such as those at Oadby and South Wigston, one could not help but notice how the rows of names under 'Leicestershire Regiment' completely dwarfed those under 'Coldstream Guards' for example, or 'Royal Artillery'. This was certainly evidence to my mind of a strong sense of local pride at that time, and a very real link between the people of Leicestershire today and the regiment. Just how many of those people, I wondered, had relatives who had served? (Some indication of the answer came to me as I researched this book – a very high number indeed)

I have always considered myself fortunate in that I am able to appreciate

Left: the former home of Pte A.Hewitt, 68 Montague Road, Clarendon Park, Leicester, and (right) the former home of Second Lieutenant F.T.Scholes, 'Park View', Mere Road, Highfields. Both of these men were wounded on the Somme in 1916.

The Magazine as it stands today, isolated on a traffic island. A sad, but oddly fitting and poignant memorial to a Regiment which has now vanished into history.

the history that is all around us every day. Driving through the terraced streets of Frog Island, Clarendon Park or Highfields, I could easily imagine the families who had been living in the area in 1914. How many of those houses in Clarendon Park and Highfields, I wondered, had black curtains at the windows in the summer of 1916? I once read in the 'Rough Guide to Leicester' that the Magazine, that mighty stone bastion which now guards Oxford Street from the hordes of traffic pouring up from the underpass, contained a 'forgettable' regimental museum. This irritated me greatly. Firstly, whenever I passed the Magazine, my thoughts trailed off to the hundreds if not thousands of men who had joined the army there. The Magazine had marked the changing point in their lives, perhaps forever (I bitterly regretted that the Victorian barrack blocks had been demolished, as this was now an additional factor which I had to conjure up in my mind's eye). The second thing which irritated me was the implication that not only the museum but also by extension the regiment was forgettable. The regiment damn well deserved to be remembered, I thought.

Each of the battalions seemed to me to have a different character; the 1st Battalion always inspired respect. The sepia photos of men with waxed moustaches and starched white uniforms made sure of that, and many of them seemed to be wearing the medals of the Boer War. The 2nd Battalion also required respect, but having spent so many years in India, had a kind of exotic quality. The Territorials were interesting. I admired the perverse way in which they were proud of the fact that they were denied the honour of the 'Hindoostan' bar accorded to the Regulars. They seemed to have an *esprit de corps* all of their own. I also felt sorry in an odd way for the Terriers, because the 1/4th had been so devastated by casualties at the Hohenzollern Redoubt action, that it was never the same again. The Service battalions however seemed to me to be the most dashing of all, representing a cross section of the county, with their hosiery workers and miners in the ranks, and the sons of the local aristocracy and meritocracy in command. They too had had their Calvary, at Bazentin, but unlike the Hohenzollern Redoubt affair they had captured their objectives, in spite of the bitter losses. They were also playing a part in something far bigger, which interested me as much as the Leicesters did - the battle of the Somme, which gripped the nation that summer of 1916. I visited their graves in Flat Iron Copse, and walked their battlefield, near Mametz Wood.

So it was the 6th, 7th 8th and 9th Battalions, of the 110th Brigade, which captured my attention the most, but oddly for units with such fine records, they were provided with little or no history. No one had written up their triumphs and tragedies, and provided thumbnail sketches of some of the personalities involved, as Milne had done for the 1/4th Battalion in his *Footprints*. The voices of the Tigers of the Service battalions seemed to be growing fainter as the years distanced me from those events so long ago, and no one seemed prepared to speak for them. Kelly had written his *39 Months With the Tigers*, but that was as much a personal narrative as a history of the 110th Brigade. There were other accounts, like Read's well-respected *Of Those We Loved*. There were the local newspapers from the time, which had almost preserved the society of those days in aspic, and which occasionally carried fascinating glimpses of life at the front. Then there were the official War Diaries, but these latter were very much the bare bones of the story, devoid of the flesh of eyewitness, first hand, heart-pounding detail.

If only I could bring all of these diverse sources together I thought, I would have something resembling the history of the battalions which I had always longed to read! In attempting to do this in the pages which follow, I have tried to strike a balance which I hope will appeal to most people. I have stuck as far as is possible to a rigid chronology, whilst equally attempting to avoid producing a desiccated glorified railway timetable of movements. I have brought in personal accounts where I thought they added colour and life to my description of an event. At the same time I have tried to restrict myself to those sections of experience which might have a general quality and wider relevance to the experiences of the whole or most of the battalion concerned.

If this book stands as any form of memorial to the Tigers, then my task will have been worthwhile.

Matthew Richardson, Leeds 1999

Cpl Charles Speddings, 1st Battalion, shortly after the Boer War. He was a Regular soldier who took part in the Relief of Ladysmith, eventually meeting up with his brother who was part of the garrison.
Mrs S.Kendrick

Captain Paulyn Rawdon-Hastings of Ashby de la Zouch, 1/5th Battalion. He was to fall at the Hohenzollern Redoubt in October 1915.
Peter Abney-Hastings

Chapter One

Kitchener's Army

The Leicestershire Regiment – the old 17th Regiment of Foot – goes back into history to the days of William of Orange, and before. It was actually raised in London on 27 September 1688, in the last days of the reign of James II. This was at the time of the creation of the first true standing army in Great Britain. Previously, for example during the Civil War of 1642-49, regiments were raised by colonels or disbanded as the need arose, but the 17th in the following year of 1689 swore its allegiance to the newly enthroned King William III, and became a permanent regiment of the line. One of its earliest campaigns – rather prophetically as later events would show, was in Flanders. Here the regiment earned its first battle honour, 'Namur', for its part in the capture of the French fortress of that name. Later it fought in the Wars of the Spanish Succession, serving with distinction in the Netherlands under the Duke of Marlborough, and in Spain itself. After this, the regiment was for 25 years part of the garrison of the Balearic island of Minorca.

In the Seven Years War of 1756-1763, the 17th Foot served in Canada, and formed part of General Wolfe's famous Brigade. As part of this force it took part in the capture of the French fortress of Louisberg, on the island of Cape Breton in the Gulf of St Lawrence, earning its second battle honour in the process. Afterwards the regiment took part in the operations which led to the conquest of French-held Canada. The Grenadier Company remained with Wolfe, and was with him at the Battle of Quebec when he fell mortally wounded at the moment of victory. For many years afterwards, the Leicesters honoured his memory by the wearing of black edging on the officers' mess dress, and by laying a black crepe ribbon on the mess table. After this, the regiment served in the West Indies against the French, winning the honours 'Martinique' and 'Havannah.'

In the American War of Independence, the 17th Regiment formed part of the garrison of New York. In 1778, just outside Princetown, the regiment found itself confronted by a far superior force, under the command of General George Washington. Nevertheless, they at once attacked, disregarding the overwhelming odds against them. Surrounded, the 17th fought their way through the enemy ranks, carrying their Colours to safety. For this action King George III awarded the regiment the insignia of an unbroken laurel leaf, which was worn in later years surrounding the Tiger on the regimental collar badge.

In 1782 came the first connection with Leicester, when regiments were allocated districts with which they were to build links, for the purposes of improving recruiting. The 17th came to the county, and one of its earliest

The 17th Foot break out from Princetown, 1778.

depots was at Hinckley. It was further ordered to adopt the additional title 'Leicestershire', and thus began the long connection between the two.

The City and County of Leicester, to which the 17th were allotted, boasted a history which was ancient even then. A Roman city, Ratae Coritanorum, stood on the site early in the first millennium. With the withdrawal of the Romans, and the Anglo Saxon invasions, it had fallen into disrepair, the Saxon place name component 'cester' or 'caester' indicating the ruins of a Roman settlement or fortress at a site. The early Saxons were suspicious of towns, and both for reasons of religion and tactics it seems they preferred an existence on the outskirts of old cities. But, by the time of the Viking conquest, Leicester was thriving once again. It was one of the so-called 'Five Boroughs' (among the others were Stamford, Nottingham, and Derby) whose enormous wealth at this time was probably generated by the production of cloth from wool. This wealth and power made Leicester and the other boroughs almost city-states, and the Vikings demanded control over them in return for peace with the remainder of England. Leicestershire now lay in the 'Danelaw', using the Danish legal system and currency, and the Danish language, a fact which is reflected in the many place names of Norse origin in the county.

Following the Norman Conquest of England in 1066, many manorial estates were handed over to the newly arrived Norman aristocracy. Numbers of other local place names – Ashby de la Zouch for example – reflect the new French influence, as do the many fine Norman castles in the area, at Ashby and elsewhere. Simon de Montfort, Norman baron and feudal lord of Leicester, played a prominent part in the crusades to recapture the Holy Land from Islam, but earned odium by expelling the Jews from Leicester.

The 1300s saw the strengthening of the defences of Leicester, with much

The Magazine, taken from an engraving from about 1820.

building including the 'New Works' later to become corrupted as the Newarke. These were constructed by Henry, Earl of Lancaster and were extended by his son Henry, Duke of Lancaster between 1330 and the 1360s, and it is not clear to which period the part of this work (including what was to become known as the Magazine) dates. This gatehouse in the city walls faced out towards the buildings on the site of the present De Montfort University, also begun by the first Henry. The building was to become Regimental Headquarters of the Leicestershire Regiment, and acquired the name 'Magazine' around 1642, when it was used for storing weapons and gunpowder during the English Civil War. Indications that it was also used as a prison at this time come from graffiti carved into the stonework, whilst evidence of the battering sustained by Leicester in the Civil War comes from the marks made by cannon balls on the surviving portion of the city walls in the Newarke.

One hundred years or so after the building of the Magazine, in 1485, Leicestershire played witness to a great moment in history when the crown of England changed hands once more. Richard Plantagenet, crowned Richard III, and champion of the House of Lancaster, spent the night at Leicester before meeting his rival Henry Earl of Richmond at Bosworth Field. It is said that as Richard crossed the Soar on his way out of the city his spur struck the side of the bridge. Following upon the battle in which Richard lost both his crown and his life, his naked body was brought back into the city draped over a horse. His head struck the bridge at the same point.

Another early view of the Magazine.

In the eighteenth Century the Magazine was used as an administrative centre for the county militia. As more land was purchased around it, the Magazine came to form one corner of an open square of buildings. In the Nineteenth Century barrack blocks were built on to one side of the Magazine, the complex forming the Headquarters of the Leicestershire Militia (3rd Battalion

Leicestershire Regiment). These Victorian barrack blocks were demolished in 1967, during the construction of Waterloo Way and the underpass road system.

The Leicesters almost entirely missed the French Revolutionary and Napoleonic Wars, save for a part in the Duke of York's expedition to the Netherlands in 1799. They were ordered to India in 1804, and took part in much of the fighting there, including battles at Bundlekund in 1807, on the Sutlej in 1808, and in Nepal against the Gurkhas at a time before these warrior people had offered their services to the British crown. Sources indicate that around this time the title of the Regiment, semi-officially at least, was 'The Royal Bengal Tigers'. The prefix 'Royal' was not granted officially however until 1946.

A derelict hosiery factory in Leicester today. It was this industry above all others which was most closely identified with the city in the 19th and 20th Centuries.

Having spent the best part of twenty years in India, in 1825, in recognition of this sojourn in the East, His Majesty King George IV was pleased to approve the Regiment

> *bearing on its colours and appointments the figure of the 'Royal Tiger' with the word 'Hindoostan' superscribed, as a lasting testimony to the exemplary conduct of the Corps during the period of service in India from 1804 to 1823.*

In 1838 the regiment returned once more to India, this time to take part in the First Afghan War, earning the battle honours 'Ghuznee', 'Khelat', and 'Afghanistan'. Still as the 17th (Leicestershire) Regiment of Foot, the 'Tigers' served in the Crimea, winning one of the newly instituted Victoria Crosses, when Corporal Philip Smith brought in a wounded officer whilst under fire, in front of the great Redan at Sebastopol. After this, a second battalion was formed, which served in Canada, whilst the 1st Battalion went back to India. Both Battalions served in India together in the 1870s

The Magazine, in the Newarke, Leicester, as it appeared around 1914. Horses and carts used the larger archway as a thoroughfare until around 1905. The 14th Century gatehouse is all that remains of a system of works, and their defences, built by Henry, Duke of Lancaster.

and 1880s, as the 1st Battalion fought in the Second Afghan War, and the 2nd Battalion went into Burma to take part in operations against King Theebaw of that country, and the murderous Dacoits who proliferated under his reign. This campaign ended with the annexing of Burma as part of the British Empire.

It was in 1888, with the Cardwell Reforms – named after the Secretary for War at that time – that the numbering system for British Regiments was dropped. The new title 'The Leicestershire Regiment' was adopted. It is the regimental system, with its love of tradition, history and ceremony that has done so much to foster esprit de corps in the British army. From his first days as a raw recruit, the soldier was made to feel aware that he was different from other soldiers. He was not a Buff or a West Kent or a Grenadier. He was a Welsh Fusilier, a Scots Guardsman, or a Leicester. He was instructed in the history of his regiment, the actions in which it had fought, and tales of heroism – often at the expense of other regiments – were related in the wet canteens when off duty.

It has often been remarked that to many recruits, and especially to those who came from an impoverished or

A scene around the Clock Tower, Leicester, sometime prior to the outbreak of the Great War.

Gallowtree Gate, Leicester, around 1910.

a broken home and who had known little in the way of stability beforehand, the regiment was more like a family. It would not be an exaggeration to say that this system has been the envy of the world. It is a system which many other countries have tried to emulate – mostly unsuccessfully. One cannot simply create 200 years of history overnight. It might indeed be argued that it was this framework of tradition, esprit de corps, sense of family and comradeship which saw the British army through the enormous strains of the First World War.

Leicester in the early years of the twentieth century was a prosperous city, its economy based largely on the hosiery or knitwear trade, which was then

Church Lane, Desford, in 1914. Desford was the home of 2nd Lieutenant Donald Johnson Pickard, 6th Battalion Leicestershire Regiment, killed on 17 July 1916.

Church Street, Lutterworth, around the time of the First World War.

by far the biggest employer in the city and the county. Other important industries were boots and shoes, production of which was probably second only to textiles, light engineering (including occupations related to the hosiery business, such as the manufacture of machinery) and trades connected with the various railways which passed through the city. In the county at large, in the southern districts, agriculture was still a major employer, and Market Harborough was the administrative centre for the fertile lands of the Welland Valley bordering Northamptonshire. In the north, particularly around Coalville, heading up towards Ashby and the Derbyshire border, mining provided work for large numbers of men. Loughborough was also a major industrial centre, with a strong economy again based on textiles.

In the west, Hinckley was another major hosiery and footwear centre. In

Oakham Market Square, before the First World War.

Loughborough High Street, early in the 20th Century.

the east the ancient county of Rutland was incorporated into Leicestershire for administrative purposes, with Uppingham and the market town of Oakham being the two major population centres. Here, farming and stone quarrying were the two prime employers.

In 1899, the county had its first, albeit limited, experience of citizens taking up arms during the South African (or Boer) War. As the conflict dragged on into 1900 and 1901, the War Office allowed the county

5504 Pte Mark Holmes of Sileby (left), with his cousin Pte Isaac Kidger, taking a rickshaw ride, sometime after the Boer War. Both were Regular soldiers of the 1st Battalion Leicestershire Regiment. Mr G.Jones

Volunteer battalions and Yeomanry to provide drafts for service on the veldt. A Volunteer Company of the Leicestershire Regiment was sent to South Africa, and two units of Imperial Yeomanry were formed. However, the bulk of the fighting was still undertaken by hard-bitten regular soldiers – the regular 1st Battalion Leicestershire Regiment was in the country at the outbreak of hostilities, and quickly found itself besieged by Boer forces in the town of Ladysmith. The garrison held out for several months, until a relief force arrived. Numbered among the relief column was a sizable contingent of recalled reservists who reinforced the depleted 1st Battalion, which then fought its way on to the end of the war, at the Battle of Lydenburg.

Field Marshal Horatio Herbert Lord Kitchener.

Field Marshal Horatio Herbert Lord Kitchener of Khartoum, was arguably the nation's greatest living soldier in 1914. Of an Anglo-Irish background, he had first been commissioned into the Royal Engineers, and gained his earliest military experience in the campaigns of the late Victorian era. His exploits in the Boer War had elevated him to the peerage, but it was more especially for his part in commanding the Sudan expedition of 1898 that he had attained the status of folk hero to a sizable portion of the population. In trouncing the fanatical Dervish forces at Omdurman, he had in the eyes of most Britons avenged the murder of General Gordon at the hands of the Mahdi in Khartoum some years previously. Some of Kitchener's actions on that campaign, however, led others to question his judgement. He deliberately had the Mahdi's tomb shelled by British artillery, and had offered to send his skull back to the Royal College of Surgeons for examination – a move which they considered to be in poor taste.

In 1914 the outbreak of the First World War caught Great Britain without a Secretary of State for War. The Prime Minister, Herbert Asquith, was taking responsibility for the post in addition to his usual duties. Kitchener, home on leave at the time from his position as 'Sirdar' or commander of the Egyptian Army, was the natural choice for War Minister, so public opinion and the popular press thought. Asquith bowed to public pressure, and installed the 64 year old Field Marshal at the War Office. It was not a happy arrangement. Many felt that Kitchener had passed his best, and that he had gone to seed. Others maintained that he had never been as brilliant as it was claimed anyway. What is well known is that those elements which make a great military commander in time of war are seldom those which make a good cabinet minister, and vice versa. Kitchener for his part disliked politicians, whom he felt were unable to be trusted with military secrets. He was apt to be taciturn during cabinet meetings, and his government colleagues often left his briefings as mystified about the current military situation as before they went in.

Kitchener, however, if he had done nothing else before he died when HMS *Hampshire* struck a mine off the Orkneys in 1916, had shown one final flash of brilliance. In 1914 he – and scarcely anyone else – had seen that it would not be 'all over by Christmas,' but instead there would be a

In many ways idyllic beforehand, rural life (seen here in 1914) was to be turned upside down by the First World War. Joe Higgs, the Smeeton Westerby Carrier, waits outside the Fox & Goose Inn at Great Glen. As well as goods, the Carrier would often take passengers on his frequent journeys to and from Leicester. Seated behind Higgs, wearing a white blouse, is Mrs Isabella Holyoak. Her brother-in-law Harry was to be killed with the 9th Leicestershires in 1917, whilst her husband William spent much of the First World War in Mesopotamia.

long war of three or more years. Accordingly, Britain would need to expand her tiny professional army of 300,000 to match the armies of several million men fielded by Germany, Russia and France. Britain at this time was under Liberal rule and a tradition of 'laissez faire' government stretching back into the nineteenth century meant that conscription was not an acceptable option. For the moment at least, participation in this life-or-death national struggle was to be a matter of personal choice for the individual. Kitchener gained cabinet approval to call for one hundred thousand volunteers, followed shortly by another hundred thousand, and then another.

With news of the British army's plight following the Retreat from Mons in August 1914 fresh in their minds, willing recruits flocked to join the Colours. Kitchener, meanwhile, had succeeded in living up to one of his nicknames, 'K of Chaos' (this was a play on his title Kitchener of Khartoum, which was usually abbreviated simply to 'K of K'). By snubbing the Territorial system which was already in existence, he had thrown the army into administrative confusion. The Territorial Force had been created in 1908 from the old volunteer battalions. The idea behind it was that in time of war or national emergency, each territorial battalion by dividing itself would throw off exact duplicates complete with administration and organisation in place, which could then absorb new recruits, and divide once more, and so on. In 1914, the Leicestershire Regiment had two Territorial Force battalions, the 4th, based at the Magazine, in Oxford

Pte Charles Hatter 1/5th Battalion .

Mr Michael Kendrick

Pte Jack Sinfield, 2/5th Battalion, killed in action in April 1917.

Mr David Sinfield

Street, Leicester, and with companies in Leicester and its immediate environs, and the 5th, with its headquarters at Loughborough, and with companies dispersed across the county. True to the plans laid down before the war, the 4th Leicesters, shortly after mobilisation in 1914 divided to form a 1/4th, and a 2/4th. Further division produced a 3/4th, and the 5th Battalion likewise formed what was known as a first line, second line, and eventually a third line. In theory, this sub-division could go on and on, to create as many new battalions as were needed.

Kitchener had long distrusted the Territorial Force in general, and had no confidence in their abilities. When he was appointed Secretary of State for War he chose to disregard the carefully laid plans, and called for the formation of an entirely new force. Accordingly, he set about creating the New Army or 'Kitchener's Army' alongside the Territorials. This resulted in recruits pouring into depots for new battalions, which had as yet no organisational structure and no officers. Furthermore, the Territorials and New Army competed not only for volunteers, but for equipment also. Leicestershire was no exception to this. However, what might be considered amazing is that out of this confusion four battalions emerged whose camaraderie, *esprit de corps*, and indeed when the time came, ability and bravery were second to none. They were the 6th Battalion, Leicestershire Regiment, raised in September 1914, the 7th Battalion, the 8th Battalion, and the 9th Battalion, all raised in quick succession afterwards.

Pte James Ward, 1st Battalion Leicestershire Regiment, with his wife and children, around 1900. He was in many ways a typical Victorian soldier.

Much has been written of the 'Pals' battalions, which were raised by the Mayor and Corporations in a number of cities in 1914. As an inducement to volunteer, men who elected to join these formations could do so in the knowledge that they were enlisting with, and could expect to serve in action beside, the friends and work colleagues that they had known in civilian life. What is less well known is that numbers of other 'Kitchener' battalions formed in places like Leicestershire in 1914 were also 'pals' battalions, in all but name. Men from the same works or street, friends, colleagues, and even relations, joined together.

Before the Boer War, when he went to enlist, 18 year old James Ward of Smeeton Westerby had given his trade simply as 'labourer', and there were precious few among the men who joined the Regular Army up to 1913 who could claim any better. In the City of Leicester in the late Victorian and Edwardian eras, the army had drawn its

23

A map of Leicester, around 1911. Before 1914 many of the recruits for the Leicestershire Regiment came from the slum areas of St Margaret's (now mostly demolished). In the First World War, recruits tended to come from the more prosperous working class areas of Knighton Fields, Belgrave Gate, and Clarendon Park.

recruits predominantly from the poorest areas – St Margaret's, the largest parish in the city, where much of the housing could only be described as slum dwellings, and St Matthew's. Shortly after Kitchener's call for his first Hundred Thousand in 1914, came the rush to enlist which followed the shock news of the Retreat from Mons. It was now to be a new kind of soldier, for a new kind of warfare; in the autumn of 1914 volunteers from a different class of society came forward, men with skilled occupations – hosiery hands, engineering apprentices, clerks and office boys. For the first time the recruits came from the upper working-class areas of Clarendon Park, Knighton Fields, and Highfields, where prim net curtains twitched behind bay windows if it was rumoured that a woman had not kept her front step scrubbed to perfection. There were miners from the collieries of Ibstock and Coalville, industrial workers from Loughborough and Hinckley, and farm workers from Rutland. These recruits were predominantly taller, fitter, and better fed than their pre-war counterparts, and, more significantly, they were used to a large extent to thinking for themselves – this indeed was after all what had led them to enlist in the first place. Properly led, they were capable of displaying an initiative which the pre-war recruit was likely to have had square-bashed out of him by an endless stream of orders from NCOs on a parade ground.

In Leicester, engineering apprentice Dick Read and three of his workmates made the short walk to the recruiting office in Humberstone Gate to volunteer. Dick was to serve with the 8th Battalion, Leicestershire Regiment. In Rothley, schoolmaster George Sleath and his brother both volunteered, also for the 8th Battalion. In Kibworth, near Market Harborough, brothers John

Slum housing, around a court in St Margaret's, Leicester. The Victorian expansion and industrialisation of the city produced areas like this, populated by the poorest of the working class.

The Horn of Plenty, a pub on Little Garden Street, off Belgrave Gate, before the First World War. Old Leicester as typified in this photograph has all but vanished.

I.L. 'Dick' Read, in 1914 an engineering apprentice, perhaps typifies the new kind of recruit who volunteered in 1914. Chester Read

An appeal published in the Leicester Evening Mail, September 1914.

Holyoak and Fred Holyoak, together with their cousin Harry Holyoak and eleven other local men joined up together on the same day in September 1914. They enlisted for the 9th Battalion. At the same time across the county, in historic Rutland, the Nutt brothers of Uppingham were also enlisting, Benjamin joining the 6th Battalion, while his brothers David and William joined the 7th. The story was the same in factories, offices, mines and farms across the county that summer and autumn, as comrades from civilian life became comrades in army life. Often they were under the command of young officers from the families who owned the farms, the mines and the factories, and who prior to the war had been their employers.

What was perhaps unique about these four Leicestershire service battalions was the fact that they were kept together, formed into what became known as the 110th Brigade, of the 37th Division. Unlike many other formations, which were raised elsewhere, they were not parcelled off individually to brigades and divisions as they were needed. Not surprisingly, the 110th was to become known as 'The Leicestershire Brigade'. It retained its identity and contained a Leicestershire contingent through four years of war on the Western Front, though this was gradually diluted by conscripts from other parts of the country, as the battles took their toll. There were reorganisations also. As the chronicler of the brigade, David Kelly, wrote in his book, '39 Months With The Tigers', by mid-1918

> *despite constant reinforcements, there were only three battalions, all woefully under strength, and only two of these were of the Leicestershire Regiment*[1].

None the less there remained a fierce pride in having belonged to one of these battalions, which persisted even after the end of the war and into old age. It manifested itself in the reunions, which were arranged in the 1930s, and in the memoirs and autobiographies which the survivors wrote. There may have been anger at the neglectful and shameful treatment received from ungrateful post-war governments, or disenchantment with the political outcomes and results of the Great War, both domestically and abroad. Yet aside from this was something else, which was perhaps the only positive aspect which the ex-servicemen had; this thing was the memory of that comradeship which they had experienced in the war, and both the sense of belonging and the sense of purpose which it brought with it. This is the story of those four battalions, but more importantly, it is also the story of the men who made them.

1. D.V.Kelly, '39 Months With the Tigers', (Ernest Benn, 1930) p16

Chapter Two

We Band of Brothers

The rush to enlist was spurred on by the feeling that the war might well be 'over by Christmas', and most of those who were prepared to join up wanted to do so quickly in order that their efforts would not be wasted, and their services still required. Many working-class men were keen followers of international events, and quite aside from the propaganda, there was a strong feeling that what Germany had done in violating Belgian neutrality was wrong, and the country's stance was right. One such individual was D.A.Bacon, a clerk in a hosiery firm in Leicester. Influenced by the gallant stand made by the Belgians, but equally concerned that the German armies were perilously near the Channel coast, he decided on 6 September 1914 to enlist. He wrote after the war:

13267 Pte J.J. Sharpe, an early recruit for 9th Battalion, of Burley, Rutland. He joined the Battalion on 7 September 1914, and was a former member of the Leicestershire Yeomanry, in which he had served for eight years. In this photo he wears the Yeomanry full dress uniform.

> *It was that night that I, who had always had a great aversion to soldiers and soldiering, made up my mind to join the Colours.*[1]

The diversity of occupations from which the would-be volunteers came was breathtaking. There were school masters, like George Ward Sleath and Jack Quincey, both of the 8th Battalion, who enlisted as private soldiers. There were clerks and office boys, engineering workers, miners from Northwest Leicestershire, quarrymen from Rutland, agricultural workers from the farmlands near Northamptonshire, and there were many, many hosiery workers. A typical story was that of Albert Smith, from Worthington, near Ashby de la Zouch. A coal delivery driver employed at the Old Glory pit in Newbold, he had been made redundant shortly before the war, when the pit was flooded. Together with a friend Charlie Platt, he walked to Ashby to enlist on 3 September 1914. The age range of recruits that would be accepted was officially 19 to 37 years, but recruiting posters stated that this

The Curzonia knitwear factory, Leicester. This building was in use as a hosiery factory before the First World War, and would have employed many of the men from the adjacent (but now demolished) houses in Curzon Street who joined the Leicestershire Regiment in 1914.

The former Vulcan Foundry engine works, on Vulcan Road, Highfields, Leicester. The Vulcan Foundry employed many of the recruits of 1914, who lived in the surrounding streets near St Saviours Road.

An 'old soldier' re-enlisted. Right: 15743 Pte William Tidmas, 7th Battalion, wearing what looks to be a kind of stopgap uniform, in September 1914. Above: Tidmas during his initial service with the Leicestershire Regiment – in the 1st Battalion around 1910 (standing, 2nd from left) Mrs D.M.Tidmas

Bill Wilson, of Leicester. He enlisted for the 7th Battalion at the Magazine, in September 1914, despite being under age. He was given the number 11727.

Mrs Clare Hawkins

was increased to 45 years for those with previous service in the army and no longer on the reserve, who wished to re-enlist. Many ex-soldiers did so, including William Tidmas of Leicester, who had served with the 1st Leicesters, and Albert Brewin of Nottingham Street, Melton Mowbray. Albert had also served with the 1st Leicesters, in his case during the siege of Ladysmith, and was employed at the Holwell Works in Melton when war broke out again. He at once rejoined.

At the other end of the scale, such was the fervour not to be left behind when so many others were joining, that there were many cases in which young men tried to enlist whilst still under age. In a good many instances, if the youth in question looked as if he could pass for 18, recruiting sergeants would turn a blind eye - the army attestation form after all asked only for 'apparent age upon enlistment'. One such case was that of Bill Wilson, 7th Battalion, of Leicester. He enlisted at the Regimental Headquarters, the Magazine, in September 1914 by adding a few months to his correct age of 17 years. He was quickly accepted and given his fare for the tram ride to Wigston Barracks.

Few of the men had any doubts that they were doing their patriotic duty by enlisting. One of those first recruits in August and September of 1914 was Charles Monk, of Mowsley, who also joined the 7th Battalion. Many years later, Charles recalled his almost pacifist family background, but also his strong feeling that he should serve his country in its hour of need:

Charles Monk, of Mowsley, who enlisted in 1914 despite the misgivings of his Non-Conformist family. Sonny Monk

September 1914: after signing attestation papers at Market Harborough, fourteen volunteers for the 9th Battalion from Kibworth wait at on the platform at the village station for a train to take them to Wigston barracks, Glen Parva. Back row: Third from left Arthur Freer (killed on 27 May 1918), fourth from left Bert Freer, extreme right R.G Lewis. Front row from left: Leonard Buckby, Fred Holyoak, Harry Holyoak (his cousin), R.G Iliffe, unidentified, and J.W.L Holyoak (brother of Fred) Rose Holyoak

> *Well I was brought up in a very good Non-Conformist home. My mother said I wasn't to fight boys at school, it's wrong. She said you could perhaps win, but it'd be because you're the best fighter, not because you were in the right, and it's the wrong way of solving things. And yet in spite of that atmosphere that I was brought up in ... I was just turned 18, and I went and enlisted.[2]*

Across the city and county in the autumn of that year, men either alone or more often with groups of friends, were presenting themselves at recruiting offices. Sometimes workmates joined in groups. On other occasions brothers enlisted together. We have already heard of the Holyoaks of Kibworth, of whom two brothers and a cousin, along with a number of friends, all joined together. There were many other similar instances: John and Joseph Goundry, who joined the 7th Battalion, or the Nutt brothers of Rutland. In Castle Donington, Everard Barker joined the 8th Battalion, while his brothers Fred and John joined the 9th Battalion. Perhaps the family with the strongest claim to have turned their battalion into a 'family business' were the Pritchards of 12, Leicester Lane, Great Bowden. Brothers

George, Harry, and J.H. Pritchard all enlisted for the 6th Battalion in September 1914, while another brother, Albert, joined the 8th Battalion later on. A fifth Pritchard brother served with the 10th (Reserve) Battalion, although it is not known if he served in France. The results of this willingness, indeed almost insistence, on the part of the men, that they should be allowed to serve with those that they had known so closely in civilian life, could be devastating for the communities and families from which they had come. On the Western Front, a battalion might suffer casualties numbering hundreds in a single attack. In the case of the Barkers, all three were tragically destined to die within weeks of each other on the Somme in 1916.

D.A.Bacon, having made up his mind to enlist, had now to tell his firm of his decision:

> Being then on holiday, and that having run its course, I returned to Leicester during the evening, and on reaching the firm's premises next morning I found that three others had already decided to enlist during the morning. Having work to clear up myself, I waited until the Tuesday morning, and informed my employer of my intentions and ascertained his views on the subject; he appeared to think I had decided on the right course and promised that my position would be open for me on my return to civil life.[3]

Another of those early recruits was I.L.Read, known as 'Dick', an engineering apprentice at Gimsons (a firm which was principally engaged in the manufacture of machinery for making boots and shoes) in Leicester. In common with many other manufacturing firms in the city, the outbreak of war had resulted in the cancellation of orders (Germany in 1914 was Great Britain's largest single overseas market) and hands being thrown onto short

An early recruit for the 6th Battalion: 10400 Pte Alf Warner, with his family, photographed outside their house in Church Gate, Loughborough, in 1915. Alf was to survive the war, reaching the rank of sergeant and earning considerable distinction in the process. Yvonne White

232027

Leic 4130
G.S.

(8 58 57) 116,000 8/14 H W V
Form
H. 2065

Army Form B. 2065.

New AF, SHORT SERVICE
(Three years with the Colours.)

ATTESTATION OF

No. 11006 Name *Thomas Henry Dono* Corps *Leicestershire Regt.*

Questions to be put to the Recruit before enlistment.

1. What is your name? ...... 1. *Thomas Henry Dono*
2. In or near what Parish or Town were you born? ...... 2. In the Parish of *Hanazwell* in or near the Town of *Stoke on Trent* in the County of *Stafford*
3. Are you a British Subject? ...... 3. *Yes*
4. What is your Age? ...... 4. *21* Years *7* Months.
5. What is your Trade or Calling? ...... 5. *Signalman*
6. Have you resided out of your Father's house for three years continuously in the same place or occupied a house or land of the yearly value of £10 for one year, and paid rates for the same, and, in either case, if so, state where? ...... 6. *No*

You are hereby warned that if after enlistment it is found that you have given a wilfully false answer to any of the following seven questions, you will be liable to a punishment of two years' imprisonment with hard labour.

7. Are you, or have you been, an Apprentice? if so, where? to whom? for what period? and, when did, or will, the period of your Apprenticeship expire? ...... 7. *No*
8. Are you Married? ...... 8. *No*
9. Have you ever been sentenced to imprisonment by the Civil Power? ...... 9. *No*
10. Do you now belong to the Royal Navy, the Army, the Royal Marines, the Militia, the Special Reserve, the Territorial Force, the Army Reserve, the Militia Reserve, or any Naval Reserve Force? if so to what unit and Corps? ...... 10. *No*
*11. Have you ever served in the Royal Navy, the Army, the Royal Marines, the Militia, the Special Reserve, the Territorial Force, the Imperial Yeomanry, the Volunteers, the Army Reserve, the Militia Reserve, or any Naval Reserve Force? If so, state which unit, and cause of discharge. ...... 11. *No*
12. Have you truly stated the whole, if any, of your previous Service? ...... 12. *Yes*
13. Have you ever been rejected as unfit for the Military or Naval Forces of the Crown? if so, on what grounds? ...... 13. *No*
14. Are you willing to be vaccinated or re-vaccinated? ...... 14. *Yes*
15. Are you willing to be enlisted for General Service? ...... 15. *Yes*
16. Did you receive a Notice, and do you understand its meaning, and who gave it to you? ...... 16. *Yes* {Name *Col. Sg. Grocott* Corps *6th N. Staffs*}

17. Are you willing to serve upon the following conditions provided His Majesty should so long require your services? ...... For a term of three years, unless War lasts *less* ~~longer~~ than three years, in which case you will be retained until the War is over. If employed with Hospitals, as Clerks, etc., you may be retained after the termination of hostilities until your services can be spared, but such retention shall in no case exceed six months. 17. *Yes*

discharged with all convenient speed

I, *Thomas Henry Dono* do solemnly declare that the above answers made by me to the above questions are true, and that I am willing to fulfil the engagements made.

Thomas ~~Henry~~ + Dono SIGNATURE OF RECRUIT.

N. Coakley Signature of Witness.

OATH TO BE TAKEN BY RECRUIT ON ATTESTATION.

I, *Thomas Henry Dono* swear by Almighty God, that I will be faithful and bear true Allegiance to His Majesty King George the Fifth, and that I will, as in duty bound, honestly and faithfully defend His Majesty, His Heirs, and Successors, in Person, Crown, and dignity against all enemies, and will observe and obey all orders of His Majesty, His Heirs, and Successors, and of the Generals and Officers set over me. So help me God.

CERTIFICATE OF MAGISTRATE OR ATTESTING OFFICER.

The Recruit above named was cautioned by me that if he made any false answer to any of the above questions he would be liable to be punished as provided in the Army Act.

The above questions were then read to the recruit in my presence.

I have taken care that he understands each question, and that his answer to each question has been duly entered as replied to, and the said recruit has made and signed the declaration and taken the oath before me

at **BURTON-ON-TRENT** on this *31st* day of *Sept.* 191*4*

Signature of the Justice

If any alteration is required on this page of the Attestation, a Justice of the Peace should be requested to make it and initial the alteration under Section 8 (6), Army Act.
The Recruit should, if he require it, receive a copy of the Declaration on Army Form B. 2065A.

The usual Attestation Form for Kitchener volunteers: for three years' service unless the war ended earlier. This is the attestation of 11006 Pte Thomas Henry Dono, 7th Battalion.

Cameron Coxon-Smith

time. At the end of August he returned to Leicester from a visit to his parents in Eastbourne to discover that:

> *the works would not be re-opening on the Monday morning, and we were to register at the local Labour Exchange for Unemployment Insurance Benefit. Thus, in my case, the British declaration of war simply added confusion to a situation already chaotic in many respects ... At the end of the second week we were told to report for work on the Monday morning, and for a fortnight worked hard to complete machines needed for the manufacture of army boots. Life proceeded thus until one morning we read that von Kluck - already famous - had reached the outskirts of Paris...*[4]

One of Dick's cohorts at Gimsons had some experience of army life already, having enlisted into the 10th Hussars before the war after an argument with his father, and had been bought out. He suggested that they should enlist, and so it was that Dick and several other apprentices found themselves that lunchtime in the queue at the recruiting office in Humberstone Gate. In the event, only Dick and one other man, Taylor, were passed as fit:

> *Spiers and Wade returned with us to the works, where we told the foreman that we were going and had to be sworn in at three o'clock that afternoon. He called us 'a pair of silly buggers' as he vigorously expectorated bits of chewing tobacco around the surrounding floor. Then, softening a shade, he said that if we came back Gimsons might have a job for us.*[5]

A different response was encountered by Arthur Cave when he left his employers, Messrs Hart and Levy Ltd, Wholesale Clothiers, of Leicester, to

Right: **Arthur Charles Cave in 1914.** *Below:* **His home at that time, 25 Melbourne Road, Leicester.** Col. Terry Cave

enlist on 1 September. He recorded in his diary: 'The firm made me a present of £2, and wished me luck.'[6]

Arthur was 21 years of age, and was the son of a London Midland & Scottish Railway engine driver. At the time of his enlistment he was living at the family home, 25, Melbourne Road, Leicester. His experience in the accounts department of his firm would in time lead to his appointment as Company Quartermaster-Sergeant (CQMS) and ultimately Regimental Quartermaster-Sergeant (RQMS). Cave joined the newly formed 7th Battalion of the Leicestershire Regiment at the Magazine. Bacon, reporting there a few days later, was to be posted to the 9th Battalion. He remembered the anxiety which prevailed, that one might in fact not be accepted by the army:

> *The following morning, Tuesday, I went down to the 'Magazine' ... and after being medically examined, weighed and passed through several other formalities, was duly sworn a soldier of the King and received the King's Shilling and an additional 1/9 for a day's keep. It was not very pleasant having to strip among a lot of other men and those strangers and of all classes; and then there was the fear of being rejected, which would have been a great disappointment in those days. However, I passed through safely, as did the others who went the day previous, though that was rather surprising as one of them, an apprentice, was quite a little chap about 5 feet three inches in height and only 17¹/₂ years old – for that reason it would have been particularly galling had I not have passed.[7]*

Bacon presented himself at Wigston Barracks only to be told that he was not

A slightly different view of the Magazine in 1914, this time looking roughly north towards what is today the location of the underpass.

New recruits in Magazine Square, at the rear of the great bastion, in September 1914. It is possible that Bacon may be among these men. Courtesy of Leicestershire Record Office

required until the following Sunday. Even then he and a crowd of other men were told to report back the next day, **not** in Sunday best but in their oldest clothes. They were also told to each buy a wrist watch, which was more practical, but something of a novelty in those days. Cave continued his account:

> I reported to the regimental depot at South Wigston, where there were crowds of other men who had also just enlisted. There appeared to be nothing to be done, and I went home each night to Leicester to sleep.

Several days later,

> with a batch of several hundred recruits I left for Badajos Barracks, Aldershot. Here the first units of Kitchener's New Army were being formed, the particular units in these barracks being the 6th Battalion, forming under the command of Lieut-Col. Challenor, and the 7th Battalion, under Lieut. Col. Carleton.[8]

In fact, the 6th and 7th Battalions had left South Wigston for Aldershot to try to relieve some of the chronic overcrowding at the depot during those first weeks in September as the four Battalions came together. Read, destined for the 8th Battalion, recalled that there were,

> men sleeping on the parade ground by the hundred without a blanket between them. The sanitary and catering arrangements were

Looking along Saffron Road, with the Regimental Depot (Wigston Barracks) on the left, 1914. The Depot was also known as Glen Parva Barracks. Duncan Lucas

5528 Sgt Charles Jordan Cattell. A Regular NCO, he was posted in 1914 to the newly-formed 8th Battalion. Mr R.J.Cattell

A view inside the grounds of the Depot. Duncan Lucas

quite inadequate and soon became chaotic, with the result that, for a fortnight or so, we of the 8th and 9th were billeted in the Wigstons... as I recall, nine hundred or so of us in the 8th were commanded by a volunteer captain of the Singapore Artillery, who happened to be on UK leave, with two reservist corporals to assist him. The corporals set us a wonderful example and a high standard, and Corporal Cattell became our R.S.M.[9]

The fact that the nights were still fairly warm must have made sleeping outdoors slightly more bearable, but other aspects of the situation were less tolerable.

Recruits for Kitchener's Army at the Depot, Glen Parva, in September 1914. Duncan Lucas

D.A.Bacon in particular recalled the terrible meal times at Wigston:

> [There was] *some crush, for no proper organisation had been formed by then and there was only seating accommodation for about a quarter of the party. With a good deal of shouting and pushing the majority of us got in at last and some were lucky enough to get a seat at a table. Each was given a basin, which apparently had not been washed that week - or the previous week for that matter - and the orderlies brought round buckets of 'tea', from which they filled the basins; but it was tea by name only, not by nature certainly for grease was floating about on top of it.*[10]

He continued:

> *One could hardly blame the cooks, for the capacity of the place was only about 350 in normal times, while now they had to contend with almost 3000. I later saw some of the Wigston 'Pontoon' (stew which forms the staple portion of the ordinary army dinner) and of which I and many others got heartily sick thereafter, but it looked so uninviting that I could not bring myself to touch it – the nearest approach to this infamous mixture in civilian life being cabbage water with lumps of boiled fat floating about in it.*[11]

The administrative structure of the barracks was so overwhelmed by the

The only surviving original barrack block at Glen Parva today – one of those filled to capacity by recruits in 1914.

Another group of Kitchener volunteers, still clad in civilian clothes, at the depot in 1914. Dorothy Parry

flood of recruits that, as described earlier, they were sent home on the first two nights. It took some time to sort everyone out into the respective Battalions in which they would serve:

> *I think all our party left the barracks that day as soon as the gates were opened, less those who had previously left via the wall, and went to their own homes or lodgings with due soldierly pride and, catching the [tram] car next morning arrived at the barracks once more in time for 'Roll Call'. Finding however that by no means the larger portion turned up at this hour it was not repeated [so early]. Many in fact were absent for days, and one is loath to record the belief that some never again put in an appearance after the first day. Things seemed to be more earnest on this the second day and we found ourselves possessed by various police sergeants and old Militia Non-Commissioned Officers etc, who got us into groups of about 100 strong – each called a 'platoon'. Each one in charge of a platoon then proceeded to take the names of those in his group, entering them in their respective notebooks – ours in particular impressing upon us the fact that the roll would be called on every parade and that those failing to answer would be 'for it', which meant that they would be called to account before an officer.[12]*

One of the elderly drill sergeants found it amusing simply to double his men

New recruits are addressed by NCOs. Glen Parva barracks September 1914. Mr R.J.Cattell

More recruits at Glen Parva, September 1914. This photograph was sent home by Pte George Sleath, 8th Battalion. Courtesy of Leicestershire Record Office/Jean B.Sleath

round and round the parade square, and training at Wigston was nothing if not rudimentary in those early days. However it was here the latter two battalions, which would in due course become part of the Leicestershire Brigade, were formed in name at least:

[Drill] *and similar kinds of routine went on for about a week, during which our party regularly slept at Leicester and daily journeyed to the barracks though many coming from a distance slept at the barracks, while a few who were sufficiently fortunate obtained billets in Wigston.*

After we had been there about four days, the platoons numbered 1 to 10 inclusive were paraded together and told that they would thereafter be known as the 8th (Service) Battalion Leicestershire Regiment. Platoons numbered 11 to 20 were next paraded and informed that they would be known as the 9th (Service) Battalion The Leicestershire Regiment. That was really the official formation of the two battalions but it was not until we had moved down to the Aldershot Training Area that any real battalion organisation was carried out[13],

The rear of the Co-Op supermarket, South Wigston. It was on this patch of ground, now a car park, that tents were pitched to accommodate new recruits in 1914.

Bassett Street, South Wigston. It was here that the overspill from the nearby barracks were billeted.

Ex-Noncommissioned
Officers
(REGULARS)
Under 50 Years of Age

WANTED
FOR

Home Service Only

TO DRILL AND
INSTRUCT RECRUITS.

:o:

Apply at
GLEN PARVA

So urgent was the need for experienced NCOs to train the new Battalions, that advertisements for them were placed in the Leicester Evening Mail in September 1914. This one asks such men to present themselves at the depot.

concluded Bacon of this part of his army career.

For the local civil population, all of this sudden activity must have been quite a spectacle, and much of the overspill from the barracks was accommodated by the people who lived in streets close to the barracks. Frank Noble, in 1914 a South Wigston schoolboy, had vivid memories of:

...the invasion of the village...by Kitchener's Army. These men were not in khaki but in a dark blue uniform with a Glengarry hat, some were in 'civvies'. There must have been thousands of them. Every house had to take some in. I know there were four or five in our house. Even so there was not enough room for them all and some slept in the ...gardens in Bassett Street.[14]

It seems likely also that a small piece of grassland behind the Leicestershire Co-Operative Society shop on Bassett Street in South Wigston was also used, for a short time at least, to accommodate recruits under canvas. This piece of ground is now the car park at the rear of the current Co-Op supermarket. Another South Wigstoner, D.M. Dougherty, in his memoir 'A South Wigston Lad', recalled this time fondly, and remembered:

There was plenty to occupy our minds and a certain air of

Y.M.C.A. TENT AT GLEN PARVA.

A large marquee has been opened by the Leicester Y.M.C.A. in the barracks ground at Glen Parva for the convenience of the new recruits, fitted up with tables, writing material, magazines, books, games, and a variety of other material to enable our soldiers to feel more at home amidst their new surroundings. The tent is packed out by the men at night, and is much appreciated. Contributions toward the cost of this may be sent to Mr. H. E. Smith, Secretary Y.M.C.A., Leicester, the Chaplain at the Barracks, or to Mr. C. Moore, Music Depot, South Wigston.

ENTHUSIASTIC SEND-OFF TO WIGSTON RECRUITS.

Hundreds of people cheered the Wigston Two Steeples' contingent of 16 men as they marched from Glen Parva Barracks this morning, led by Mr. Moore's band, and entrained for Aldershot for further training. The female employees came in a body, waving flags, ribbons, etc., and the school children were also assembled. It was a magnificent send-off—one of the best ever witnessed at Wigston. One of the 16, under the mobilisation order, was married, by special licence, a day or two ago.

GOALVILLE

The leaving of Glen Parva. The 8th and 9th Battalions in particular received an enthusiastic send off as they left South Wigston.
Leicester Evening Mail

'Three Cheers for Two Steeples!' Workers from the 'Two Steeples' hosiery factory in Wigston gather outside Glen Parva barracks on 3 September 1914, to see off co-workers who had joined the 8th and 9th Battalions. Duncan Lucas

Colour Sergeant
J.T.S. Nobbs, 2nd
Battalion
Leicestershire
Regiment, about
1910.

excitement in all that was going on around us - the barracks were full, men were sleeping in tents and in houses, and we put up four young men from Loughborough in our front room for two nights. These men formed the 6th, 7th and 8th Battalions of the Leicester Regiment, and I often passed them all out on a route march led by Sergeant Cattell whom I knew well at church. Cattell had finished his time and was in the Leicester Police Force when war broke out, but was called up with the Reserves and was retained at the depot to deal with recruits. The whole lot of the men, still in civilian clothes, left for training...With their departure Wigston became quiet again[15].

New contingents of recruits would soon arrive in South Wigston to replace them, but for now the 'originals' began to train in earnest.

Around the Leicestershire battalions: The 6th Battalion, first to be raised, was composed in the main of recruits from the city and county of Leicester. Among the officers was Lieutenant John Nobbs, a former Colour-Sergeant of the 2nd Battalion, who had over 20 years of service with the Leicestershire Regiment. He had served in India, and was granted a commission in September 1914, bringing some much needed experience to the battalion. Among the second lieutenants were James Hanley Hopewell, the 22 year old son of a wealthy wine and spirit merchant from Nottingham, and G.T.L. 'Gussie' Ellwood. Ellwood was the son of the Reverend C.E. Ellwood, Vicar of Cottesmore, Rutlandshire, and had been reading for Greats at Magdalen College, Oxford when the war broke out. He received his commission into the 6th Battalion on 26 August 1914. Shortly after Hopwell and Ellwood, the battalion was joined by 2nd Lieutenant William Thornton Wettenhall, who was a Cambridge Blue, and in 1910 had won the quarter mile in the Inter Universities Sports. The Quartermaster of the 6th Battalion, in the time honoured tradition of the British Army, was another old soldier who had been commissioned, Harry Lindley. Like John Nobbs he had served for a number of years as a Colour-Sergeant, including time spent in India. The Colonel of the 6th in October 1914 was Major (temporary Lieutenant-Colonel) Edward Lacy Challenor, another member of the regiment of long standing, born in 1873 and serving with the Leicesters since the age of 20. He had served in the South African War, and with the possible exception of Captain B.E. Crockett, was the only one with experience as an officer. Along later came Second-Lieutenants David Kelly, and

John Nobbs' house in 1914;
81, Blaby Road, South
Wigston, now a florist's shop.

Nobbs shortly after
receiving his commission
in the 6th Battalion in
1914.

41

George Gillet, both from a battalion of the Universities and Public Schools brigade. Kelly, recently down from Oxford, had been in Spain when the war broke out. Returning to England to enlist, he like many other potential officers had joined the UPS brigade as a private, before meeting up with Gillet. It was the latter's friendship with Colonel Challenor, which brought them both to the 6th Battalion in the autumn of 1914. Commissioned in October 1914 was J.W. Burdett, one of the two Burdett brothers who were to serve as officers with the 6th Battalion. They were the sons of Mr T. Burdett, the former manager of the Leicester branch of Lloyds Bank. Finally, Frank William Curtis, 20 years old, was another ex-member of the UPS brigade, who was commissioned in November 1914. He had managed his family estate before the war, and was an old boy of Bedford School.

In addition to Leicestershire men, the 7th Battalion boasted a sizable contingent from Chesterfield and other parts of Derbyshire. In command of the battalion was Lieutenant-Colonel G.D. Carleton, who had been 'dug out' of retirement for the post. One of his officers was Captain F.W. Woolnough, until recently a lieutenant in the British West Indies Regiment. Among the newly joined second-lieutenants were Edward Kingsley Wakeford, and Noel Compton Burnett, who were to be killed on the Somme, and Arthur Aubrey Clarke, who was to gain the Military Cross in 1916, but fell at Passchendaele the following year. Wakeford was the son of Mr Edward Wakeford, the

Lieutenant Colonel E.L. Challoner, commanding officer of the 6th Battalion. He is shown here as a Major, just before the war.
Courtesy of Leicestershire Record Office

Harry Lindley, as a Sergeant with the 1st Battalion in India before the First World War This photograph was in fact taken on his wedding day. He was to become Honorary Lieutenant and Quartermaster of the newly raised 6th Battalion in September 1914. Leicestershire Record Office

Harry Lindley as Lieutenant and Quartermaster of the 6th Battalion, with his family. He died in Leicester in 1916, and is buried in Welford Road cemetery. Leicestershire Record Office

2nd Lt. Frank
William Curtis,
'A' company, 6th
Battalion, 1915.
He was
commissioned in
November 1914,
and later served
with the Kings
Shropshire Light
Infantry. He was
killed at Polygon
Wood in
November 1917.
Courtesy of Beryl and
Stuart Blythe

superintendent civil engineer at Gibraltar Royal Naval dockyard. Prior to the war and being commissioned, he had lived with his grandfather, the Reverend Edward Atkins, Vicar of St Nicholas and Master of Wyggeston Hospital in Leicester. Wakeford was also a mathematics scholar, and was studying at Cambridge. Another second lieutenant was John Gordon Hollis, son of Mr and Mrs T. Hollis of the Barncroft, Kirby Muxloe. He had studied at university in Düsseldorf, Germany, before the war, and like so many other second lieutenants in the Leicestershire battalions, he had enlisted as a private soldier before being offered a commission in October 1914. In November 1914 they were joined by second lieutenants Alan E.G. Mason, son of Dr and Mrs Mason, of London Road, Leicester, and Charles James Stuart Wright, who as his name suggests was of an old Scottish family. Born in 1891, he was the grandson of the late Captain James Cummin Burnett of Monboddo, Kincardinshire.

The 8th Battalion, raised approximately one month after the 6th, was composed to a far greater extent of recruits from the outlying towns and villages of the county of Leicestershire. It also had a fair sized minority of Nottingham men. The battalion was commanded initially by Major H. McEwan until the middle of October 1914 when Lieutenant-Colonel H. de B. Hevell DSO arrived to take command. He was quickly succeeded by Colonel C.H. Shepherd DSO, after Hevell took over the command of a battalion of the Worcestershire Regiment. In December Shepherd retired from the army, and was succeeded by Lieutenant-Colonel H.P.Bell, who was in turn succeeded by Lieutenant-Colonel F.J.Radford the following June. Among his subordinates was a Reserve officer, Major H.R.Manley. Another officer senior in years was Captain R.T.Knowles, late of the Singapore Artillery, also 'dug out' of retirement. The captains and company commanders at this time included A.L.Morris, an Indian Army officer home on leave. He was a captain in the 17th Infantry (IA) and his skills would prove invaluable. Another reserve officer was Captain E.F. Griffin, as was Captain G.W. Capper, a retired regular officer with North West Frontier and Boer War ribbons, who was able to bring his considerable experience to the infant battalion. Few of these elderly officers would serve in France with the 8th, but some of those younger men who would

Frank and Jack Breacher (8th Battalion) with their father Captain J.B.Breacher. Mrs S.Chatham

do so and who would gain distinction in the process, were already with the battalion. These included Lieutenant H.L. Beardsley of Loughborough and Second-Lieutenant T.L. Warner. Warner was the son of the late Mr Charles Warner, and his home was 'Willowdene', on London Road, Leicester. Also present by October 1914 were the Breacher brothers, also of Leicester. Second-Lieutenants Frank and Jack were the sons of Captain J.B. Breacher, a regular Leicestershire Regiment officer of many years standing who now held a post connected with recruiting. Finally, the battalion was shortly joined by Second-Lieutenant I.L. Berridge. He was a member of the well-known Leicester hosiery machinery manufacturing firm, I.L. Berridge & Co.

In the 9th, last battalion of the future 110th Brigade to form, there was a good sized Rutland complement, although men from Oakham, Uppingham and elsewhere were dotted through the other three battalions. A CO was already in place – Lieutenant-Colonel H.R. Mead, also of the Indian Army. His second-in command was Major J.G.Mignon, until recently a Captain in the Reserve of Officers, who had been a staff officer in the Boer War. At the end of June 1915 he was promoted to Lieutenant-Colonel and took over command of the 8th Battalion. Mead himself would be replaced in due course, by Lieutenant-Colonel C.H. Haig, who took the 9th Battalion to France. The battalion had scarcely any company commanders in place by October 1914, but among the fifteen or so second-lieutenants who had already been appointed was Alexander Charles Nicholas March-Phillipps de Lisle, a member of an old county family. Second-Lieutenant de Lisle was the son of Mr E.J. de Lisle, who was for a number of years Member of Parliament for the constituency of Mid-Leicestershire. Other early members of the 9th included Frederick Herbert Emmet, the youngest of the six sons of the Reverend W.E. Emmet of Oxford, and 25 year old Henry Yarde Martin. He was the son of Paymaster Rear-Admiral Sir W.E.R. Martin CMG RN, and before the war had worked for the London & Westminster Bank. He joined the Public Schools Battalion of the Middlesex Regiment as a private soldier, before receiving a commission into the Leicestershire Regiment at the beginning of December 1914.

2nd Lt. Henry Yarde Martin, 9th Battalion, early 1915. He was educated at Bedford School and worked at the London and Westminster Bank. He was commissioned from the Public Schools Battalion Middlesex Regiment in December 1914, and was killed later in the war with the East Lancashire Regiment.

Courtesy of Beryl and Stuart Blythe

1 D.A.Bacon. Typescript memoir, Leicestershire Record Office (LRO) p2
2 Charles J.Monk. Interview with author, 1989.
3 Bacon, *op cit.* p2
4 I.L.Read, 'Of Those We Loved' (Pentland Press, 1994) p501
5 Read, *op cit.* p502
6 A.C.Cave, unpublished typescript diary. 1.9.14
7 Bacon, *op cit.* p2
8 Cave, *op cit.* 2.9.14 & 5.9.14
9 Read, *op cit.* p504
10 Bacon, *op cit.* p3
11 Bacon, *op cit.* p3
12 Bacon, *op cit.* p3
13 Bacon, *op cit.* p4
14 F.Noble. Typescript Memoir held in Wigston Archives of Mr Duncan Lucas.
15 D.M.Dougherty, *A South Wigston Lad*. Privately produced typescript memoir.

Chapter Three

Forging a new Brigade
Training at Aldershot and on the South Coast

NCOs were required both for the training of recruits at home, and to accompany the battalions abroad, as indicated in this appeal placed by the 6th Battalion. A number of old soldiers did in fact accompany the battalions to France, but a good few did not, being simply not up to the physical hardships entailed.

Leicester Evening Mail

By the autumn of 1914, the 8th and 9th Battalions had left Wigston, and had joined the 6th and 7th Battalions in the vicinity of Aldershot. Kitchener's Army formations from all over Britain were converging on the town and accommodation was at a premium. The 6th and 7th were cooped up in Badajoz and Salamanca Barracks, and Arthur Cave noted that:

The two battalions were occupying the accommodation normally occupied by one, and most of us were sleeping on the floor. I shall not forget the dreadful scramble there used to be for every meal, and the miserable conditions under which we were expected to live. Still, the novelty of it all compensated for it to some extent, and we were ready to put up with anything if it would get us any quicker to France, for we were convinced, as most people were, that it would all be over by Christmas.[1]

The combination of cramped, overcrowded living conditions, along with young men and boys who might have come from quite isolated backgrounds on farms or in the countryside, mixing with city dwellers for the first time, was quite likely to promote the spread of infectious disease. In fact, in late September 1914 the movements of the men of the 6th Battalion were curtailed for a time in order to try to prevent the further spread of scarlet fever, which had indeed broken out in the battalion. The outbreak was not as serious as it might have been, however, and there were apparently no fatalities as a result.

Meanwhile, the newly arrived 8th and 9th were now allotted Bourley Camp, just outside Aldershot, about midway on the road to Fleet. Bourley Camp was situated in a hollow between a hill known as Caesar's Camp, and the Long Valley. The main camp was on the north side of the Aldershot-Fleet road, whilst the mess tents were on the south side. On the east and

The camp of the 8th Battalion Leicestershire Regiment at Bourley, Aldershot, September 1914. Note the washing hanging out to dry between the tents.
Chester Read

west sides, the camp was bounded by thick woods. D.A. Bacon described
the scene in September 1914:

> At that time and on first sight especially, the camp made a pretty
> picture, for the country round was beautiful and the grass was <u>green</u>
> (underlined because it did not long remain so). The first few weeks
> spent here were very much enjoyed - camp life was a novelty to most
> and the whole thing seemed romantic.[2]

However, things were not to remain so tranquil for long. Two days after the
arrival of the two Leicestershire battalions at Bourley came the 9th Battalion
South Staffordshire Regiment, who were to share the camp accommodation
with them. Shortly before their arrival, the mess tents had been laid out
ready for the afternoon tea of the Leicestershire men. The South Staffords
upon reaching the camp quite naturally assumed that this was welcome
refreshment prepared in order to revive them after their lengthy journey, and
proceeded to clear the lot. The resulting fight, which occurred when the
Leicestershire men reached the now-denuded mess tents, was only halted by
the timely arrival of Major Mignon. Bacon continues the story:

> There was a battle royal, which only ceased when Captain [sic]
> Mignon arrived on the scene, explained the situation and promised to

Recruits of the 8th Battalion at Aldershot, September 1914. They carry long Lee-Enfield rifles, and Boer War vintage equipment. The rifles appear to have white paint on the barrels, possibly to indicate that they are no longer safe for use with live ammunition. Back row (l to r) S. Hooton, C. Cook, A. Killingley, S. Foxon, I.L. Read, A.Taylor. Front row: (l to r) W. Johnson, E.Withers, A.Lewin, E.Simmonds. Chester Read

LIFE IN KITCHENER'S ARMY.

Leicester Recruit's Experience at Aldershot.

We have, this morning, received an interesting letter from a Leicester recruit in Lord Kitchener's Army, who is stationed at Aldershot, and who, judging by the spirit in which his letter is written, is perfectly happy.

ALDERSHOT, Thursday.

"The 8th and 9th Battalions of the Leicester Regiment (Kitchener's Army)," he states, "left Glen Parva at 4 a.m. on Monday last, after being on parade from 8.45 p.m. Sunday. Despite the standing, through which many were perished, the Battalion left in good spirits, to the accompaniment of the Y.M.C.A. band playing ' It's a long way to Tipperary.'

"Each man had a sandwich of bread and cheese to last him on his journey, and we arrived at Aldershot at 9.30 a.m. Then we had about four miles to walk to our camp, and on arrival, we were marched into huge marquees for breakfast. We went in to breakfast in separate companies, which is very different to Glen Parva, where thousands are fighting to get a look in.

"We had dinner about 2 o'clock, and a good meal it was too—a leg of mutton between twelve men, a large plate of potatoes, and about ½lb. of bread. We were also supplied with a knife, fork, spoon, plate and a cup. If the recruits at Glen Parva could read this they would drop dead!"

The King and Lord Kitchener visit Aldershot to-morrow (Friday).

There have been several aeroplanes flying about to-day. We have just been dished out with our blankets (two for each man), and a waterproof sheet to lie on.

There was such a skirmish this afternoon, when about half the Battalion set up the yell that a German prisoner had escaped. I got up and ran after them, and when I got to a spinney somebody said, " He has beaten you and has got up the tree." When I got close up I found the " German prisoner " was a squirrel.

There are all sorts of soldiers here. Some are wearing half khaki and half " civies," while some are in khaki suits but wearing bowler hats.—Yours,

F. A. ISAACS.

The life of a Kitchener's Army recruit at Aldershot, recounted in the Leicester Evening Mail.

get some more tea for the battalion. That of course could not be done in a hurry, and after a lengthy wait, on the Captain's appearance at the door of the Food Store, everyone crowded round him like they would round a cheap jack in the market place. After a great deal of scrambling and fighting to get there first, loaves were given out one between four men and 7lb jars of jam between so many and slabs of margarine likewise; and another mashing of tea was made. Unfortunately for most, owing to the rush many fellows had 7lbs of Jam and loaves to themselves while others had hardly any. The whole camp was in uproar and all through the evening odd fights between our men and those of the S.Staffs continued. This sort of thing could not have happened later, but at this stage it must be remembered, there was practically no discipline and very few officers or NCOs.[3]

After this unfortunate incident, meal times went more smoothly, but hardly a day passed whilst the 8th and 9th Battalions were at Bourley without at least one fight in the mess tents.

Dick Read remembered that the authorities tried to remedy the shortage of officers and NCOs as quickly as possible:

On reaching Aldershot we were formed successively into platoons and companies. Reserve officers appeared...while newly-commissioned second lieutenants

A 9th Battalion group at Bourley, Aldershot. This group are fully dressed in Kitchener Blue. Standing back row third from left is 14934 Pte Arthur Sturman. Pete & Sue Sturman

Another 9th Battalion group around the same time. They too wear the Kitchener Blue uniform. Front row, 2nd from left is Frederick Webb, of Croft. Joan Poultney

> *from public school O.T.C.s joined us daily. Somewhat elderly reservists with Boer War ribbons put up 'stripes' soon after joining, as quartermaster sergeants and sergeants.*[4]

Other NCOs, lance-sergeants, corporals and lance-corporals, were appointed from among the men who had volunteered. Generally, the army way was to ask anyone who had ever been in charge of anyone else, or who wanted to be, to make themselves known. In this way, works foremen and other working-class men who had held positions of some authority in civilian life took up similar posts in the army. Dick also remembered that others had been members of either the Boys' Brigade or one of the many other forms of cadet corps, which had flourished before 1914 in response to the perceived German menace. However, he and his friends had a pact that none would take a stripe or stripes whilst in the army, in order that they should all remain together during their service. This attitude, whilst perfectly understandable, made the appointment of NCOs from among the brighter recruits like Read doubly difficult for the army. Eventually he, like many others, did accept stripes, but it took months to wear down the resolve of these determined groups of friends. Whilst the companies were being formed here at Bourley, the 'Pals' ethos of the battalions which had been recruited from the same streets and district was further reinforced. Those men who wished to swap companies or platoons to be with their chums were given the opportunity to do so, provided that they could find an equal number of persons to swap with them. This could have potentially disastrous results for a town or street when the battalions reached the front, as later events would show.

Soon more officers began to arrive, mainly from University and Public School Officer Training Corps. Some had served briefly in the ranks of the Public Schools battalions which were being formed at the time, before being plucked from obscurity and groomed for a commission.

Up till that time there had been about 8 officers in the [9th] Battalion all told, but one morning about 8 days after our arrival at Bourley we were surprised to see about 20 or 30 smartly dressed young men standing in a group outside the orderly room; they were all aged about 18 to 20. We soon learned however that they were our new officers straight from College or OTC, not yet having obtained their kit. These young officers were distributed throughout the Battalion, one to each platoon (and a few over). At first they were rather inclined to be 'superior' but as time wore on and they got to know the men better, they assumed more of the 'comrade spirit' and got on with us very well. Naturally they had little or no experience and had to learn just as we, and each evening they were put through the training in

Another 8th Battalion group at Aldershot. This photograph was probably taken by the same photographer, possibly on the same day as that on page 46. As there are ten men in each photograph, they are possibly the occupants of individual tents. The man on the back row, extreme left is George Sleath, whilst his brother kneels front row second right.

Courtesy of Leicestershire Record Office/Jean B.Sleath

which they were to take us the following day, by the few regular officers we had; therefore chiefly in training us they reaped their own knowledge and experience,[5]

recalled Bacon. Soon afterwards there arrived with the 9th two of the most important figures in the organisation of an infantry Battalion - its commanding officer, and its most senior NCO. Bacon continued:

Our Colonel made his appearance in quite the early days of training. He was seen on the parade ground strolling very unconcernedly. An oldish rather slight gentleman with very bronzed features. It was at first thought that he was one of the well to do civilians who were interested in the raising of the New Armies, but news soon came round that he was our colonel to be. The next day he arrived in uniform with an appearance much more military and wearing a whole row of medal ribbons. He (Col. Meade) had seen much service in India and Egypt, and he it was that transformed us from being a mere mob of men into a thoroughly organised and efficient Battalion of Infantry, and right well he did, though of course it took no little time...In striking contrast to the arrival of the Colonel was the arrival of the 'Battalion Sergeant Major' in the camp, albeit he was first seen strolling around the parade ground in civvies. He was a heavily built man with quite an air of authority, in fact one would almost have thought he had been Colonel as he not only used to grouse at the men but also at the officers, constantly ordering them to put more 'ginger' into their movements.[6]

The emphasis at Aldershot was on individual training, squad and platoon drill. The first stage was to learn the elementary parts of parade-ground drill, including forming fours. The new recruits also needed to master the art of marching in lines and columns and to gain an understanding of the meaning of instructions such as 'left wheel', 'right turn' and so on. After this, came more detailed instruction, on weapons and on skills such as visual signalling. However the battalions were dogged at this stage by shortages of the most basic equipment (a situation which was repeated across virtually the whole of Kitchener's Army) and it was some months before production of items such as rifles caught up with demand. The 6th and 7th Battalions due to their earlier formation were more advanced in musketry, and received some rifles quite early on, whilst the 8th and 9th Battalions could only wait and drill with wooden dummies. In fact the 9th Battalion did not 'fire its course' as musketry training was called, until shortly before departing for France. This led to much crowing from members of the 6th Battalion that they would be posted abroad first, and it was to the great satisfaction of members of the 9th that all the battalions were eventually ordered to embark on the same date.

Only the 6th Battalion at this early stage had a khaki uniform. The 7th had been issued with old full dress parade tunics - scarlet with colourful facings – and blue trousers, obtained from various reserve stores. The

Recruits of the 8th Battalion in training. The Kitchener Blue uniform, coupled with the fact that there are still leaves on the trees, suggests that the location is Bourley Camp, in September 1914. The man leading the second column is George Sleath. A school master, he was a natural choice for an NCO, and was later commissioned. Courtesy of Leicestershire Record Office/Jean B.Sleath

'Kitchener Blue' – it was an often ill fitting stopgap uniform of dark blue serge. Soldiers complained that it left them looking more like postmen or tram drivers !

condition of these once smart uniforms, in the circumstances of training for active service, quickly deteriorated. The 8th and 9th Battalions meanwhile were clothed with 'Kitchener Blue'. This was typically an ill-fitting uniform, rushed into production as a stopgap and made from supplies of blue serge material. Often shapeless and baggy, the tunic and trousers were topped off with a blue sidecap. Soldiers complained that the uniform left them looking more like postmen or tramdrivers than soldiers, and these uniforms were eventually consigned -via the good offices of the Red Cross - for the use of British prisoners of war held in Germany. D.A.Bacon had a great deal to say in his memoirs about this garment, little of it being favourable:

> *One monstrosity we did have issued at Bourley [was] the Kitchener Blue uniform. One does not like to comment too much on that hasty measure, being, as they were, an emergency issue but though I have never had the doubtful pleasure of being in prison, it was impossible not to think that the affair far more resembled the prison garb than His Majesty's uniform. I do not think that anyone looked even passable in them as they were invariably of an awful cut, but of course the funniest part of all was the cap, and quite a lot had little or no idea as to what size to wear a cap of the forage description or as to how they should be worn. The consequence was that some were worn pulled right down over the head while others resting on top of the head, looked like an upturned boat on the ocean. In addition to this was the fact that when it rained, all the blue dye in the cap came out and ran down the face and neck, completing the miserable picture of uncomfortable uniformity.[7]*

51

The men were compensated for their own clothes which they had worn out in the period before the arrival of the blue, at a rate of 4/- for boots, 6/- for a suit and 6/- for an overcoat.

Arthur Cave, of the 7th, as a Lance-Sergeant concerned with quartermaster's stores, was better placed than most to keep his uniform in some sort of presentable condition. On the shortage of equipment he recorded in his diary for 27 November:

> It looks as though all the boots in England have been bought up, as they now began to arrive for issue; boots of every description and colour, until the regular army pattern could be supplied in sufficient quantities.[8]

He added later:

> Uniforms of various kinds also began to arrive, and we were a motley crew. No doubt I looked very resplendent in a full dress red tunic which fell to my lot, and very proud I was when I went home in it for Christmas. The cap was minus a badge, these being at

Right: 11766 L/Cpl Harry Shillaker, 7th Battalion, photographed in December 1914 at Aldershot. He wears the old red full dress tunic. Supplies of these tunics were issued to the 7th Battalion only in 1914, and were worn until Khaki became available in the Spring of 1915. Below: The reverse of Harry's portrait, with a message to his sister. Mrs Freda Nicholson

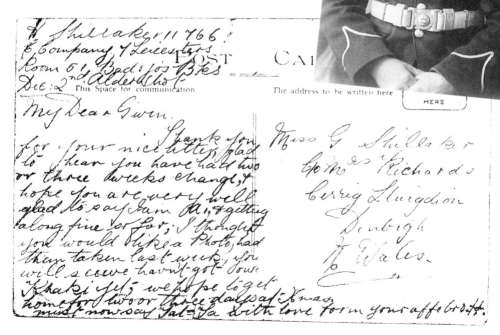

a premium, and fetching, when obtainable, half a crown.[9]

The civilian overcoat mentioned previously completed the outfit until November 1914, when white buckskin Slade-Wallace pattern ammunition pouches, and Lee-Metford rifles of similar Boer War vintage arrived at Aldershot. Around the same time winter weather also arrived, with the consequence that Bourley camp became a quagmire. Anyone who has ever spent time under canvas in the autumn or winter can imagine the difficulties which the men of the Leicestershire battalions faced. Dick Read remembered another unpleasant aspect, in addition to the chill of the damp ground, and the wind howling under the canvas tent flaps:

> *Although Latrine buckets were placed in position every night, occupants of the crowded tents had great difficulty in emerging without treading on someone, and in bad weather anything could happen in the dark, if the culprits thought themselves unobserved. On paynights, with strong beer at only a few coppers a pint, this evil was at its worst.*[10]

David Kelly, by now a second-lieutenant with the 6th Battalion, also recalled that

> *It was a dismal winter of mud and rain, and the overcrowding led to occasional friction among both officers and men - the latter once engaged in a mass combat we had to quell - the dividing line apparently being blue trousers against khaki.*[11]

The friendly rivalries between units, which in wartime breed both renewed effort and greater efficiency, had here under the trying conditions of training boiled over into aggression and in-fighting.

Shortly before Christmas 1914 the 8th and 9th Battalions, which had been under canvas, moved into vacated barrack blocks at Aldershot. The conditions at Bourley had become so bad that the military authorities finally had to act.

> *The chief trouble we had to contend with at Bourley was mud - pure unadulterated mud. After a fine summer we had a wet autumn and the constant rain on the very soft ground coupled with the never ceasing tramp of feet in the camp, quickly turned the once fair camp into a large mud bath with tent islands dotted about in it. This took place in the latter part of October and gradually got worse until at last it was so bad that we were forced to evacuate. It is most objectionable to be in tents, as thick as 12 to 14 in a single tents and have 2 or 3 inches of mud right up to the tent. One could never go out without getting up to the ankles in it and the consequence was that the mud was nearly as thick inside the tents as outside – it got on everything, blankets and kit, and yet under these circumstances one was expected to turn out on parade clean and smart in every particular – the army takes no excuses; it had to with regard to boots in those days, however, for the use of stilts would have been the only way to obviate it. Anyone in the Aldershot district or in Aldershot, could always tell from which*

camp we came as the boots always wore the trade mark even after polishing them in some grass en route. It simply would not come off. The other numerous camps in the neighbourhood were pitched for the most part on sandy or gravelly ground.

During the last few days at the camp conditions grew from bad to worse and rumour came round about the end of November that we were to move into barracks at Aldershot on December 3rd. It was mighty cold camping out at this time of year, though we had three blankets apiece and for the last month or so floorboards were installed in the tents - and they were needed.

By the last day of November, the mud everywhere near the camp was a full six inches deep and during the night there was a most violent rain and wind storm. This put the 'tin hat' on the camp entirely; most of the tents were torn and shattered and on going down for breakfast, everyone cold, wet and miserable, with rain still falling fast , one found that the whole of the Mess Tents were blown down and looked a sorry sight indeed, and we had to carry our meals up to our own tents from the cook house. This seemed to decide the authorities for we struck tents that day, during the afternoon, and took over one half part of Talavera barracks[12],

recalled Bacon, who added that a roaring fire in the grate of one of the barrack rooms soon cheered himself and his comrades.

Some of the luckier NCOs and men managed to obtain a leave pass to enable them to return home to their families at Christmas - one of these fortunates was Arthur Cave, who went home resplendent in the red tunic with which he had recently been issued. For most, however, the festive season was spent in the less than cheery surroundings of Aldershot. A chilly Christmas was spent by Dick Read and his comrades of the 8th Battalion,

Above: 16005 Pte Arthur Atterton Dolby, 7th Battalion, who died on 28 December 1914, the battalion's first loss. He lived at Luffenham, Leicestershire. Right: Dolby's grave in the Gun Hill Cemetery, Aldershot.

Sarah Saunders-Davis

in Buller Barracks, with a Christmas meal comprising cold tinned herrings, bread, and lukewarm tea, with a fire built from smashed wooden crates which had been raided from the coal yard of the nearby Gun Hill railway station.

Shortly before the New Year the Leicestershire battalions suffered one of their earliest casualties: Private Arthur Atterton Dolby of South Luffenham, 7th Battalion, died on 28 December 1914, of pneumonia, aged 26, in Cambridge Hospital, Aldershot. He was buried with full military honours in the nearby Gun Hill cemetery, and left a widow and two children. Other early deaths had been those of Private Henry Albert Carter, of the 6th Battalion, who died on 6 December 1914, and Private Henry James Williams, also of the 7th who died on 26 December 1914. Like Dolby, Williams too was laid to rest in the Gun Hill cemetery. There can be little doubt that the harsh conditions which had been endured during the autumn and early months of winter contributed to much illness among the men before they had even proceeded upon active service.

One pouring wet afternoon in January 1915, Lord Kitchener arrived at Aldershot to see the New Army formations raised in his name. Dick Read recalled:

'A' Company, 6th Battalion, photographed in January 1915. The officer seated second from right is 2/Lieut J.H.Hopewell. John Taylor

thousands of us, drawn up on the Queen's Parade, stood for hours in ankle deep mud and water in our makeshift civvy overcoats, soaked to the skin. At length there were shouted commands from somewhere in front, then more shouting. Our new officers drew their new swords and stood at the 'present'. We had no arms; we just tried to stand to attention. No one had the faintest idea what it was all about. Then, through the driving rain, we glimpsed the bobbing upper portions of a cloud of what must have been horsemen passing in front ... and they were gone. Officers sheathed their swords through the slits made for the purpose in their new, soaking wet greatcoats - all except our platoon officer, Ward. He pushed the point of his sword through the side of his coat, thus making a new slit several inches long. It was the only bright spot in our day. Later we learned that Kitchener had been showing the French War Minister, Millerand, some of his New Army.[13]

At the beginning of 1915 the battalions began route marches and more strenuous training, including a march to Reading where the Huntley and Palmers Biscuit factory provided a billet for the 8th Battalion for a night. The 9th also proceeded to the Reading area for a short spell, being billeted in Swallowfield and Arbourfield. It was here that the men of the 9th at last received their khaki uniforms. To the critical eye of D.A. Bacon, with a background in the textiles and garments trade, these first uniforms were less than spectacular in quality:

January 1915. Soldiers of the 6th Battalion on a route march. Note the diversity of equipment, including Boer War vintage Slade Wallace equipment, and both long and short model Lee Enfields. Only the 6th Battalion were dressed in Khaki at this time. John Taylor

A platoon of 'A' Company, 8th Battalion, practising trench digging under the watchful eye of their officers, during the battalion's brief stay in the Reading area. Greg Drozdz

> *These [uniforms] arrived in great crates and platoons were marched up to them one at a time to be fitted under the supervision of the Quartermaster and Quartermaster-Sergeant. I say fitted, though really those first outfits and caps of Khaki were awful affairs, ranging in colour from yellow-brown to bright green and one had the greatest difficulty in getting the two garments to match. As regards the cut of the coats in particular, it was terrible, and the wonder was that any men could be found to fit them; some of the collars diverged at all sorts of angles and often one side was as much as an inch lower than the other. This was perhaps the expected result of clothes being made at an unprecedented rate and by people who had largely never made clothes before. Still, fit or no fit, we were all very pleased to get into Khaki.*[14]

Then, in March, developments began apace. The 6th Battalion, which had been earmarked for the original 9th Division, the 7th which had been destined for the 15th Division, and the 8th and 9th Battalions which were part of the 23rd Division, were now officially drawn together, and were soon to become the 110th Brigade of the newly formed 37th Division. At the same time the four battalions loaded supplies and stores and entrained for Kent and south Hampshire to begin serious exercises and manoeuvres.

The 6th Battalion went into billets in Liphook, the 7th in the Andover area, while the 8th went to Folkestone and the 9th to New Romney. Men of the 8th were billeted in private houses in the Leas and along Sandgate Road, and likewise the men of the other battalions were placed among ordinary families in their respective areas. Arthur Cave, with others was put up by a Mr Cooper, a confectioner, of Old Winton Road, Andover. Civilians who had rooms to spare in their houses were often given little say in the matter when billets were required, but could expect to receive handsome financial recompense from the army for their trouble.

At the same time uniforms and equipment began to arrive - khaki serge for those who did not already have it, supplies of the modern SMLE rifle, and stocks of the new 1914 pattern leather harness and equipment

Old Winton Road, Andover. Houses on this street provided billets for men of the 7th Battalion including Arthur Cave. Sarah Saunders-Davis

A 7th Battalion route march, Andover spring 1915. Whilst the officers wear khaki, the NCOs and men here are still clad in the red tunics issued to the 7th Battalion at Aldershot. Sonny Monk

A photograph taken on the same street, some weeks later. Headed by the drums and fifes, the 7th Battalion marches to church parade, Andover, spring 1915. Red tunics have now been replaced by khaki. Steve Law

This 7th Battalion group in Andover in late 1915 now wear newly issued khaki uniforms, but only one man has a cap badge. 15743 Pte (later A/Sgt) William Tidmas is seated on the upturned bucket. Mrs D.M Tidmas

A 9th Battalion group photographed at Romney in Kent, 1915. Rose Holyoak

9th Battalion men drawn up on parade outside their billets in Kent, Spring 1915. Note the fact that still not everyone possesses a complete uniform. The Lance Corporal nearest the camera is Walter Partridge of Loughborough. Yvonne White

The 9th Battalion marching to church, Romney in Kent, early spring 1915. Rose Holyoak

An 8th Battalion route march through Folkestone, March 1915. Mrs S.Chatham

Above left: The top of the Dover Road, leading up to the 'Valiant Sailor'. Above right: The pub 'The Valiant Sailor' in Folkestone, at the top of the hill on the Dover Road. Many times, weary and exhausted during a route march, the men would pass this location in the spring of 1915. Roger Lewis

Former 8th Battalion billets in Folkestone in Sandgate Road (left) and on the Lees (right). Roger Lewis

Machine gun section, 8th Battalion, in Kent in the Spring of 1915. Note the wooden guns. The soldier back row sixth from right is Dick Read. At the left-hand end of the seated row is 14372 L/Cpl J.E.Price who was killed on 14 July 1916, and who lies in Flat Iron Copse cemetery. John Taylor

(identifiable in photographs by its 'S' shaped buckle in the style of a snake). Now at last, the men of the Leicestershire Brigade began to feel like real soldiers. Dick Read remembered:

> We now paraded proudly and with redoubled smartness, and marched incessantly for long route marches in full equipment. Our Battalion band became a reality, and I'm sure that survivors of the 110th Brigade will never forget the long and arduous ascents of the hill on the Dover Road, with the 'Valiant Sailor' at the summit, and the Capel turn.[15]

Strenuous route marches such as this served to harden the men's feet to marching, and to improve the general physical fitness of those who were out of condition.

At the end of April 1915, the 110th Brigade came together officially for final training at Perham Down camp, on Salisbury Plain, near Tidworth. David Kelly now encountered the new brigade commander for the first time:

> We had now become a Leicester Brigade - 6th, 7th, 8th and 9th battalions - under the command of Sir Guy Bainbridge who had served with Kitchener in the Sudan and with the Mounted Infantry in the Boer War. Bainbridge, who was by temperament an old-fashioned Cavalry officer, came to my Colonel as CO of the Senior Battalion and asked him for a 'Galloper'[ie. a mounted officer who carries messages] ... it was precisely because I was almost the only Oxford man in my Battalion that I was transferred to Brigade Headquarters, and thereby had an infinitely more interesting as well as more comfortable war. My Colonel had probably decided that I would never be much use as a regimental officer; the Brigadier was able to boast that he had 'an Oxford double-first' (an exaggeration, but his words) on his personal staff, while I obtained a tent to myself, a groom and a batman, and had little to do but ride about with the Brigadier and make notes of regimental deficiencies; so everyone was satisfied.[16]

16112 Pte Thomas Hall, 8th Battalion photographed in a Folkestone studio, 1915. Steve Law

Life in the ranks at Perham Down was somewhat different. Here the activities included firing one's musketry courses on the ranges. Those with an aptitude for this could hope to gain 3d per day extra proficiency pay, if their standard of musketry was sufficient for them to be rated as a First Class Shot, or a Marksman. It was also here at Perham Down, that the 110th Brigade's unique scheme of battle insignia was probably devised. There seems to have been no precedent for this outside of the brigade, and little has been written about it, so in consequence its origins are not clear.

Tents of the 9th Battalion camp at Perham Down, around April 1915. Jim Briggs

A platoon of the 7th Battalion at Perham Down, 1915. 12544 Pte A.E.Smith, back row third from left, was to serve from 1914 to 1918 with this Battalion without being wounded. Mr S. Smith

Nevertheless it appears fairly certain that the system was composed of pieces of different coloured cloth, which were sewn on to the left hand side of the wearer's collar. The 6th Battalion apparently wore a black patch, those of the 7th a red one, the 8th green, and in the 9th a yellow patch was worn. This system, like all such schemes devised in the First World War, was

Below: A Lance Corporal of the 9th Battalion, from Northampton. The light coloured collar patch is clearly visible in this studio portrait.
John Taylor

Below: By contrast, the patch on the collar of this private soldier is darker, possibly the red or green of the 7th and 8th Battalion, but not as dark as the distinctive black patch of the 6th Battalion. The scheme adopted in the early part of the war is not well documented, but it would seem likely that the 6th Battalion wore black collar patches, the 7th red patches, 8th green patches, and the 9th a yellow or white patch.
Steve Law

Below: As this photograph shows, any scrap of material would seem to have been deemed adequate to serve as collar insignia, provided it was of the correct colour! It seems likely that the men were told off to find material for the patches, rather than it being issued, due to the inconsistencies in size, shape, and position. Steve Law

intended to deprive information of the wearer's formation to the enemy. However, it had further uses: Charles Monk, of the 7th Battalion, recalled many years later that:

> *If you were in trouble and were caught by the Military Police, and you had a Tiger on your [badge], well they asked you which battalion you'd come from, if you were in the 6th you could say 8th, or if you were in the 8th you could say 6th. But if you had a red or a green patch, they knew where you were from. Ours in the 7th was a red patch.*[17]

Much of the training covered field work, crossing the countryside at night on a compass bearing, and individual skills such as signalling. One old soldier who had re-enlisted in the 6th Battalion wrote home to Leicester where his sisters and brother-in-law were still living, from Perham Down, in April 1915:

> *Dear Brother & Sisters,*
>
> *Just a few lines in answer to your letter I am please [sic] that you are in good health & got papers all right & [I] don't remember what you mean about my medals they are safe if I do go out and get knock [sic] over I am left everthink [sic] to Lizzie so you will have to ask her for them I am glad things are all right we are on night operations 3 nights [a] week beside field work in the day it is getting hot again. How is Doris getting on at school I hope she likes it Jack how do you like Swedish Drill I see Fosse is about bottom I was surprised Sheffield won the cup do you hear anything off Bill I cannot get in touch with him & I hope he is all right I think this is all this time from your loving brother Jack.*
>
> *No 11776 Sgt J.Carr D Coy*
> *6 Service Batt Leic Regt*
> *Perham Down Camp*
> *Salisbury Plain Hants xxxxx for Doris*[18]

The fact that Carr had completed his army will in his pay book, leaving his medals to (presumably) his wife, indicates that the thoughts of the men were turning more seriously now to active service. Leicester Fosse, of whom Carr was obviously a keen follower, later became Leicester City Football Club.

Dick Read remembered those last days spent in England, and the finer weather at last, with some degree of fondness:

7th Battalion at dinner, Perham Down, 1915. John Taylor

6th Battalion at dinner, Perham Down 1915. John Taylor

> *In lovely summer weather we trained as a Division, the scheme being an advance on, and the storming of, the old town of Newbury, the defenders being one of our brigades. On the return exercise to Tidworth, our 110th were the defenders. It was all good fun, and may have been of some use to our officers. To augment our numbers, several pairs of us had to carry pole targets - silhouettes of six or more soldiers in the 'prone' position, fixed at intervals along a long pole. Across sometimes thickly wooded country, this became really hard work at times.*[19]

Also whilst at Perham Down, the final deficiencies in equipment were made up. For months, Dick Read as a member of the 8th Battalion machine gun section had trained with wooden models of the Vickers machine gun. Now, at last American made Lewis machine guns began to arrive. Initially disappointed at not receiving the weapons which they had studied for so long, Dick and his comrades quickly came to appreciate the merits of the Lewis gun. It was lighter and more portable than the cumbersome Vickers, and its ammunition was carried in a drum magazine with a 47-round capacity. This again had advantages over the canvas belts used to feed the Vickers, being easier to change in a hurry, particularly in the heat of battle.

With these last details now being attended to, it could not be long before the battalions proceeded overseas. The men of the brigade were inspected on 25 June 1915, by HM King George V, a sure sign that they had reached the level of competence required for the army to feel comfortable showing them off. Speculation as to the destination of the Leicestershire battalions was rife in the final weeks, with the rumour-mongers favouring a destination in the

Middle East, or perhaps Gallipoli. In the event, it was to be France. The news that the 110th Brigade was leaving Perham Down came suddenly, and no embarkation leave was granted. A number of men, especially those who were married, attempted to leave camp or 'break out' that weekend, but most of those who did so were quickly detained by the Military Police either on their way or at home. The home addresses of the men were of course known to the army, and in some cases the Redcaps were even waiting to pick them up as they alighted from the trains that they had caught. The final evening before embarkation, some members of the 7th Battalion were seen serenading their colonel outside the officers' mess marquee, with the refrain, 'You've got a kind face you old bars-tard, you ought to be bloody well shot'. Under different circumstances the culprits might have found themselves on a charge of insubordination. However, with active service only hours away, and with officers and men welded now into a fighting machine (in so much as officers and men could be welded together, without yet having experienced the shared dangers of real warfare), the incident was taken in the good spirit in which it was intended. The only results were hoots of laughter.[20]

Through out the spring of 1915, as the battalions of the 110th Brigade trained and route marched across southern England, back in Leicestershire recruiting continued apace. In February and March German machine guns were brought back to Leicester following a trench raid by the 2nd Battalion in December 1914. They were a familiar sight at recruiting rallies, and curious onlookers jostled for a better view. New recruits continued to come forward. Jack Horner of Leicester, not yet 18 in 1915, was to join the 8th Battalion, and remembered:

It was a cold grey day on March 12th 1915 when my pal Bill Hill and I were going back to work in the afternoon. I was in the engineering trade, Billy in the shoe industry. I was working 48 hours per week for a wage of 7 shillings per week, and one and a half pence a day for going in at 7 o'clock in the morning to light the fires - that was my spending money, spent in riotous living - a piece of fish with chips, on a plate and eaten in a fish

There is a place called Tidworth
In the wilds of Salisbury Plain
If I could only but escape
I'd ne'er go back again

The place is noted far & wide
A depot for recruits
Trench digging and route marches
What wear out all your boots

The scenery is beautiful
You should see 'Nine Tree Hill'
Where we go through a performance
Which folks call 'Swedish Drill'

We rise each morn at half past five
Just when 'Reveille' blows
And practice rapid marching
In charge of NCOs

Sometimes we go shooting
To try and earn our bounties
But some of the shots I fired myself
Could be found in several counties

Tidworth is alright in its place
With its valleys and its dells
But I would rather be in France
Or else the 'Dardanelles'

To find a place like Tidworth
Many miles you'd have to roam
But I wish the war was over
And I was back at home

G.W.Sleath 19/7/15

George Sleath's poem, Tidworth. Jean B.Sleath.

A 9th Battalion group at Perham Down camp, Summer 1915. This group are clearly ready for action, and the photo illustrates the soldiers' kit which was now complete. Note the SMLE with long bayonet, large haversacks on the back, and leather equipment rig. Pete & Sue Sturman

The mascot of the 6th Battalion: the youngster is John Nobbs, aged about 5, the son of Lieutenant J.T.S.Nobbs. He wears a miniature version of his father's uniform. This photograph was taken in the back garden of Nobbs'house, 81 Blaby Road, South Wigston.

Margaret Nobbs

and chip shop in Churchgate, all for two pence, then later, seated in the Gods at the Palace...The doors opened, and there was a race for the front seats, to see all the great stars of variety. I was just over 17 years old at that time, and on the way to work, we were discussing things in general, when one of us, I don't recall who, suggested that we go and join the army. No sooner said than done![21]

Horner and his pals walked to the recruiting office in Humberstone Gate. There a recruiting sergeant gave them each the two pence to get a tram to Saffron Lane, and thence to Wigston Barracks. Instead, they walked the three and a half miles, and pocketed the two pence.

A sergeant soon took a few of us in hand, and took us to the clothing store to be kitted out.

The Quartermaster Sergeant, QM: 'Your name ?'

'Horner, J.W.'

'Your number is 17411, and that stays with you as long as you're in the Army' One of his assistants took me in his care.

'Take your coat off' He

67

RECRUITING OFFICE

5,000 "LEICESTERS" Now at the FRONT ASK 2,000 MO[RE]
LEICESTER MEN TO JOIN THEM

Spring 1915 – this banner outside the town hall in Leicester leaves citizens in no doubt that their country still needs them. Courtesy of Leicestershire Record Office

measured chest, shoulders, leg length, and went behind the counter and produced a suit [of Khaki].

'Try this on - not bad, see the tailor this afternoon.'

Then all the other items of kit were issued, shirts, socks, shaving kit, old-type razor, brush and soap...Every item had to be stamped by stencil with indelible ink, except the knife, fork and spoon, ie eating irons. All that lot, boots included, were put in a kit bag, already stamped with your name and number, so with our great-coats hanging on our arms, we marched off to the barrack block.[22]

Another lad who enlisted later in 1915, also eventually to serve with the 8th Battalion, was George Holt, a young porter with the Ashby and Nuneaton Joint Railway. Having trained as a Lewis gunner in England, he was to reach the 8th with a reinforcement draft in early 1916.

From November 1914 through to the spring of 1915, hundreds more recruits like Jack Horner and George Holt continued to volunteer. With the 6th, 7th, 8th and 9th Battalions already at or near their full establishment, these men were in the main at first posted to the newly raised 10th Battalion at Portsmouth. Originally conceived as a service battalion like its sisters, the 10th

17411 Private J.W. Horner, 10th (later 8th) Battalion, shortly after his enlistment in March 1915. He has no cap badge, and wears an ill-fitting suit of khaki.

Ernest Edgar Durrant (later 17811, 9th and 7th Battalions) in 1914. He was a railwayman on the Great Central Railway, and joined the army in June of 1915. Fergus Durrant

George Holt, left, a porter with the Ashby and Nuneaton Joint Railway at Snarestone station, photographed in 1915 shortly before his enlistment. Right, Holt shortly after his enlistment in late 1915. Mr Ken Holt

was however soon re-designated as a Reserve Battalion. It acted as a pool to train and hold reinforcements for the other four. Many of these men would soon cross the Channel, in the wake of the 110th Brigade, to fill gaps in its ranks as the casualties began to mount.

In March 1915, Private William Buckingham of the 2nd Battalion Leicestershire Regiment won the Victoria Cross at the Battle of Neuve Chapelle. He returned to England to recover from the wounds which he had

Left to right: Pte Togo Bolesworth DCM, Pte William Buckingham VC, L/Cpl T.Newcombe DCM & Russian Cross of St George, a local dignitary, and Sgt Payne of the depot, at a recruiting rally at Barwell. Buckingham eventually tired of his role in recruiting, and elected to return to France. He was killed on the Somme in September 1916. Mrs K.Best

received in the action, and from the summer of 1915 through to early 1916, along with other 'Leicestershire Heroes' who had been decorated, he toured the county and assisted the campaign for recruits. Buckingham's story was a poignant one. He was an orphan, and had been brought up in the Cottage Homes in Countesthorpe. As soon as he was old enough, he had enlisted in the army. During his period of convalescence he also found time to return to visit the orphaned boys in the Cottage Homes, who were thrilled to see him. However, like many others, Buckingham was a reluctant hero who eventually tired of his role in recruiting, and asked to return to active service. Posted to the 1st Battalion, he was killed on the Somme in September 1916. His presence in the county during the time he was back in Leicestershire was undoubtedly an inspiration to many of those who subsequently enlisted for service with the 110th Brigade.

1 A.C.Cave, unpublished typescript diary. 5.9.14
2 D.A.Bacon. Unpublished typescript memoir, LRO, p5
3 Bacon, p5
4 I.L.Read, 'Of Those We Loved', (Pentland Press, 1994) p505
5 Bacon, op cit. p7
6 Bacon, op cit. p7
7 Bacon, op cit. p11
8 Cave, op cit. 27.11.14
9 Cave, op cit. 27.11.14
10 Read, op cit. pp505-506
11 D.V.Kelly, The Ruling Few (Hollis & Carter, 1952), p90
12 Bacon, op cit. p12
13 Read, op cit. p120
14 Bacon, op cit. p14
15 Read, op cit. p507
16 Kelly, op cit. p90
17 Charles J.Monk. Interview with author, 1989.
18 Sgt J.Carr, original manuscript letter. LRO DE 4136/21
19 Read, op cit. p508
20 Quoted in Read, op cit. p5
21 J.W.Horner, typescript memoir, author's collection.
22 Horner, op cit.

One of the 'Leicestershire Heroes' who accompanied Buckingham VC on his recruiting tour: 11159 L/Cpl A.G.Robinson of Hinckley who had been awarded the Russian Medal of St George for bringing in a wounded Gurkha officer, under fire, during the Battle of Neuve Chapelle in 1915. Mrs K.Best

New recruits at the regimental depot, Wigston Barracks, in the summer of 1915. Duncan Lucas

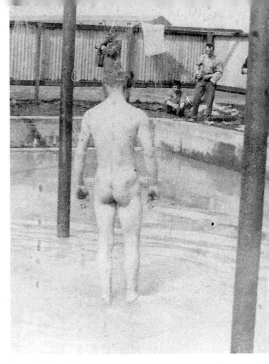

Officers with a motorcycle. Margaret Nobbs

Scenes at the 6th Battalion camp, Perham Down, Spring 1915: Who is the mysterious nude bather ?!
Margaret Nobbs

Lieutenant Nobbs on his motorcycle. Margaret Nobbs

Lieutenant G.E.E. Strong. Margaret Nobbs

Captain W.P.Deane. Margaret Nobbs

Captain C.G.A.Cox. Margaret Nobbs

Lieutenant J.W.Burdett (Transport Officer). Margaret Nobbs

Battalion transport and field cookers. Margaret Nobbs

A 6th Battalion group at Perham Down, Spring 1915. This photograph shows 10990 Pte John Shorthouse of Hinckley, who was later killed on the Somme. Greg Drozdz

A group (possibly 'A' company) from the 8th Battalion Leicestershire Regiment, 1915. The completeness of the uniforms, and the fact that everyone now seems to have a SMLE rifle, suggests that this was taken at Perham Down. Steve Law

Another 8th Battalion group, taken around the same time. Mr Eric Kellaway

8th Battalion Machine Gun Section football team, Perham Down 1915. John Taylor

Officers of the 9th Battalion Perham Down, around April 1915
Back row: Lieut. A.C.N.M.-P. deLisle, Sec-Lieut. S.T.Hartshorne, Sec-Lieut. P.E.Bent, Sec-Lieut. W.A.Barrand, Sec-Lieut. W.J.Wright, Sec-Lieut H.J.Barrand, Sec-Lieut. C.E.N.Logan, Sec-Lieut. O.J.Hargraves, Sec-Lieut G.G.Hargraves, Lieut A.V.Poyser (RAMC).
Third row: Lieut H.F.C.Anderson, Lieut A.S.Bennett, Sec-Lieut. F.A.Barrett, Sec-Lieut S.W.Sheldon, Sec-Lieut. B de H. Pickard, Sec-Lieut H.S.Rosen, Sec-Lieut F.E.Papprill, Sec-Lieut.F.C.Warner, Sec-Lieut M.L.Hardyman, Sec-Lieut. F.Cresswell, Sec-Lieut H.Y.Martin, Lieut H.E.Milburn, Sec-Lieut A.G.E.Bowell.
Second row: Capt. J.B.Baxter, Capt. A.W.L.Trotter, Capt. C.R.Dibben, Capt. G.C.I.Hervey, Major J.G.Mignon (2nd in command), Col. H.R.Mead, Major R.B.Unwin, Capt & Adjt. F.N.Harston, Capt. A.E.Boucher, Capt. F.H.Emmet, Lieut & QM W.Hunt.
Front row: Lieut G.E.G.Tooth, Sec-Lieut A.A.D.Lee, Sec-Lieut F.Scott, Lieut H.M.Henwood.

Warrant Officers and sergeants. Note the Regimental Sergeant Major, front row, fourth from left.

Machine gun section 9th Leicesters Perham Down. The weapons are Lewis guns, the item in the middle is a Barr & Stroud range finder, for calculating distance.

The cooks and pioneers, 9th Leicesters.

Battalion Scouts, 9th Leicesters.

Stretcher bearers, under the command of the Medical Officer, Lieut A.V.Poyser RAMC attached 9th Leicesters.

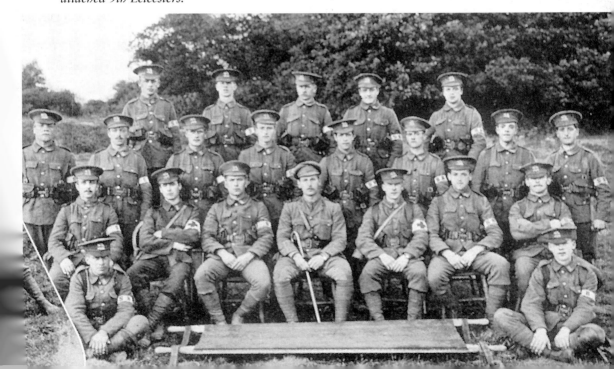

Number 1 platoon (A Coy)

Number 2 platoon (A Coy)

Number 3 platoon, A Coy (Sec.Lieut Pickard)

Number 4 platoon (A Coy)

Number 5 platoon, including front row Capt C.R.Dibben, OC 'B' Coy.

Number 6 platoon

Number 7 platoon

Number 8 platoon

Number 9 platoon (Lieut Hargraves)

Number 10 platoon

Number 11 platoon (Lieut Hartshorne). Present in this group are: Pegg, Robertson, Rydall, Milne, Rilett, Munn, Ringrow, Roberts, Martin, Ireland, Mears, Bates, Pick, Martin E.H., Lockton, Leadbetter, Moore, Gilliver, Morris, Marriot, Leeson, Riddington, Morrall, Muddimer, Roach.

Number 12 platoon, 9th Leicesters, Perham Down, Pte J.W.L. Holyoak of Kibworth fourth from the left on the third row from the back. Next to him, third from the left is Pte Harry Holyoak, his cousin who was to be killed at Croisilles in 1917. Note the battle insignia on the collars of the enlisted men.

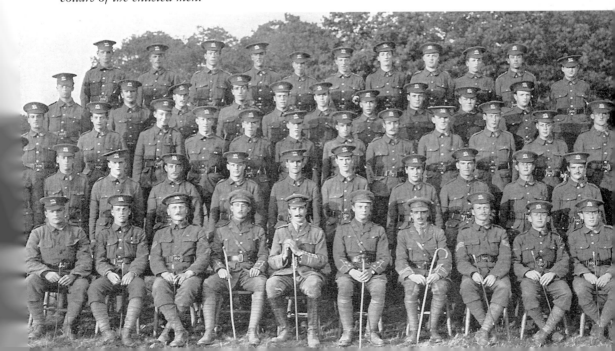

Number 13 platoon

Number 14 platoon

Number 15 platoon

Number 16 platoon. Seated extreme right, front row, is Bugler Fred Webb, who was to be killed on the Somme in 1916.

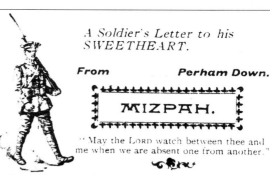

The dark shade of battle insignia worn on the collars identify this group as part of the 6th Battalion, Perham Down, 1915.

A card sent to his sweetheart by Pte Jack Holyoak, 9th Leicesters, from Perham Down Camp. Rose Holyoak

Drums of the 8th Battalion. John Taylor

Chapter Four

Foreign Fields

France at last

On 28 and 29 July 1915, the Leicestershire Brigade moved in stages to Ludgershall Sidings, not far from Tidworth, on Salisbury Plain. They began to load field cookers, transport wagons and other equipment on to railway carriages, and the 9th Battalion War Diary for 28 July 1915, reads as follows:

> *7.30am: The whole of the transport entrained at Ludgershall for Southampton, proceeding to Havre. The party numbered 3 officers, 107 other ranks (including 4 ASC attached) 78 horses, 19 four wheeled vehicles, 4 two wheeled. The personnel included Machine Gun Section, Transport, grooms, 9 signallers (with 6 bicycles) etc.*[1]

This gives some idea of the sheer scale of the undertaking, and it is perhaps rather surprising that according to the diary this voluminous amount of equipment took only an hour to load aboard the trains.

The Will of 12544 Pte Albert Smith, 7th Battalion, contained in his paybook and made out on 28 July 1915, immediately prior to embarking for France. Mr Sid Smith

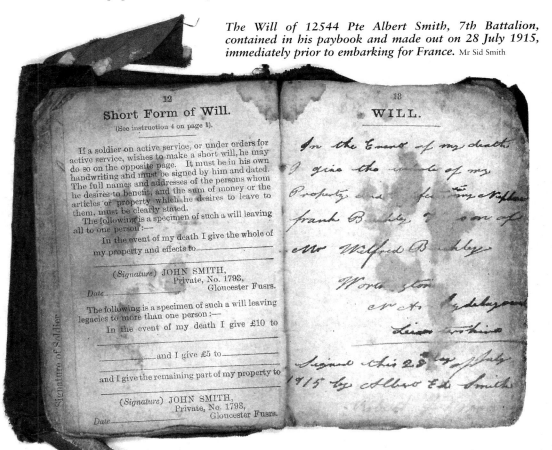

On the following day came the men themselves, who were bound for France at last. At Ludgershall the 9th Battalion alone required two express trains to accommodate its four companies, B and D companies travelling aboard X581, while A and C were on X582. As indicated by the 9th Battalion War Diary, some men, mostly cooks and transport men needed to prepare a reception for the brigade, travelled ahead of the main bulk of their battalions. Dick Read and a small contingent of the 8th Battalion crossed on 29 July, but unlike the rest of their comrades, travelled from

> GOD BLESS YOU AND BRING YOU SAFELY HOME AGAIN.
>
> Thoughts for our Soldiers and Sailors.
>
> "The Lord lift up His countenance upon thee and give thee peace."—*Numbers vi. 26.*
>
> "Be thou faithful unto death, and I will give thee a crown of life."
> —*Rev. ii. 10.*

This small card was given to Pte Jack Holyoak, 9th Battalion by a well-wisher on Guildford station on 29 July 1915, as the battalion proceeded to France. Rose Holyoak

Southampton to Le Havre. As the troop train from Ludgershall arrived in the traditional home port of the Merchant Navy, he remembered:

> [we] *were passing the backyards and streets of Southampton, waving to the girls and feeling thrilled generally. As we disappeared into the maze of the docks, we felt ourselves to be real soldiers at last; but our khaki was still very new and our buttons shone in the sunlight.*[2]

All afternoon Dick and his mates sweated and struggled to get limber after limber down from the goods wagons of the train to within reach of the cranes on the dockside. The cranes then lifted and swung them into the hold of a medium sized steamer, the Ellerman Line boat, SS *City of Dunkirk*. Horses, mules, limbers and supplies of every description were being loaded by similar parties up and down the dockside, until at last, around 4pm, the men themselves paraded for inspection, and then filed up the ship's gangway. With a destroyer escort, the *City of Dunkirk* edged out into the Solent and beyond the Isle of Wight. As Southampton disappeared into the sea mist, a sombre mood settled over the troops onboard. Many began to sing softly. Dick recalled:

> *In the gathering twilight of the summer evening the engines stopped; the pilot went down the ladder and jumped into the dinghy which came alongside from his waiting launch. As he jumped, he waved and shouted 'Good luck, boys!' The engines restarted, and as bells tinkled on the bridge and below, we all sang, 'The Anchor's Weighed'. To the sustained farewells of this old song, his little boat and the English coast were lost to view. For many who sang, it was in truth their vale to their native soil.*[3]

This last remark is particularly poignant, for of the original Leicestershire brigade which crossed that night some three thousand strong, nearly a half would be killed. Of these, a goodly proportion would not have returned to see England again after July 1915.

14967 Pte C.H.F. Barrowcliffe, 9th Battalion, in 1915. He left the battalion later, after being selected for officer training and receiving a commission.

John Taylor

Lieut D.V.Kelly, 6th Battalion, 1915. He was to become 110th Brigade Intelligence Officer, and later wrote '39 Months With The Tigers'.

By 10pm on 29 July the bulk of the remainder of the brigade had arrived at Folkestone docks, and began to load aboard troopships. The 7th Battalion was accommodated by the SS *Onward*, while the 8th Battalion boarded the SS *Golden Eagle*, and the 9th took the SS *St. Seiriol*. David Kelly recalled that the Leicestershire Brigade,

> *embarked and sailed from England in utter darkness and complete silence.*

It was, he observed, full of contrast with what one might have expected:

> *As the crowded troopships moved off in the night I remembered the illustrations of fourteen years before, showing South African troopships lined by cheering soldiers waving to the band and crowds ashore.*[4]

There was no fanfare, and there were no musicians, or cheering civilians to see off the 110th Brigade. Even were it not for the lateness of the hour, the people of Folkestone had by this stage of the war seen too many ships full of 'Tommys' bound for France to 'do their bit', for this kind of spectacle still to arouse excitement.

After what was for the most part a calm and uneventful crossing, on a beautiful and balmy summer's night, the majority of the Leicestershire men disembarked at Boulogne, between 11.30pm and 1.30am. However, a few other transports arrived slightly later as dawn was beginning to break, affording a good view of the docks of Boulogne to the curious Tommies on board. Few except the very enterprising among them would have travelled much beyond their own home district before this time, and scarcely any would have had any knowledge of France. They lined the gangways of the ships, craning for a better view of this strange and unfamiliar place. For

Boulogne docks and harbour – for many men of the 110th Brigade it was their first sighting of France. Ruth Broadhurst

A scene in Rue Thiers, Boulogne. Ruth Broadhurst

Dick Read, arriving in Le Havre that same morning, there was much of interest to be seen:

> With a blast from her siren, the City of Dunkirk got under way once more, drawing nearer to the forest of cranes and sheds and finding a channel through which we glided by a kind of esplanade into the dock system. We crowded to the ship's side to get our first close-up of France. The cafés with their chairs and tables outside, the quaint tramcars, the blue of the French soldiery and the darker blue of the police - the shuttered windows, the unfamiliar sounds and smells - all these intrigued us immensely.[5]

The first destination of the Leicestershire Brigade, as the men filed down the gangplanks of the ships and through the sleeping and still deserted ports, was a rest camp in the hills behind Boulogne. In the afternoon of 30 July they entrained once more, this time in enormous trooptrains pulled by the huge black locomotives of the 'Société du Chemin de Fer du Nord', and headed eastwards, towards the Franco-Belgian border. The officers and senior NCOs travelled in first or second-class passenger carriages, but the enlisted men would soon become used to the standard method of moving troops around on the railways of northern France: in cattle trucks marked *Hommes 40, Chevaux 8*. The destination of the locomotives was Watten, in the Pas de Calais. Dick Read, having acquired fresh straw for the floor of the truck shared by himself and a few mates, settled down to write a quick postcard to his parents, informing them that he was now of the BEF - British Expeditionary Force. Having scrounged a little hot water in some mess tins from the fireman of the engine, he and his comrades were able to wash and

11903 Sgt J. W. Matthews, 8th Battalion. An experienced NCO with Boer War service, he accompanied the battalion to France in July 1915.
Violet Matthews

An enormous troop train, of the Chemin de Fer du Nord.

shave for the first time in France. Then,

> *feeling fairly clean once more, we slid the doors back and sat down in the sunshine, dangling our legs over the side, and taking in as much as we could of the French countryside. All day we jogged along thus, living on bully beef, biscuits and tinned butter, and about four in the afternoon passed through Boulogne, then Calais.... It was dark when we were shunted into a siding near a station on which we read dimly 'Watten.'*[6]

Billets for troops in northern France were usually found in quiet villages some miles behind the lines, officers often in farmhouses or other large private dwellings, men in barns, factories, warehouses or even schools. Marching out of the station yard that night, Dick and his party of the 8th Battalion took a circuitous route to the village of Houlle, where the rest of the battalion was to join them. Here they were billeted in an empty brewery. Weary, footsore and hungry, but posted as sentry at the gates, Dick had his first opportunity to meet a French civilian:

> *A door opened behind me, in a house corresponding to the porter's lodge of the brewery, and I heard the clamp, clamp of wooden shoes over the stones of the yard as a girl carrying a pail went to the pump nearby. Straightening up, I watched her with interest and as she returned to the house she saw me, and bid me bonjour. Somewhat confused, but pleased, I returned her greeting as best I could...A few minutes later she returned with a basin of hot coffee and a long narrow slice of crusty bread. I don't think I had ever tasted anything more delicious and I told her so with many bons, whereat she smiled and pointed at my shoulder badges. 'Lei-ces-taires-hein? Leices-taire*

The 'PH' or Phenate Hexamine gas hood, used by the British army in France in 1915 and 1916. The correct method of wearing it involved tucking the bottom inside the collar of the tunic, to prevent the entry of gas. Taylor Library

Squairr?' She pronounced awkwardly. 'Long way to Tipperary-hein' with a laugh which disclosed a fine set of teeth. As she disappeared into the house, France was tolerable again I thought.[7]

For the next three days the Leicestershire Brigade remained at rest, inspecting kits and more importantly, learning gas drills and how to wear the grey flannel 'ph' gas hood. The Germans had first used poison gas the previous April, and now it was an unpleasant but accepted part of trench warfare. Then began a series of marches of about 20 kilometers a day, billeting each night in a different village. On 4 August, QMS Arthur Cave of the 7th Battalion noted in his diary,

The war is now 12 months old and we had not seen anything of it yet...My billet was a barn, but very comfortable as straw was plentiful.[8]

Over the next four days the brigade marched by stages up towards St Omer, then beyond to Eecke, where they rested for two days. In the hot August sun and on the uneven French pave, the last stage of the march had been a gruelling one. Thick khaki serge uniforms and puttees wound around the lower legs did not help matters, and dust thrown up by passing motor lorries added to the mens' discomfort by coating the back of already dry

L/Cpl Walter Partridge of Loughborough, 9th Battalion, in 1915. His brother, 10050 Pte H.C. Partridge was to die whilst serving with the 6th Battalion in 1917. Yvonne White

92

throats. By noon, many waterbottles were empty, and in the villages the men passed through could be seen stragglers and men who had fallen out from columns which had passed through earlier, waiting to be picked up by battalion transports later on. Dick Read noted that some were even prepared to flout standing orders and to chance their own lives in the process:

> One or two we even saw at cottage doors asking for water and tendering their bottles. We speculated as to whether it was worth the Field Punishment No.1 we were warned would be meted out, to men caught, in view of the danger of contracting typhoid and enteric from drinking water so obtained. Most of us were sufficiently intelligent to appreciate the good sense prompting this order. Moreover, we had seen the primitive sanitation prevailing, according to our standards, and already the taste of chlorine in our drinking water and the smell of chloride of lime were necessary accompaniments and guarantors of our daily lives.[9]

The next day, whilst the Brigade was bivouacked at a farm near Eecke, two men of the 8th Battalion were indeed awarded Field Punishment Number One, after having been caught filling water bottles on the line of march.

Left: 12496 QMS Joseph Ball, 9th Battalion, in 1915. He joined the battalion aged 43. Like many other Quartermasters in the Kitchener's Army battalions, his background in storekeeping (in this case with the accounts department of the GPO in Leicester) made him a natural choice for the appointment. Right: QMS Ball's son, 22074 Pte Joseph Reginald Ball. He served with the 7th Battalion for a time in 1917, before transferring to the DLI, in which uniform he is seen here. This is the only known documented case of a father and his son serving in the 110th Brigade, albeit in different battalions. Mrs M.Packwood

F.P.No.1 involved the individual concerned being tied to the wheel of a wagon for two hours each day, and was applied each day that a Battalion was out of the front line, until the sentence was complete. One of these two individuals in particular was destined to end his career in the army in sadness and ignominy.

By 9 August the men were bivouacked at Dranoutre, in the Kemmel district in Belgium, a short distance from the front line. The area took its name from Kemmel Hill, a fairly modest prominence by most standards, but which in this flat low lying part of Flanders dominated the countryside around. There was also a village of Kemmel, situated at the foot of the hill. In this sector the men were to receive instruction from experienced Regular battalions in the ways of trench warfare. Half a battalion at a time went up, with each company dispersed among a different unit to receive tuition. After a trip to the trenches near Locre on 11 August, Arthur Cave of the 7th Battalion noted in his diary:

Lieutenant Arthur Ernest Eaton, 7th Battalion. His home was on Evington Drive in Leicester, and he was an Old Wyggestonian. In 1915 he was battalion Bombing Officer.

> *First casualty in the battalion – L/Cpl Billings, wounded in the shoulder. Remaining two companies to the trenches. My first experience of delivering rations to the front line...Arrived firing line about midnight, bullets whistling past all the time, and everywhere ruins. The trenches were built up of sandbags, the ground here being too boggy for the ordinary underground trenches. Verey lights being sent up every few seconds on both sides turned night into day. Just as we were about to leave the line there was a terrific explosion which turned out to be a German mine, but which caused no damage.* [10]

In fact the first fatal casualty due to enemy action in the entire Leicestershire Brigade was sustained on this day, 11 August 1915. Private George Coates, a soldier of the 6th Battalion from Cheadle, Staffordshire, was killed in action probably by a sniper whilst under instruction in the trenches.

For Dick Read, the memory of moving up to the trenches for the first time was, in later years as an 'old hand' a source of amusement:

> *Afterwards we sometimes joked about it; how our Lewis Gun section followed the rear platoon of 'C' Company in single file across the dark fields; how tense we were and how anxious each of us was not to lose touch with the man in front; how we ducked involuntarily when the first stray bullets whined overhead or ricocheted; how by the light of a German Verey light we saw, thrown into eerie relief, the British graveyard and the wooden crosses – and how lost we felt in the blackness as the rocket petered out. Then – our first casualty, as we were crossing the last of the fields at the edge of a spinney, just before entering the communication trenches. As we passed him we heard the wounded man gasping as stretcher bearers tended him. He had been hit in the stomach and subsequently we were told that a sniping rifle was laid on this point by day and fired at intervals during the night.* [11]

David Kelly likewise recalled with wistful irony his feelings on entering the front line for the first time:

The first man of the entire 110th Brigade to be killed in France was 11534 Pte George Coates, of the 6th Battalion, whose death occurred on 11 August 1915.

John Taylor

94

I received my own baptism of fire during a first tour of the line, in the course of which exactly two bullets whined overhead. Perhaps no amount of subsequent experience can give the same thrill as the first exposure to fire, for nature, as the war so often proved, makes all things in time seem normal and stale. Otherwise...of all that week I retain chiefly the memory of swarms of greedy flies which haunted the filthy farm occupied by Brigade headquarters to which I had just been attached.[12]

Each company spent about a week in the front line, during which time, as well as learning to duck at the appropriate moment, the Leicestershire men were employed by their hosts for whatever fatigue work needed to be done to improve their positions. In this part of Belgium, with its high water table, trenches were rarely dug, and sandbag barricades or breastworks were the norm. These could be seen snaking across the flat countryside for quite a distance if one was prepared to put one's head over the top to have a look. With snipers so active, this was not advisable.

Dick Read's company of the 8th Battalion were in the vicinity of Wulverghem, in the care of the 3rd Battalion Royal Fusiliers, and 3rd Battalion Middlesex Regiment, of the 85th Infantry Brigade. At this stage in the war they still retained a high proportion of pre-war Regular soldiers, most of whom were Cockneys. The Leicestershire men could not fail to be impressed by the easy confidence of their hosts. For their part, the Middlesex men and the Fusiliers seemed only too willing to take the newcomers under their wing and to pass on valuable and potentially life-saving pieces of knowledge.

A group of Regulars from the Royal Fusiliers, Belgium, 1915. Liddle Collection

When the troops came out of the line, they found some of the first reinforcement drafts from the 10th Battalion waiting for them. These soldiers had crossed to France in the wake of the 'originals' about a week later. One of those men was Private Jack Horner, of Leicester, who was to be posted to the 8th Battalion upon his arrival in France. He recalled,

> *Having found the Battalion Headquarters, the Quarter Master Sergeant (QMS) blandly informed us that the battalion was having instruction in the trenches. It was on August 12th 1915 that we, the first reinforcement, of about forty men [reached] the battalion...We drew some rations, including corned beef (ie bully-beef) our staple food for months to come. We slept rough for the next two nights, in the fields, or the ditches around it, and no-one amongst us knew how to light a fire to brew up. In due course the Battalion arrived, on Shank's Pony, of course...having survived the baptism of fire, the first introduction to life in the trenches...We Rookies were soon drafted to our companies.* [13]

Horner's was but the first of a number of drafts from the 10th Battalion, which arrived over the next few months (the largest was probably that which arrived in France on 9 September 1915) in order to bring the brigade up to its full fighting strength.

The reinforcements were soon introduced to an unpleasant but undeniable truth of army life – if they spent any length of time overseas in France, they would certainly soon be infested with lice. The very fact that troops were continually on the move, being billeted in barns and sleeping in straw that had housed troops both British and French from a host of different units in the preceding weeks, made this almost inevitable. When out of the line, soldiers did the best they could to delouse themselves – Dick Read and his mates tried

> *all methods available, the favourite being the glowing end of a cigarette run along the inside seams of the trousers or jacket. When accompanied by a steady cracking, the cigarette end was doing its job. Now and again, one of us would exclaim at the size of one detected, such as 'I've got a cap badge! – What a beauty – Match this one!* [14]

The Leicestershire Brigade spent about a week in the Kemmel sector, and then, in the last week of August, entrained once more. This time, their destination was the pleasant undulating country south of Arras, with green fields, villages as yet untouched by the war, and clusters of woods and orchards. They detrained at Doullens on 26 August, and marched at night through deserted villages and misty fields to the village of Mondicourt. Here they were billeted for about a week, being among the first British troops to pass through this area. They were now in the sector of the front line held by the French Army. Signs of French military activity were all around, from cheery *Poilus* wandering around behind the lines, to batteries of the famous '75' or *Soixante-Quinze* field guns in woods and fields, and the latter attracted considerable interest on the part of the Tommies. The time at

16474 Pte George Wyman. An agricultural labourer from Ridlington, he was to be posted to the 7th Battalion in the autumn of 1915, after joining the 10th Battalion in December 1914.

A British No1 Mk III stick grenade, of the type which caused the tragedy at Mondicourt.

Mondicourt was occupied in yet more training, and on their last day spent in the area, tragedy struck the 8th Battalion. In a field outside the village, one of the recently formed bombing sections was receiving instruction in throwing the early pattern of British stick grenade, which pre-dated the more familiar Mills Bomb. One man, who was being shown how to throw a live device, accidentally dropped it. The grenade went off among a crowd of men, the result being that one officer, Lieutenant D.A.Baldwin, and five men were killed outright. Several others were wounded, three of whom died later that day.

The Leicester Brigade was now set to take over a stretch of trenches from the French, a short distance to the south. These positions faced the ruined village of Monchy-au-Bois, which lay immediately behind the German line, some distance to the north of the Somme sector. David Kelly was not the only member of the brigade to find both the appearance and the apparent attitude of the French Army in this area bemusing, particularly the possibly superficial air of negligence towards both military discipline, and to the condition of their trenches:

I made a preliminary tour of the whole line with Taudieres, a young French officer similarly attached to the headquarters of the French regiment we were relieving, and so received my first impression of the French at war, a spectacle which always fascinated me. Mr Belloc remarks somewhere that a French farmer will plant thorns where an

French soldiers, prepared for the cold, in the winter of 1915. The 110th Brigade took over its earliest positions from pragmatic little 'poilus' such as these.

Berles au Bois circa 1915: Rue Verte. Annie Damiens

Berles au Bois in 1915: The Marie. Annie Damiens

Berles au Bois. Rue du Moulin. Annie Damiens

English farmer will spend £4 on a gate, and that both methods keep out cows, and I often had the same feeling about the two national methods of waging trench warfare.[15]

Sentries seemed slack, and working parties rare among the French, and in many parts of this sector, the *Poilus* seemed to have adopted a live and let live approach to the Germans opposite. They rarely fired or attacked first when not engaged in a major offensive, but retaliated vigorously when fired upon.

Berles-au-Bois, the village taken over behind the lines as billets by the 6th and 8th Battalions, had previously been home to a French unit, the 69th Chasseurs á Pied. Dick Read and his comrades in one of the Lewis gun sections were allotted rooms in the courtyard of a large farm:

We now had leisure to examine our billet and make ourselves comfortable, if possible, before night fell. As neither house or barns were inhabited there was plenty of room, and we soon saw that our predecessors had known how to make the best of their good fortune. There was a profusion of wire-netting beds in the room our gun team had bagged, and as we threw down our equipment and stood our rifles and Lewis impedimenta against the walls, we marvelled at the many clever crayon and pencil sketches upon the walls – of girls either in the nude or in ravishing states of dishabillé. *There was not any doubt that the unknown artist was a professional; perhaps, we speculated, on the staff of* La Vie Parisienne *or* Pêle-Mêle. *Apparently most of the other rooms had received similar treatment. This alone put everyone in high good humour...*[16]

Jack Horner, also of the 8th, found Berles an equally charming place:

[It] appeared to be a small community of farm houses, and about 300 people. There was a road running straight through for about half a kilometre, which then forked, leading to two other villages, Pommier, right fork, Bienvillers au Bois left fork. A cul de sac almost in the centre, and on the left of the main road, were four or five farm houses, a few ordinary houses, and believe it or not, a small shop which sold everything – just like the Corner Shops back home, and a

An estaminet in Berles au Bois. Annie Damiens

pretty young Mademoiselle, about my age, used to serve us, and she didn't lack customers...[17]

However, Horner's billets were by no means as luxurious as those of Read!

Our platoon was billeted in a farm house...Each of us made sure that we had a good sleeping place, warm, and out of the draught. Myself and my mate Woody bagged an outhouse that was warm, dry and comfortable, but too near the midden in the centre of the forecourt, which smelt like Hell. Ah well! We didn't expect everything to be perfect.[18]

War time buildings in Berles as they appear today: This building (No 7 Rue Verte), viewed from two different angles, was once an estaminet frequented by Dick Read and his pals. Chester Read

About two kilometers to the south lay the village of Bienvillers-au-Bois, home to the 7th and 9th Battalions. Arthur Cave, as part of a company Headquarters staff, was able to bag a room in one of the best billets, a large villa which had been abandoned by its inhabitants. He described the situation in his diary for 4 September 1915:

It had apparently been left in a hurry by its owners, who had left behind beds and furniture. The Company Officers were

16783 Pte George William Joyce, 9th Battalion, of Ketton, Rutlandshire. Killed on 4 September 1915.

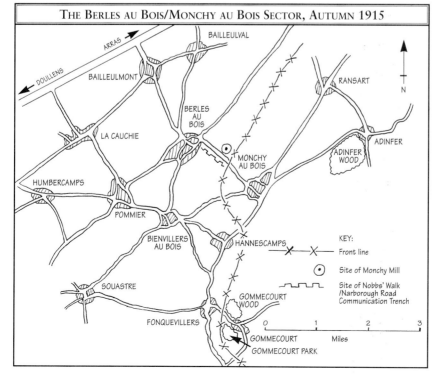

THE BERLES AU BOIS/MONCHY AU BOIS SECTOR, AUTUMN 1915

BAILLEULVAL
ARRAS
DOULLENS
BAILLEULMONT
RANSART
N
BERLES AU BOIS
LA CAUCHIE
ADINFER
ADINFER WOOD
MONCHY AU BOIS
HUMBERCAMPS
POMMIER
BIENVILLERS AU BOIS
HANNESCAMPS
SOUASTRE
GOMMECOURT WOOD
FONQUEVILLERS
GOMMECOURT
GOMMECOURT PARK

KEY:
Front line
Site of Monchy Mill
Site of Nobbs' Walk /Narborough Road Communication Trench

0   1   2   3
Miles

John Nobbs, by now a Captain and Adjutant of the 6th Battalion, photographed in late 1915.

Margaret Nobbs

Lieutenant D.V.Kelly (later Sir David Kelly), accompanied by the 110th Brigade's French liaison officer. This sketch was penned by the Frenchman.

accommodated in one half of the house upstairs, and the company staff in the other half, while the Company office was downstairs. The house was only a mile away from the front line at Monchy-au-Bois, and stood at the junction of the Monchy-Bienvillers Road. Bullets frequently hit the house. The village, including the church, was mostly in ruins, though quite a number of inhabitants remained.[19]

For the months that followed, life followed a familiar pattern in the trenches near Berles - the 6th and 8th Battalions relieved each other after a tour in the trenches, and the 7th and 9th did likewise. Here the Leicestershire Brigade, being in the same area for a number of months continuously, had the opportunity to name the trenches and saps in the locality according to their own tastes, and thus Narborough Road, Humberstone Gate, Gallowtree Gate, High Cross Street and Nobbs' Walk (after Captain J.T.S.Nobbs of the 6th Battalion), came into general use. In this sector, from the front line trenches the dark mass of Adinfer Wood could be seen (if one was careful) down the slope of No Man's Land and away in the distance. Before it lay the village of Monchy, in German hands. Behind the more northern British positions, held alternately by the 6th and 8th battalions, lay the ruins of Monchy Mill, which was occasionally used as a hide by snipers. Through the long grass of the now abandoned fields ran a path, from Monchy across no man's land to the Mill. This led to rumours around the battalions that the French who had previously held the sector had fraternised with their German opponents. In fact the path, which was rapidly becoming more overgrown, was a pre-war track once used by the villagers of Monchy.

These were in some ways idyllic times for the Leicestershire Brigade. The countryside was beautiful, and dotted with woods and orchards. Birds sang, and the only indication of the wholesale destruction which would characterise the later years of the war, came from the occasional shell. Apart from tours of duty in the front line, time could be spent walking, or in one of the estaminets in the villages. Here one could get a drink of *ving-blong* as the Tommies called it, or a simple meal. David Kelly wrote in his memoir:

> My chief memory of that golden autumn and hard winter in the trenches south of Arras is one of peace - peace that is in comparison with what came after. There was little shelling from either side (though enemy trench-mortar fire began to be annoying after November) trench raids had not become an obsession, and casualties were few, except in the depth of winter, from trench feet and trench fever.[20]

Kelly spent much of his time touring the front line, acting as liaison between the battalions and 110th Brigade headquarters. On many occasions this had meant wading through waist deep mud in communication trenches, but

101

A 'West' Bomb throwing engine, in the trenches in 1915.

Lieutenant (later Captain) F.E. Breacher, photographed by a French officer on 13 October 1915. Steve Law

on one particular tour, with his old battalion the 6th, Kelly went out on a patrol:

I went with the company commander on an eerie walk in Nomansland - which was however about one hundred and fifty yards wide there - and inspected the bodies of French territorials, in the old pre-war uniforms, which had lain out there for perhaps a year close to a sunken road leading [from Berles] *into the German held village of Monchy-aux-Bois. By some curious freak of nature one of them had been completely preserved as though turned to stone, with clearly marked features and a beard.*[21]

Here at Berles, the 8th Battalion was joined by an officer with a pedigree more unusual than most. Lieutenant Wallace McCutcheon was an American actor and dancer. With the USA still neutral at this time he like a number of his fellow countrymen, had decided to join the army of one of the Allied powers in order to fight against Germany. However, McCutcheon seems to have had some difficulty in mastering the system of orders in the British Army; he once ordered his men to 'Stack Guns', when what he meant to say was 'Pile Arms'.[22]

For the battalion officers and the men in the ranks, as the autumn of 1915 turned into winter the routine of one week in the front line trenches, followed by another in the reserve positions, continued. Static warfare such as this encouraged the development of trench mortars and bomb throwing engines, as over a period of time with the enemy in a fixed position, they could be adjusted to give a high level of accuracy. The German trench mortars were particularly feared, and the Leicestershire Brigade replied with a variety of engines for hurling grenades, such as the West Bomb Thrower,

Lieut. G.T.L. Ellwood, 6th Battalion, severely wounded while on a night wiring party on 18 October 1915. His home was the Rectory, at Cottesmore, Rutland.

and other similar catapults. Such machines could be extremely unpredictable, and at least one 7th Battalion man, Sergeant Cyril Mellors, received a Distinguished Conduct Medal for his quick thinking when dealing with the emergency when one misfired.

Casualties were light enough still to be a cause for comment in diaries and letters. One member of the 9th Battalion, Private W. March, recorded in his pocket book for 15 September:

> Trench digging at night 1 Harborough chap killed named Brotherton just in rear of firing line while digging.

The following day he noted: 'Brotherton buried went to the funeral.'[23]

It was not until November that the 6th Battalion suffered its first fatal officer casualty. Lieutenant John Dalrymple Champneys had taken a patrol out into No Man's Land in a fog. They had encountered some Germans, and had been fired upon, Champneys being mortally wounded. He had been left behind and as the fog lifted he was taken prisoner by the Germans. Shortly afterwards a German soldier shouted across No Man's Land that the English officer had died of his wounds in Monchy. The Germans buried his body, and marked it with a cross bearing details of his regiment, and when Monchy finally fell into British hands in 1917, the grave was still being tended. Whether by presentiment of his coming death, or perhaps simple common sense, Champneys had emptied his pockets of personal effects before going on patrol.

10976 Pte John Thomas Chater, 6th Battalion. He wears one of the goatskin overcoats, which were issued during the winter of 1915/16 to men of the 110th Brigade. The most prominent feature of these garments it was generally agreed was the appalling stench that they gave off when wet. Katrina Robson

Towards the end of the year the men were issued with goatskin jerkins to be worn over the khaki tunic, for added warmth. Dick Read's section were issued with theirs in Berles before leaving for a spell in the front line:

> As it was very cold we revelled in their warmth, and the village street looked like a scene in Lapland or Alaska. When the warmth engendered reached the skin coats, the smell became almost too strong for our stomachs in the billet. Nevertheless...we all wore our coats under our equipment as we set off to relieve the 6th Battalion once more for a four day tour of duty.[24]

As heavy winter rains fell, the condition of the trenches deteriorated steadily. As early as 2 November, Private March of the 9th Battalion noted:

> Relieved from the trenches by the 7th batt. Waist deep in water coming out in places arrived in billets in a nice mess.[25]

Meanwhile on the same day Arthur Cave recorded in his diary that,

> The trenches were now so bad that it was necessary to pave them with duckboards, and brace the back and sides with expanded metal, iron stakes and wire.[26]

By the end of that month, a number of hard frosts, combined with the rain, had made some communication trenches impassable. In these conditions, the health of the men was bound to be affected, goatskin coat or not. Private John Lord of Countesthorpe was 37 years of age when he enlisted for the 6th Battalion in 1914, making him among the oldest of the men who proceeded on active service. His diary for the end of 1915 serves to document not only the terrible weather endured in the line during this time, but also his own steady deterioration in health. The rigours of active service in these conditions were simply too much for him:

Sun 3 Oct: *Cold all day especially in our dugout I have a bilious attack not very bad. Frost again.*

Wed 20 Oct: *Cold bilious. Letter & parcel from Patience and letter from George.*

Thu 21 Oct: *Come out of trenches and go to 6th Leic. Cold & draughty.*

Fri 22 Oct: *Still at 6th Leic. The cold catches me and at night and get cramp in stomach. Sent 10 Francs home. White frost.*

Sat 23 Oct: *Cold settles in my back. Capt Weirmouth comes to see me.*

Thu 28 Oct: *Wet day trenches in very bad state, cannot get about without getting up knees in mud.*

Tues 2 Nov: *We come out about 2pm get wet through & I have another bilious bout. Write in green envelope to Patience, rain all day.*[27]

15617 Pte J.T.Lord, 6th Battalion, of Countesthorpe. He died on 17 January 1916. John Taylor

The bottoms of the trenches were now regularly flooded with several inches of water, and in places the duckboard pathways had floated away. What was worse, the sump holes of two or three feet in depth which had been dug beneath the boards with the intention of draining away some of the water, now became dangerous mantraps for the troops struggling with equipment up to the front line. In some cases, the only option was to leave the safety of the trench, and advance to the front line along the top. On one occasion, Read and his Lewis gun team were forced to take this dangerous step, only to discover once they had left their trench that they could see swarms of tiny figures clad in Feldgrau moving about in the distance. The Germans, whose trenches at some points near Monchy were lower than those of the British opposite, were in a similar predicament, and for some time, each side was

The ruins of Monchy Mill, around 1915. Annie Damiens

too concerned with its own problems to fire at the other. Dick took the opportunity in relative safety to examine the remains of Monchy Mill, which had been the site of a battle between the Germans and French cavalrymen in November 1914. The skeletons of both men and horses were both much in evidence. Later on that day, having reached the front line and relieved a party of 6th Battalion men, he remembered:

> As they left we heard shouting opposite, and saw a group of German soldiers trying to attract our attention. Hurriedly, therefore, we dumped our kits, cleaned up the [Lewis] gun, mounted it on the emplacement and got on the top again to see what transpired, our sodden feet and clothes forgotten. In the bright sunshine the scene before us was of enthralling interest. From the top of our actual trench we could not understand what the Germans to our front intended to convey to us, as the thick wire thrown out by both sides largely obscured our view of one another. But about 150 yards to our left, where the distance between the trench lines increased and there was a distinct No-Mans-Land, we saw a number of our men clear our wire and advance to meet a party of German soldiers there. They met, and groups were soon deep in conversation, gesticulating and laughing in efforts to understand one another. We saw the Germans stroking the hairy coats worn by our chaps, mud-encrusted though they were. Cigarettes were exchanged, and we observed several Leicesters smoking cigars. The Germans offered their water-bottles which, we were told afterwards, contained Schnapps or coffee.[28]

Jack Horner was also present on this occasion, and posted as a sentry had a full view of the incident, though a healthy respect for military discipline prevented him from leaving his post. After perhaps ten minutes this rather strange pre-Christmas truce was ended abruptly by a shot fired from the British lines, which apparently hit one of the Germans who were present. The incident is described by the German writer Ernst Jünger, who in 1915 was serving in one of the units facing the Leicesters at Berles, in his book *Storm of Steel*.[29]

On Christmas Day itself, there was no truce – a volley of shells from British gunners helped to ensure that there would be none of the week-long fraternising that had characterised the Christmas of 1914 on some parts of the British front. Arthur Cave was one of those fortunate ones who had secured a leave pass at Christmas the previous year, and was granted the same privilege in 1915. On December 24 he wrote in his diary:

> I arrived in Leicester to the great joy of my parents, to whom I had been unable to give notice of my being granted leave. I considered that I was extremely fortunate in being allowed to be home for Xmas. Had a quiet time as all my pals were by this time in France, and of course not so lucky as I to be home.[30]

For most of the Leicestershire Brigade, Christmas of 1915 was spent in France. In his diary, Private March of the 9th Battalion recorded:

Just prior to Christmas 1915, Lieut J.B.Breacher (left) went on leave to England. As this leave pass and railway warrant (right) shows, he had to return to his battalion by 22 December. Mrs S. Chatham

Saturday Dec 25th: Xmas Day relieved the 7th batt at 4am strong bombing party went out at night and did useful work had a fine sight in the afternoon 2 airmen looping the loop over enemies trenches worth seeing.[31]

At other points along the 110th Brigade front that Christmas night, patrols of the Leicestershire battalions found themselves out in No Mans Land in parties repairing barbed wire entanglements. From the enemy trenches, the eerie sound of singing could sometimes be heard, as the Germans held impromptu carol services in the front line.

In January of 1916, winter really arrived in the Monchy sector, with freezing weather making life doubly difficult for the troops in the trenches. To gauge a little of the damage to the health of the men in general from continually standing in near-freezing water for days at a time, one can examine battalion War Diaries over the winter of 1915-16. In this way it is possible fully to appreciate the number of men who returned home listed as 'sick'. One of these men was Private John Lord, whose health deteriorated

Lieut. Eustace Fowler Smart, 7th Battalion, killed in February 1916. The battalion's first officer casualty.

rapidly after he was invalided home in early January. He died later that month, of a chill contracted whilst in the trenches. (Today Lord's grave can be seen in Countesthorpe churchyard, whilst his grandson began the family firm of Lord's Electrical Goods, which can still be found in Wigston). Belatedly, tours in the trenches were reduced from four days to two. Whale oil was issued to rub on the feet, and thigh-length waders provided as trench stores, but after each tour in the trenches, the sick parades lengthened. As well as trench-foot (a fungal growth caused by continual exposure to moisture), other illnesses linked to exposure included pneumonia and rheumatic fever. Dick Read in his memoir provides a gripping description of the effects of the weather that winter:

The cold was intense. No one who has not done sentry-go under the same conditions, in the watches from midnight to 'stand-to' can have an adequate idea of the numbing effect on the senses of such a January dawn. Stamp our feet and flail as we might, the cold gradually gained on us. Our ears, deprived by instructions from above of the protection of ear flaps or balaclava helmets (as these were held to prevent sentries hearing a creeping enemy) had long since ceased to have any feeling in them at all. We nudged one another frequently to keep alert. A muttered word or a cough, and the breath made a miniature cloud of steam in the frosty air. With 'stand-to' and first light, we would cock our frozen ears in an effort to catch the first faint footfalls of the dixie carriers coming up the communication trench from the cookhouse in the ravine, their load of hot tea well laced with rum, and the bacon – alas – sadly congealed. The very sound quickened our numbed senses, and as the dixie drew nearer, though still at a distance, the aroma of the rum reached us across the now-white-topped sandbags. How welcome, when eventually it arrived and put new life in us to face another day. If we could, we used to stand over the steaming dixie and breathe in deeply through our running noses, until the carriers replaced the lid and, stolidly shouldering it again, staggered off around the traverse.[32]

In February 1916 the 110th Brigade began to take over more sections of trench from neighbouring French units. This was partly due to the increasing strength of the BEF in France as a whole, and partly due to the increasing pressure on French manpower far to the south at Verdun, where a fearsome struggle was raging. These new trenches eventually included those in front of Bailleulemont to the left of the existing positions, and to the right as far as Hannescamps. Also in February, trench routine changed, to cope with the extra amount of line to be garrisoned. From now on, three battalions would be in the line at once, with one out resting, and the four would rotate. Periodically the entire brigade would be out of the line, being relieved by another brigade of the 37th Division. This system also afforded battalions at rest the opportunity to march as far back from the line as Pommier or Humbercamp for billeting, away from the shells which were increasingly beginning to fall in Berles. As winter wore on and spring approached, time during the periods spent out of the line was more often occupied with intensive training courses, in bombing, Lewis gunnery, visual signalling and a host of other activities.

However, there was also time to visit the divisional concert party, which had recently been formed, and which had drawn men with a talent for performing from across the division, including a number from the Leicestershire battalions. One of them was 'Sandy' Reeve, formerly of 'C' Company, 8th Battalion, who with a deep bass voice performed popular numbers of the day such as *Asleep in the Deep*. Other songs performed by the troupe were parodies of popular West End show tunes. One was called *You're Here and I'm Here, So What Do We Care ?*, and the new lyrics were a play on the fact that being selected for the divisional concert party was considered a cushy number, arousing the envy of the front line troops:

> You're Here and we're here
> We Hope you've been amused
> Now you've seen what we've done - well
> We hope you won't abuse us
> 'Cause we'll tell you straight and true
> That we are soldiers just like you
> And though
> We're not in the trenches just now
> Its because our gallant staff
> Has sent us around here
> To try and make you laugh
> But one and all
> We're ready at the call
> To join our Regiments ![33]

As March led into April, the weather gradually began to improve. At the end of March, the Brigade was relieved from the front line trenches, and marched to rest billets in the area of Sus-St-Leger and Warluzel, then after a couple of weeks, moved to the Doullens area. They would spend six weeks there in total, cleaning up, resting, and training, as well as reorganising. About this time, for the first time in several months, the men were able to have a bath. For Jack Horner, this was a prospect full of excitement:

> *we were told to Fall In, and bring the towel, soap, and all dirty clothes. This could only mean one thing: we were going to the baths. By God! How we needed it! I joined the battalion on August 12th 1915, and it was then mid April 1916, but visions of*

A wounded soldier's autograph – Pte. G. Scothern, 6th Battalion, wounded in February 1916.

Regimental Sergeant Major C.J. Cattell, of the 8th Battalion (seated centre) with some of his NCOs. France, early 1916.

Mr R. J. Cattell

SERGT. A. T. PRITCHARD.

Sergt. A. T. Pritchard (27), for about two years goods clerk at the Midland Station, Syston, succumbed to wounds received in the trenches March 13th. His death has caused intense regret among his colleagues and friends in Syston. Volunteering soon after the outbreak of war, Mr. Pritchard joined the "C" Company. —— Leicesters. and by his ability and application rapidly attained the non-commissioned rank. He leaves a wife and two children.

14780 Sgt
A.T.Pritchard, 9th
Battalion. Leicester
Evening Mail

a long soak in hot water, followed by a shower and a swim, were soon dispelled. After a long march, we were shown into a very large barn, no swimming baths, just six halves of huge wine vats, each capable of taking 10 or 12 men, filled with lovely steaming hot water, and so each batch left their dirty clothes in a heap and clambered in, splashing, pushing, ducking, and generally acting like a lot of school boys; you scrub my back, I'll scrub yours. But how wonderful it was to feel clean again, after all those months. Before we were ordered out after 10 minutes Operation Lice was put into effect – 4 executed.[34]

However, even with shirts washed and pressed, some of the eggs remained in the seams, and with the heat of the human body to incubate them, lice were soon back in large numbers.

The number of Lewis guns per battalion was now doubled to eight, and training had to be given to those detailed to form the new sections. Battalion bombing sections had been established for some time, but more men were selected for training in visual signalling, with heliographs if the weather was good enough, with flags if it was not. On 30 March, as a finale, the brigade was inspected by the General Officer Commanding the 37th Division, Major-General Count Gleichen.

They also formed working parties to cut down trees and prepare brushwood bundles for use in the front line, as well as repairing the support trenches in the area. After this short stint at Warluzel, on their last day in the area the 110th Brigade held a sports competition, attended by the Commanding Officers of all four battalions. Many of the events carried a distinctly martial theme, with bayonet fighting on the list of competitions. The following day the Brigade moved again to Bouque-Maison, Neuvillette, and St Amand, in the Doullens area, where for a fortnight in glorious weather they practised attacking exercises. As May arrived, the 7th Battalion was occupied in building a new railway from La Bret to Bienvillers. Those not employed building the railway found working parties for the trenches, or continued to practise bayonet fighting, musketry, or gas helmet drill.

Towards the end of May, with the rest period over, the brigade returned once more to the trenches in the Bienvillers-Bailleulmont sector. The weather was now fine and warm for much of the time, but military activity in this previously quiet sector was beginning to pick up also. Dick Read's 8th Battalion now found themselves much further south than they had been the previous autumn, within sight of the village of Gommecourt. He noted:

The road from Bienvillers to Bucquoy and Achiet-le-Grand – now a grass track barricaded at a dozen points – crossed our trenches near our gun position, but we could follow its course into the valley along *one side of the osiers, then into and past the German trenches up the slope to Les Essarts, where it disappeared behind the ridge. At night we could hear what at first we took to be the German ration limbers trundling up on the reverse side; but as May turned to June, we felt pretty certain that new German batteries and their attendant ammunition columns were responsible for at least some of the nightly rumbling over the pave. Looking across to our left, we could see the broken trees around Monchy, and beyond, at a new angle, the dark green mass of Adinfer Wood; to the right that of another wood, the more sinister because of its proximity to the trenches there - the Wood of Gommecourt.*[35]

June became a series of nightly excursions into no man's land, with patrols out in the long grass which lay between the two sets of trenches, attempting

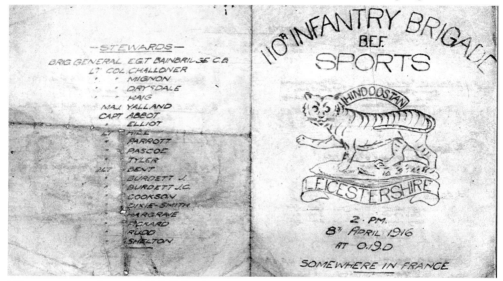

The programme from a 110th Brigade sports meeting in April 1916. By the time the summer was out, Mignon, Abbot, Hill, and Pickard had been killed.

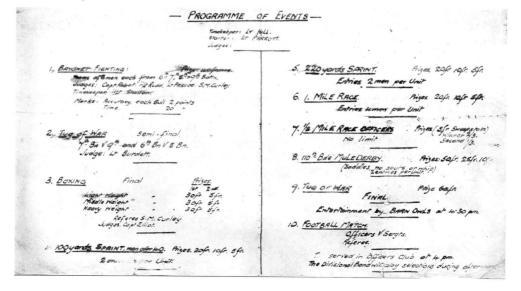

A fire burning in Bailleulmont, after the village was struck by German shells. The mounted figure is either a French officer or possibly a Gendarme. Annie Damiens

21897 Pte Ezra Baum, 9th Battalion. Killed on 23 May 1916. He was from Stoney Stanton.

John Taylor

to gather information on the German dispositions. On other occasions there were working parties out repairing the British barbed wire entanglements, and most nights later in June parties of the 6th Battalion worked to dig a new front line trench, closer to the German positions, along with its attendant communication trenches. They were covered by parties of Lewis gunners who went out with them, and who lay in the grass watching for any signs of a German attack. The situation became increasingly hazardous as the month wore on, as the Germans began to use a new and more accurate type of trench mortar. However, the commencement of the Battle of the Somme lay only weeks away now, and a few miles to the south, the offensive which was to tear land and trenches and trees asunder as it blundered forwards, was about to begin.

An 8th Battalion group, in the spring of 1916. Seated front row extreme left in this group is 27170 Pte Alfred Shooter, of Leicester. Neville A. Easingwood

This photograph shows a bombing section of the 9th Battalion (identifiable by the cloth grenade badges sewn on to the upper sleeves), in the spring of 1916. Back row (l to r): L/Cpl Hurston (Melton), L/Cpl Knott (Oakham), Pte Alcock (Castle Gresley), Pte Brewin, (Castle Donington), Pte Whitbread (Market Harborough), Pte Taylor (Oakham), Pte Percival (Loughborough). Seated: Sgt Partridge (Loughborough), Pte (?) Hallam, Sgt Goodman. 14867 Pte John Charles Taylor, and 15020 Sgt Ernest Knott were both to be killed on 14 July 1916 during the Bazentin Ridge battle. Yvonne White

1 War Diary, 9th bn Leicestershire Regt, LRO. 28.7.15
2 I.L.Read, *Of Those We Loved* (Pentland Press, 1994) p5
3 Read, *op. cit.* p6
4 D.V.Kelly, *39 Months With the Tigers* (Ernest Benn Ltd, 1930) p15
5 Read, *op. cit.* p8
6 Read, *op. cit.* p10
7 Read, *op. cit.* pp11-12
8 A.C.Cave, unpublished typescript diary 4.8.15
9 Read, *op. cit.* p14
10 Cave, *op. cit.* 12.8.15
11 Read, *op. cit.* pp16-17
12 Kelly, *op cit.*t p16
13 J.W.Horner, unpublished typescript memoir. Author's collection.
14 Read, *op. cit.* p16
15 Kelly, *op. cit.* p17
16 Read, *op. cit.* p36
17 Horner, *op. cit.*
18 Horner, *op. cit.*
19 Cave, *op. cit.* 4.9.15
20 Kelly, *op. cit.* p19
21 Kelly, *op. cit.* pp20-21
22 Captain McCutcheon is mentioned on a number of occasions in Read's account.
23 Pte W.March, 9th bn Leicestershire Regt. Manuscript diary, LRO, 15.9.15, 16.9.15.
24 Read, *op. cit.* pp88-89
25 Pte W.March *op. cit.* 2.11.15
26 Cave, *op. cit.* 2.11.15
27 Pte J.T.Lord, typescript copy of diary. J.Taylor collection.
28 Read, *op. cit.* p93
29 E.Jünger, *Storm of Steel* (1929 reprinted 1994) pp51-53. Jünger comments, 'From the English cap badges we were left in no doubt after that day that we had the 'Hindustani' Leicestershires opposite us.'
30 Cave, *op. cit.* 24.12.15
31 Pte W.March, *op. cit.* 25.12.15
32 Read, *op. cit.* pp109-110
33 Quoted in Read, *op. cit.* pp111-112
34 Horner, *op. cit.*
35 Read, *op. cit.* p119

Chapter Five

'Thou hast brought his strongholds to Ruin...'
The Battle of Bazentin Ridge

By the late Spring of 1916, Kitchener's Army formations had begun to arrive in France in such numbers that, at long last, the B.E.F. (now under the command of Sir Douglas Haig) could begin to contemplate taking an equal share of the fighting in the western theatre. Up until that point this weight had largely been borne by the French Army. Yet in spite of this steady increase in manpower, Britain remained on land the junior partner in the alliance with France. The French commander, Joffre, wanted an Anglo-French offensive to be launched as soon as possible in that summer of 1916, to relieve the pressure on the French troops around the city of Verdun, who had been locked in a life or death struggle since February. The logical place for this Anglo-French offensive was, in Joffre's mind, at the point where the British and French sectors met, astride the River Somme. In this rolling, pretty and peaceful countryside, the Germans had constructed two formidable defensive lines, and were working on a third. It was not Haig's ideal choice of ground. He would have preferred to attack at Ypres where - in that year of 1916 - the German defences were not as yet so elaborate. However, such are the political realities associated with coalition warfare, that Haig had little choice but to comply.

The 110th Brigade, still part of the 37th Division, was destined not to participate in the ill-starred first day of the Somme offensive, 1 July 1916. They were still holding trenches to the north, beyond Gommecourt, and were concerned with providing diversions to distract German attention away from the main area of the assault. On 29 June at 4.30am a group of 4 officers and 70 other ranks from the 7th Battalion, together with

General Sir Douglas Haig, Commander in Chief, B. E. F.

French commander General Joffre

113

Royal Engineers and parties from other units, raided the German trenches near Bailleulmont. The 7th Battalion War Diary for this date states that:

> Gallantry was displayed by No. 1 section B Squad, altho' nearly all wounded, continued to fight until their objective was reached. 2nd Lt Pickering-Clarke, Sgt Jordan, Cpl Toogood, Ptes Bennett, Brewin & Parker were especially good. Our total casualties were 1 officer died of wounds [2nd Lt A.E.G. Mason], 2 men killed (1 RE) 28 wounded (25 slight) - all were brought in except Pte Cross A Squad (killed). The total estimate of damage done to the enemy was 60 killed (including those in the dug-outs) 30 of which were counted in the trench.[1]

Two days later, the waves of British infantry broke against the German defences from Gommecourt in the north, down past Serre and Beaumont Hamel, to Montauban beside the French in the south. The soldiers of the Leicestershire Brigade were held in reserve for the Territorial 46th (North Midland) Division's unsuccessful attack, and as a result were not required. Quartermaster-Sergeant Arthur Cave, of the 7th Battalion, was able to watch the attack on Gommecourt (which involved the Leicestershire Regiment Territorial battalions, 1/4th and 1/5th) as it unfolded, from a field near Souastre.

Nevertheless, the events of 1 July 1916, would impact upon the 110th Brigade in a quite unexpected way. Elsewhere on the morning of the main assault, one of the brigades of the 21st Division had been so badly hit that it was decided that for some considerable time it would have to be rested. Indeed, it would have to be rebuilt, practically from scratch, and on 6 July 1916 the brigade selected to replace it in the 21st Division was the 110th. The men of the Leicestershire battalions were now ordered to adopt the colour scheme of their new parent formation - yellow circles, rectangles,

LIEUT. A. E. G. MASON.

Lieut. Alan E. G. Mason, son of Dr. and Mrs. Mason, London Road, Leicester, who has died of wounds in France. Some biographical details of the deceased officer appeared in the "Leicester Mail" yesterday.

Lieutenant Mason's obituary.
Leicester Evening Mail

German defenders, photographed behind their lines on the Somme in 1916.

A British gas barrage blows across German positions on the opening day of the Battle of the Somme, 1 July 1916. Liddle Collection

squares and triangles for the 6th, 7th , 8th and 9th Battalions respectively. Dick Read remembered that one fine summers morning,

> *after breakfast, in general parades, each man received [four] pieces of yellow material about 2 ¹/₂ inches square, and was shown how and where to sew them on his tunic: one square...on each upper arm immediately below the shoulder strap, and one on the back below the collar ... we spent most of the morning getting these fixed - it certainly gave us something to do.*[2]

The other piece was generally sewn onto the hessian sacking covering the helmet. Later on, orders were given to pack up, and,

> *By midday we were on the march with full packs, in column of route, heading south west. The whole 110th Brigade, in fact the 6th, 7th, 8th, and 9th Battalions of the Leicestershire Regiment, were on the move...It was late that evening that we marched, aching and tired out, into the village of Talmas. Here we slept in a barn which had recently housed troops. The straw wasn't too clean either.*[3]

The Brigade marched south by stages, and Dick continued:

> *We were on the move in good time on the following morning, having drawn constituents of a haversack dinner. The day promised to be hot and sunny. After marching four or five hours through Vignacourt and Flixecourt, with the usual 'fall out on right of t'road' for five minutes every hour, we began to feel the strain...Colonel Mignon rode to and fro along the ranks continually, joking with us and exhorting us to stick it for the honour of the regiment. Heartened by him, we determined grimly to keep going.*[4]

A private of the 6th Battalion, from Market Harborough. Note the black collar patch.
Squire de Lisle

1/5th Northn. General.

Form# I. 1237 / 10

Army Form I. 1237.

MEDICAL CASE SHEET.*

No. in Admission and Discharge Book.	Regimental No.	Rank.	Surname.	Christian Name.
T 5542	14934	L/Cpl	Sturman	A.

Year	Unit.	Age.	Service.
23.7.16	9 Lesters	21	1 $\frac{10}{12}$

Station and Date.

Disease. Shell wound near left knee.
A.T.S. given in France
Wounded near Mametz wood on Jul, 13th
C.P.H. small wound nearly healed
For & X ray exam—.

N. E. Spragg
Capt. R.A.M.C.

X rays disclose small F.B.
ant to head of Tibia . 1·6 cm deep
N. Es

" 29 Operation. The fragment of shell was found embed-
-ded in the patellar tendon removed. N. E. Spragg
Capt. R.A.M.C.

Long Eaton

Admitted on Sept 2.

Sept 11. 16 General Improvement. Better movement.

" 14. 16 Better movement of knee joint. Quadriceps still
weak at Insertion.

Oct 4. 16 General Improvement. Knee joint still weak

18. Transferred to Leicester.

N.L.P. Beard

L/Cpl Alfred Sturman, of the 9th, was one of the 50 other ranks of this battalion to be wounded between 11 and 13 July. The injury was to keep him out of the forthcoming battle. Also shown is Sturman's medical history sheet.
Pete & Sue Sturman

At length the battalion reached its destination, Soues, where the men bivouacked, but in that arduous march both officers and men had shown some of the qualities of mutual respect and reliance which would stand them in good stead, and which they would certainly need, in the coming battle:

> We would have dropped in our tracks that day rather than have straggled. It would have been letting him [Colonel Mignon] down. Such an attitude may seem naïve and outdated...[but] we knew in those moments that in Colonel Mignon and his officers we had real leaders.[5]

By 11 July the brigade had reached the vicinity of Bottom Wood, around Quadrangle Trench and Quadrangle Support. Here for the next two days, they suffered the effects of intermittent German artillery fire, as they held the line. 9th Battalion headquarters were in a deep dugout in a copse, which like the whole area around had been captured from the Germans only a few

13265 Pte Ernest Henry Jeffs, 9th Battalion, killed on 11 July.

A large scale trench map, showing the ground between Mametz Wood and Bazentin le Petit Wood, over which the Leicestershire Brigade were to attack. Bazentin le Grand Wood, from which much enemy fire was directed at the 6th Battalion, is visible on the right. Further to the south is Flat Iron Copse, in 1916 the location of a dressing station. Many of the casualties of the Bazentin battle are buried here.

days previously. It was a wilderness of desolation -

the then unfamiliar scenes of slaughter and destruction, pervaded
by the equally unfamiliar "battlefield smell" of churned up earth and
rotting corpses, was dream-like in quality, and left but a hazy memory[6]

remarked Kelly. The fire of German artillery batteries was particularly
severe, and a number of casualties were suffered at this time. The War Diary
of the 9th Battalion records on 12 July 1916, the deaths of Major
A.W.L.Trotter and Second-Lieutenant A.B.Taylor, and the wounding of
Second-Lieutenant H.F.King, all as a result of shellfire. It also gives the total
casualties sustained by the battalion between 10 and 13 July as being three
officers and fifty other ranks. On 13 July the Leicestershire battalions
moved back to Fricourt, to draw the stores that they would need, and to
prepare for their part in the coming attack.

The task of the 110th Brigade was to storm the German second line
positions on Bazentin Ridge, between Mametz Wood and Bazentin-le-Petit
Wood. In the event, they were also forced to clear Bazentin-le Petit village
(though it was not in their area) owing to their right flank being exposed. It
was to be a night attack, at that point in the war a practically unheard of
undertaking. French High Command told General Sir Henry Rawlinson,
British Fourth Army commander, and author of the plan, frankly that it was
unworkable. Nevertheless, on the night of 13/14 July, in accordance with
instructions, the four Leicestershire battalions moved into position through
Mametz Wood, which had been attacked and had taken a fearful battering
about a week previously. Kelly remembered:

the wood was everywhere smashed by shell-fire and littered with
dead - a German sniper hung over a branch horribly resembling a
scarecrow, but half the trees had had their branches shot away, leaving
fantastic jagged stumps like a Dulac picture of some goblin forest ...
All the old 'rides' through the wood were blocked by fallen trees and
great shell-holes, and all over hung the overwhelming smell of corpses,
turned up earth, and lachcrymatory gas. The sinister aspect of the

The shattered remains of Mametz Wood, through which the four Leicestershire battalions
moved into position.

A German gun abandoned in Mametz Wood. The breech block has been removed so as to render it useless to the British.

> *wood was intensified that night by the incessant whistling and crashing of shells and the rattle of machine guns and illuminated by the German flares, Very lights, and the flash of bursting shrapnel.*[7]

The battalions wound their way along a blasted trench, which skirted the western edge of the wood. Arms and legs of partially buried bodies protruded from the sides of the trench, and as the men moved up in the darkness, they shook hands with these gruesome relics for good luck. One by one the companies arrived at their allotted positions, along the eastern edge. The 7th Battalion War Diary records the considerable difficulties encountered during this phase, mainly caused by German shelling: one platoon of 'C' company losing almost half of its number, and the commanding officer Lieutenant-Colonel Drysdale, being wounded as the Battalion marched up to its attack positions. He was forced to hand over command at this early stage to the Battalion adjutant Captain A.A.Aldworth, but the diary records that by 2.55am the Battalion was in position and that 'The men behaved admirably under trying conditions.'[8]

The 6th and 7th Battalions were to lead the attack, along with 'D' company of the 8th Battalion. They were drawn up in four waves, with some troops just outside the edge of the wood. The rest of the 8th Battalion, and the 9th were to follow in support and to mop up any surviving Germans in the overrun enemy positions. Those troops on the left of the attacking line (8th Battalion) were to skirt around the northern edge of Bazentin-le-Petit Wood, whilst those in the centre (7th Battalion) and on the right (6th Battalion) would enter the wood itself. The three remaining companies of the 8th and the four of the 9th would then follow them in. In the open ground in between the two woods they would encounter the German first line trench, known as Villa Trench, whilst running through the middle of Bazentin Wood was the German second line, named on British maps as

11766 Sgt Harry Shillaker, 7th Battalion, of Launde, killed on 14 July. Freda Nicholson

Forest Trench. Another significant topographical feature was a narrow gauge light railway track, which had been laid and used by the Germans for transporting supplies prior to the opening of the offensive. It ran through Mametz Wood, across No Man's Land, and in to Bazentin Wood, following roughly the direction the attackers were to take.

Waiting just inside Mametz Wood were Dick Read and another 8th Battalion comrade, Private 'Jackie' Johnson. Read and Johnson for this attack had been detailed to carry a Barr & Stroud rangefinder, and were uncertain as to how close to follow the attacking waves. At zero hour, 3.25am, Read remembered:

> we noticed that dawn was breaking. As we spoke a thousand shells seemed to whistle over our heads at once, then...pandemonium indescribable, as the preliminary bombardment of the German positions commenced. The enemy retaliated, but such was the noise that we could not hear their shells coming at all, saw great bursts quite close, and were smothered and bruised several times with earth, leaves and tree bark. To speak to Jackie I had to cup my hands and shout into his ear.[9]

18372 Pte William Noel Shelvey, of Uppingham, 8th Battalion, killed on 14 July.

All along the line, subalterns' whistles blew, and men scrambled forward into the open stretch of country between Mametz Wood behind, and Bazentin Wood in the distance. About half way between the two, shrouded in an eerie mist, lay visible the German front line trench. Almost immediately they were met with the rattle of machine gun fire and German artillery fire. Private D.A.Bacon, crouching in a trench with 9th Battalion Headquarters, recalled:

> Being our first experience of assault, we were naturally excited and expectant, and apart from the infernal noise and smoke, and the chilly air of the morning, we were not uncomfortable. The Battn Sgt Major, to uphold the honour of his rank, had bethought himself fit to fill his waterbottle with rum. - how and where he got it remains a mystery - but a share was very acceptable...[with] one continual roar of guns and shells whistling and shrieking through the air - talk was impossible - it was a perfect avalanche of destruction, and how any Boche could have been alive to withstand the infantry attack was beyond comprehension.[10]

14867 Pte John Charles Taylor, of Oakham, 9th Battalion, killed on 14 July.

He continued:

> The Headquarters crouched, as the others, in shell holes or trenches, from which could be seen troops of the attacking battalions moving forward in extended order at a walking pace...by that time

21830 Pte Frederick Bradshaw, 7th Battalion, killed on 14 July. He was from Oakham, but had enlisted at Leicester.

The open country between Mametz Wood and Bazentin Wood, as it is today. Richard Lane

Germans take shelter against the British bombardment.

10998 Pte Frederick Robinson, 6th Battalion, of Uppingham. Killed on 14 July.

most of the enemy machine guns had been silenced, though one or two, more lucky or more persevering than the rest, blazed away in solitude and desperation, and deserving the Iron Cross, it is to be hoped they received it ![11]

The 7th Battalion War Diary records that the attacking British line was in a race against time to cross No Man's Land before the Germans could man their machine guns. On the right, the 6th Battalion quickly reached its first objective, with many Germans fleeing back towards Bazentin Wood. In the centre of the attack, however, the 7th Battalion was held up for about twenty minutes by a machine gun, which the Germans had brought into action. They were able to press on only when bombers of the 6th Battalion worked their way along the German trench from the right (as the British saw it) to silence the machine gunners. In 'D' Company of the 8th Battalion,

The ground over which the 6th Battalion attacked on 14 July 1916. Bazentin le Petit Wood in the distance. Richard Lane

A German machine gun crew with their Maxim '08. German machine gunners tended to be hand picked for their initiative and ability to work alone or in small groups, and it was this weapon in the hands of such skilled gunners which caused so many casualties among attacking British soldiers.

which had gone over in the first wave, Captain F. Ward, the Company Commander, was hit almost at once. Whilst lying on the ground wounded, and receiving medical attention, he urged the rest of his company to continue going forward. His Company Sergeant-Major, Ben Stafford, was instrumental in seeing that the men did not lose direction and continued to their objective. They were met with heavy resistance and the enemy 'treated us severely with liquid fire, bombs and their devilish machine-guns'[12]. The defenders were quickly dispatched, however, mainly with grenades, as the men got into the German main trench. Now the Germans tried to force their way back in, also using grenades:

> *We had a job to keep up with them in bombs, but we had all the bombs collected from the casualties in front and the German bombs came in handy too. L/Cpl Mason fought well in this defensive action but was unfortunately killed. We were shelled fairly heavily too, on occasions and suffered a few more casualties[13],*

wrote CSM Stafford later to the wounded Captain Ward.

An anonymous private writing some weeks later to his father to describe the attack, found his letter published by the *Leicester Evening Mail*, under the heading *How the 'Tigers' fought*. Describing first the awesome nature of the shelling, and the difficulties of remaining calm whilst waiting in the wood, he continued:

> *Still we knew worse was to follow and we braced up.*

17811 Cpl Ernest Edgar Durrant, 9th Battalion. On 14 July 1916 he and a party of comrades worked their way through Bazentin Wood and emerged in Bazentin village. There, three German soldiers emerged from a cellar with their hands in the air, wishing to surrender. As they did so, a British NCO with Durrant's group shot them all. Fergus Durrant

122

14876 Pte Frederick Webb, 9th Battalion. He was from Croft, Leicestershire, and died of wounds on 14 July. He has no known grave, and so it may be that he died at an advanced aid post, and was buried on the battlefield rather than in a cemetery behind the line. Mrs J.Poultney

Presently the word came down for the first line to go forward, and having previously fixed bayonets, away forward went the first line, followed by the second and third. Up went the enemy's flares, and some men, it seemed, did not get down. The Boche spotted them, and away went their machine guns. We had covered a great deal of ground and their machine gun fire checked us, but only momentarily, for as soon as word was again given, forward we went again, until we were well in range of bomb throwing distance. Then the fighting began in real earnest, each side bombing for all they were worth.[14]

Signaller G.F.Hillyard, (8th Battalion) the son of Mrs Hillyard of Montague Road, Leicester, also had his account published by the Mail. Hillyard got into the German front line trenches, which on the Bazentin Ridge were to become famous for their elaborate dugouts, and which were often lavishly furnished with items appropriated from the local occupied villages, such as beds, tables and even on occasions grandfather clocks. He described

their dug-outs in which they had electric lights fitted, hot and cold water, baths, beds etc. There were all sorts of drinks there, and we also found a lady's pair of boots. This dug-out was over 40 feet deep[15].

Hillyard was given a message to carry back by his battalion adjutant, but was hit by shrapnel in the right ankle in the process. He managed to deliver his message before taking shelter with other wounded in a shell-hole. Both Hillyard and the anonymous correspondent were in agreement that the German troops facing the 110th Brigade (who were mostly Bavarians) were eager to fight whilst their machine guns were intact, and they could hold the British Tommies at ranges of 200 yards or more. However, they were less keen to engage in hand to hand fighting once the distance had closed to bombing or especially bayonet range, and they then tended to try to surrender. Others, commented the latter source,

German soldiers in a dugout in 1916.

turned tail and scuttled off into the open. Here our machine guns worked havoc amongst them, and it was ludicrous to see some of them struggling to get out of their equipment so as to be able to make better use of their legs.[16]

Over on the right-hand side of the battlefield, the 6th Battalion had to deal with the problem of Bazentin-le-Petit village. They had already suffered casualties whilst crossing the open ground, inflicted by Germans firing on them from Bazentin-le-Grand Wood. However, a short while later they were able to return the favour in good measure when the Germans, forced out of the latter position by the 7th Division's attack, were raked by the 6th Battalion Lewis guns. At around 6am, reinforced now by some parties of the 9th Battalion, the 6th began clearing the village. Three German officers and 200 other ranks were captured by the 6th Battalion at this point alone.[17]

The Church in Bazentin-le-Petit photographed by the Germans in April 1916.

One of those men wounded in the crossing of the open ground between Mametz Wood and Bazentin-le-Petit Wood was Private Jack Horner, in 'D' Company of the 8th Battalion. In his memoirs he recalled that:

In the far distance, on the right, we could see our objective, the village of Bazentin, or what was left of it, and on our left centre, a large farmhouse...A machine gun and four men appeared from nowhere on the left centre in front of the farmhouse, and held up the entire centre, but we on the right flank were able to push forward. From upper windows of the farmhouse the Germans were shooting us down, as if we were rabbits in a field. I had made about 200 yards and passed the rear of the machine gun which was still holding up the centre attack, and had I been given any Mills bombs I could certainly have dropped a couple amongst those Germans.

The rifle fire from the farmhouse was intense, and I got a bullet through my right forearm. If you are hit by a high velocity bullet, its rather like a red hot poker going through your flesh, and the force with which it travelled knocked me back, and flung my rifle yards away. There was not a great deal of blood, but my right hand went

Bazentin today. Richard Lane

13609 Company Sergeant-Major Robert Hancock, 9th Battalion. In this photo he wears the ribbon of the Military Cross, awarded to him for conspicuous gallantry on 16 July, when he organised survivors of the various battalions and held off a German counter-attack. Mr E Hancock

Hancock's Military Cross.

dead and immovable. I could not be of use any longer, so I made my way back with others, down the track through [Mametz] Wood.[18]

Read and his comrade Johnson, of the same battalion, were also in the vicinity. They were carrying ammunition for troops now dug in near the northern edge of Bazentin-le-Petit Wood. The RSM informed them that advanced battalion HQ was somewhere in the centre of the wood, and so they set off in that direction. They came first upon a party lining a shallow trench in the wood, under the command of a lieutenant. Shortly after Read and Johnson had dumped the ammunition with them, several of these men were killed and their lieutenant was wounded by shrapnel. After carrying him back to a dressing station on the edge of Mametz Wood, the pair returned once more to the trench but found it deserted except for corpses. They then headed off in the direction of Bazentin-le Petit village, from where heavy firing could be heard:

The trees echoed to the constant rattle of rifle and machine gun fire, punctuated by frequent explosions of grenades in the direction of the village. The shelling had slackened, probably because neither side knew where their opponents were with any accuracy...Here, near [the] village, we found that we were being sniped at from behind, and took cover hurriedly in the undergrowth. A few moments later the sniper fired again, at some

A party of walking wounded including one German, make their way to a dressing station near Bernafay Wood. Taylor Library

Regimental Sergeant Major Charles Cattell, 8th Battalion. He was instrumental in directing the operations of his battalion on 14 July, particularly after the death of the commanding officer Colonel Mignon. Mr R.J.Cattell

figures coming our way through the wood. Two 7th Battalion men, recognizable as such by their red 'flashes', were shepherding a line of German prisoners who stumbled forward with hands clasped over their heads.

Jackie and I spotted our man in the same instant, sitting in a tree barely 130 yards away. He appeared to have forgotten us, and was pointing his rifle at the leading 7th man when, having had ample time to aim, we both fired. The German toppled over backwards and fell to the ground, his steel helmet following his descent through the branches. We both rushed to the spot, as one does after potting a rabbit. He was quite dead.

Meanwhile, the 7th Battalion man and the leading prisoners had seen what had happened, and the latter were looking apprehensively at one another. It seemed to have unhinged the 7th man. This, and the strain of the last ten hours had evidently proved too much for him, for he started to laugh in a strange fashion, pointing his rifle first at the corpse and then threateningly at them. They immediately held their hands high, several shouting 'kamerad, kamerad!' His mate came up, rifle slung, but holding a Mills grenade in his right hand and the drawn pin in his left. He, too, looked scarcely responsible for his actions, as he glowered and shouted at them 'c'mon yer bastards. Keep those f.... hands up. C'mon!' and the sorry procession moved on. We left them, not giving much for the chances of the unfortunates, although just then, I'm afraid, we shouldn't have minded much.[19]

Lieutenant Alexander de Lisle was with the 9th Battalion, and went into the attack with them in support of the 6th and 7th Battalions. He and his men poured through the wood to find and link up with the 6th:

Behind the German first line of this 'second system of defence' ran the great wood, Bazentin-le-Petit, which itself was spanned at intervals by three successive lines of trenches, each with its separate wire protection. Between these lines were short lengths of trench, so it was

11086 Pte Thomas Henry Dono of the 7th Battalion was promoted to Sergeant on 14 July, in the wake of severe losses among NCOs. In some companies, every officer, sergeant and corporal was killed or wounded. This is a charcoal sketch done after he was commissioned in 1917.

Cameron Coxon-Smith

16860 Pte Harry Matts, 7th Battalion, killed on 14 July. His mother lived at 11, Alexandra Terrace, Leicester.

10931 Pte Alex Whitlock, 6th Battalion, killed on 14 July. His home was at Tugby, Leicestershire.

23780 Pte Henry Major Taylor, 8th Battalion, killed on 15 July. He was from Gaulby, Leicestershire.

14008 Pte 'Freddy' Smith, of Shepshed, 8th Battalion, killed on 15 July. He was a close friend of Dick Read.

a veritable maze. These fell into our hands, one after the other. It was impossible to march on the intervening ground at the double, so choked with fallen timber, so full of huge shell holes that it was all climbing, jumping, scrambling and sprawling. Whatever the method of going, they got there – Trust the Leicesters for that ![20]

De Lisle's men posted machine guns in the newly-won trenches to cover their comrades coming up behind them through the wood. Their eyes strained as they peered through those trees still standing and the thick undergrowth, for any signs of the field grey-clad foe. De Lisle himself noted that it was fortunate that German resistance in this area had been crushed, as enemy machine guns firing down the rides in the wood (across the line of advance) could have caused mayhem.

Late afternoon on 14 July found the Brigade in possession of most of Bazentin-le-Petit Wood, including the whole of Forest Trench (the second objective) with German troops still holding out in the northernmost edges. It was in a sadly depleted condition, having lost most of its officers who had gone over the top that morning, as well as a goodly proportion of the rank and file. In the 8th Battalion, most of Dick Read's immediate circle of friends had been killed – Freddy Smith of Shepshed, Ted Lineker and Horace Phillips, who had been hit in Mametz Wood before the attack had even started. Captain H.L.Beardsley had assumed command of the depleted Battalion. Of the officers of 'C' Company who had made it across No Man's Land, through the German trench and on into the wood, only Lieutenant Warner had remained uninjured to direct operations. By 4pm he too had been hit and was out of the battle, but his actions on this day were to play a key part in his award of the DSO the following year. Another award, this time a Military Cross, was won by Captain A.A.Clarke, 7th Battalion for his part in leading his company in the attack, consolidating Forest Trench, and gathering the men for an attack on the third objective, the German third line, although this last action was not successful. Late in the afternoon, Beardsley and the three or four subalterns with him, along with two Company Sergeant-Majors had organised the survivors of the various companies, who had been hopelessly intermingled, into defensive positions along the line gained.

Lieutenant (Acting Captain) Thomas Lovell Warner, 8th Battalion, and Warner's home, 'Willowdene' on London Road, Leicester. Warner reached the rank of Major and was decorated with the DSO, before dying of appendicitis in 1917.

127

Lieutenant de Lisle of the 9th Battalion was ordered to take a party forward to try to clear the Germans from the northern edge of the wood. He did so, but was seriously wounded in the process:

So as one man we are up and off, not knowing how far the enemy is ahead, but knowing that he is somewhere within the next hundred yards of wood right in front of us. We could only double about ten yards, for the wood was blocked by shell-split fallen trees; and other undergrowth is so thick that soon even walking is impossible. Then the whole line halts, and replies to the murderous hail of bullets still coming from unseen rifles...There is a cry: 'A German sentry on the edge of the wood!' 'Do not worry! Knock the *******out!' A shot is fired and down he goes.

Then we yell out: 'For God's sake stop this useless firing and go forward with the bayonet and bombs.' But no! [Our men] say, and I heard them: 'That is the Germans telling us to stop, and we won't for those b******s!' I get up to urge the men to stop firing; but almost as soon as I do so I receive a bullet in my neck at close range. It penetrated deep, and the blood gushed out. I fell downwards into a shellhole. One of the men quickly applied my first field-dressings as tightly as possible to try and stop the bleeding, for it was bleeding fast. In fact, I thought my number was up, as it bled so hard.[21]

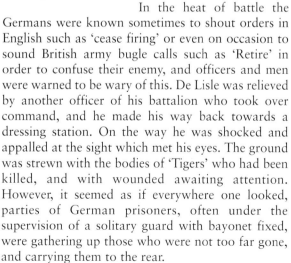

Lieutenant Alexander de Lisle, 9th Battalion. Squire de Lisle

14724 Pte Arthur Mattock, 9th Battalion, killed on 14 July. He was from Fleckney, near Market Harborough.

14982 Pte Daniel John Smith, 9th Battalion. Killed on 14 July. He was from Wokingham, Berkshire.

In the heat of battle the Germans were known sometimes to shout orders in English such as 'cease firing' or even on occasion to sound British army bugle calls such as 'Retire' in order to confuse their enemy, and officers and men were warned to be wary of this. De Lisle was relieved by another officer of his battalion who took over command, and he made his way back towards a dressing station. On the way he was shocked and appalled at the sight which met his eyes. The ground was strewn with the bodies of 'Tigers' who had been killed, and with wounded awaiting attention. However, it seemed as if everywhere one looked, parties of German prisoners, often under the supervision of a solitary guard with bayonet fixed, were gathering up those who were not too far gone, and carrying them to the rear.

At around 7pm, a final effort by the Leicester lads was made, which threw the remaining German

LEICESTERS "LIKE HEROES."

TRIBUTE BY ONE OF THEM.

A soldier in the Leicester Regiment, who was wounded in the British advance, writing from a military hospital in the South of England, asking if we will send him a "Leicester Mail" in which the official casualty list of last Friday's fighting is printed, says:

"We were in the first line of the charge. When I was wounded in the wood of Bazentin le Petit I passed lots of my comrades dead and wounded. We suffered heavy casualties. But the boys were splendid; they were like heroes, as they always have been, and the officers were grand. We lined up in "No Man's Land" just as though we were on ordinary parade. And when the order for the charge came, away we went laughing, and occasionally cursing when we fell in a shell-hole!.

"After reaching the second-line trenches, which were in the wood, I was wounded. I had hard luck—got the little finger of my right hand blown off, and the third finger smashed." (Our correspondent has written with his left hand.) "But never mind. The boys did the work they were supposed to do." Good luck to them; they deserve it.

An anonymous account of the fighting, from the Leicester Evening Mail.

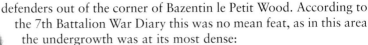

defenders out of the corner of Bazentin le Petit Wood. According to the 7th Battalion War Diary this was no mean feat, as in this area the undergrowth was at its most dense:

> the bushes and trees were very thick round this part which necessarily made progress slow, the enemy evacuating and manning a trench about 30 yards from the wood, before our men could get through.[22]

A soldier's identity bracelet, found on the Somme battlefield near Bazentin in the 1980s. The original owner, Pte Walters of the 6th battalion, survived the battle, but may have lost the bracelet after being wounded.

Paul Reed

By nightfall, calm was beginning to fall across the battlefield, and the exhausted survivors slept fitfully while a few sentries kept watch. Artillery rounds from British batteries had silenced the harassing fire of German machine gunners still shooting from the direction of Contalmaison, whilst the shells of the German artillery were now falling away in the British rear areas, hoping to catch ration parties and reinforcements moving up.

With darkness falling, Dick Read and Jackie Johnson of the 8th had time to sit and reflect as they brewed mugs of tea that night:

> We watched a fatigue party bringing up our rations, dumping piles of bulging sandbags on the ground near us, and this set us running through the names of our mates we knew already to be killed, wounded or missing. Both of us had lost all our best pals, and we sat there with leaden hearts, lost in our thoughts. Eventually Jackie broke the silence. 'Plenty of rations tonight Dick!' nodding towards the pile. 'Enough for the whole battalion, eh? About six times too many' He added bitterly. 'Christ, there'll be hell to pay in Leicester and Loughborough...and Coalville...and Melton...and Uppingham...when they know about this. The Leicester Brigade, eh? Bloody well wiped out!' and he trailed off into silence again, immersed in his thoughts.[23]

They had successfully taken all of their objectives on 14 July, but for the Leicestershire battalions the Battle of Bazentin Ridge had been a tragedy. The casualties had indeed been truly appalling, and the 110th Brigade had been dealt a shattering blow, in the worst four days of fighting in its history to date. Each battalion had suffered in the region of a hundred men killed, with around two hundred more wounded. The most senior officer to die in the attack was 46 year old Lieutenant-Colonel Jepson George Mignon, commanding the 8th Battalion, giving the lie to the idea that only young men died in the Great War. David Kelly commented,

> I grieved particularly over Colonel Mignon of the 8th Battalion, one of the most charming of the many fine men I knew through the war, who was killed leading a bombing party like a subaltern, and I remember vividly seeing him lying on his back still clutching a rifle.[24]

Lieutenant Colonel J.G.Mignon, commanding officer of the 8th Battalion, killed on 14 July 1916.

Mignon had died as he had lived, leading his battalion in the attack, and was the kind of man who would not expect his subalterns to do what he was not prepared to do himself. Dick Read too had seen him lying dead still holding his rifle, and had been equally moved by the loss of a much respected commander. Today Mignon has no known grave, being commemorated instead on the memorial to the missing at Thiepval. The 8th battalion had probably suffered the heaviest officer casualties, and came out of the battle commanded by Captain Beardsley, with only two officers unscathed. Lieutenant-Colonel Challenor, commanding the 6th Battalion, had been wounded, as, it will be remembered, had Lieutenant-Colonel Drysdale, 7th Battalion. Lieutenant J.C.Burdett, 6th Battalion, was lying injured in hospital, having received a gunshot wound to the head. He was before the war a well known Leicester 'Tigers' rugby footballer, being a regular member of the First XV. Lieutenant F.Scott, son of the stationmaster at Coalville East L.&N.W.R. railway station, had been wounded in the arm, whilst Second Lieutenant F.T.Scholes of Park View, Mere Road, Leicester, was wounded in the left wrist. Lieutenant William Head Stephens had been killed, Lieutenant-Colonel Haig (Officer Commanding, 9th Battalion) wrote to his parents to inform them that their son had been hit in the hand by a shell fragment early in the morning of 14 July. He had the wound dressed, but elected to rejoin his company, and reached them at about 10am, going forward into action with them. He was killed later that same day. Other officers killed included Lieutenants G.T.L. 'Gussie' Elwood, and J.H.Hopewell, both of the 6th Battalion. Hopewell was killed by a shell whilst leading his men over the top, early on the morning of 14 July, shortly after 3.20am. A sergeant, H.Whait, saw Hopewell fall, but was unable to reach him, being wounded by the same shell. Later on that morning a stretcher bearer, Lance Corporal. J.Booth of the 6th Battalion, came upon his body, but was also hit before he could bring him out. Neither Ellwood nor Hopewell's remains were discovered after the war, and both are commemorated on the Thiepval memorial. Company Sergeant-Major Stafford of the 8th Battalion informed his wounded Company Commander that:

> The Company suffered heavily, Sir, 4 Officers (2 killed. Messrs Greenaway and Bowells) 2 wounded, you and Lt. Ewen, and 130 other ranks. There were no Sergts killed, Sgt Kirk was very badly wounded but is in England now. Sgts Buxton, Croker, Hills were wounded badly before we reached our objective. Sgt Reed of the Lewis Gunners was killed on the last day in the trench. L/Sgt Hills was wounded by shrapnel a day or two after the attack. Cpl Rayson, L/Cpls Rogers, Wheeler, Morley G., Holyoak, Mason, E., Dunn, West, Chesham and Clarke were all killed, Sir.[25]

However, it was over a period of weeks that the news of the attack filtered through to the home front, and it was some time before the numbing weight of the casualty list could truly be appreciated by those in Leicester and Loughborough and Melton and Uppingham. The first information received was of the officers who had been killed, then of the NCOs and men. Only through their obituaries can the range, and indeed the talent and quality of these men be appreciated. Across Leicester, in street after street, the blinds

Lieutenant G.T.L. 'Gussie' Ellwood, 6th Battalion, killed on 14 July.

Lieutenant James Hanley Hopewell, 6th Battalion, killed on 14 July. His body was never found. A 6th Battalion stretcher bearer who took part in the attack, 10983 Pte J Booth, reported that the officer was killed by shrapnel whilst advancing through Bazentin Wood. Booth himself was wounded shortly afterwards, and was unable to return to the scene.

Lieutenant J.C. 'Jimmy' Burdett, 6th Battalion, wearing his Leicester Tigers jersey. Stuart Farmer

were being drawn as they had never been before up to this point in the war. At number 34, King Richard's Road, the parents of Sergeant E.Kenney, 7th Battalion, mourned the loss of their son, a member of the Great Meeting Cricket Club. His commanding officer had written to them,

> *Your loss is great, but it will be softened by the knowledge that your son died bravely and willingly.*[26]

Their neighbour at number 32 King Richard's Road, Mrs Hills, shared some of their anguish, for her husband Sergeant Arthur Hills, 8th Battalion was lying wounded in hospital at Aldershot. He had been hit by shrapnel, and was one of the men mentioned by CSM Stafford in his letter to Captain Ward. Hills had before the war been employed as a Clicker at the Co-operative Society works on Duns Lane. Another well known cricketer, CQMS Harold W.Murrell, who worked for Messrs Harrisons, seed merchants in Leicester and played for St Phillips CC, was also wounded, as was CSM Hickley (hit in the shoulder). Hickley's mother lived at 10, Waring Street, Leicester. Lance Corporal J.W.Baldwin of the 8th Battalion, aged only 23, had left a widow and young child at his home, 127 St Saviours Road East, while at number 8, Bassett Street, the parents of Privates Walter and Charles Snutch waited anxiously for further news, after learning that both of their sons had been hit. To learn that a son was in hospital was often only the prelude to tragedy, for the parents of Private Haden Bickley at 39, Regent Road learned as late as the end of July that their son, a former employee of Messrs Coleman & Lewitt's boot manufacturers, had succumbed to his injuries in hospital on 27 July, thereby depriving Enderby Town Football Club of a talented player.

15054 Pte Fred Barker, 9th Battalion (seated) killed in action on 14 July. His two brothers Everard (left) 8th Battalion and John (right) also 9th Battalion would die before the year was out. Eric Kellaway

Across the county the story was similar. In Earl Shilton, Mr & Mrs John Thompson of Hill Top had learned of the death in action on 14 July of their son, Private Gus Thompson, 9th Battalion. Mr & Mrs Kind, of Station Road had likewise received news of the death of their adopted son, Lance Corporal Jack Wheeler, 8th Battalion. In Loughborough, news had arrived that Private Jack Belton, a promising footballer who had played first for Loughborough Corinthians, and latterly for Nottingham Forest in the Football League, was wounded, as was Private George Simmons, of 7, Granville Street. Simmons, one of the first Loughborough men to join Kitchener's Army, was suffering from a gunshot wound. Private W. Tustaire, a

10976 Pte John Thomas Chater, 6th Battalion, killed on 17 July. He was born at Northampton, but was living in Leicester at the time of his enlistment. Katrina Dobson

131

former blacksmith at the Falcon Works in Loughborough, was also injured, having had one of the fingers of his left hand shot off.

In Hinckley, Mr and Mrs Wallace of Queen Street learned that their son, Sergeant Sidney S. Wallace, 7th Battalion, a former worker at the Sketchley Dye Works, was dead. Meanwhile, in nearby Barwell, news was received that 37 year old Private J.M.Chaplin also of the 7th Battalion, and a former employee of Barwell Boot Factory, had been killed, leaving a widow at his home, 37, Mill Street.

Market Harborough did not escape lightly either. Mr & Mrs Carter of East Street received a letter from their son, L/Cpl A.G.Carter, 8th Battalion, who was in hospital in England. In it, Carter informed them:

> I have stopped one of Fritz's bullets with my face. It went in against my left ear and came out just under my right eye, a very narrow escape so the doctor told me.[27]

12271 Pte William Henry Freeman, 7th Battalion, of Market Overton. Killed on 14 July.

After being hit, Carter had lain in a shell hole for five hours, before he was able to get to a dressing station to receive medical attention. The parents of Private W.H.Reedman, 6th Battalion, were relieved to receive a letter from him dated 21 July 1916, stating that he was unwounded, after a mistaken report that he was a casualty. Nevertheless, something of their son's ordeal was evident in his letter:

> Just a few lines to let you know I am well, but lucky to be alive. We have been amongst the fighting of late, and had a rough time. Thank God I was spared. It was a terrible, and I don't want to see anything like it again.[28]

In nearby villages, news was not so good: Mrs Glasscock of Highcroft Villas, Husbands Bosworth, had learned that her son Lance Corporal W. Glasscock, also of the 6th Battalion, was in a serious condition in hospital with twenty three shrapnel wounds in his body. Of the Pritchard brothers from Great Bowden, four of whom were serving in the Leicestershire brigade, George (6th Battalion) had been hit no less than five times in the right arm by machine gun bullets. Albert (8th Battalion) had received a shrapnel wound to one arm, while J.E.Pritchard (6th Battalion) was in hospital recovering from a bayonet wound.

10328 Pte Edward Walton, 6th Battalion, killed on 17 July, aged 20. He was a miner from Whitwick, and some of his family had been involved in the Whitwick pit disaster of 1911.

John Taylor

Nailstone Colliery was badly hit, with a number of families bereaved, as were other mining families in Coalville, where Private W. Ducksbury (formerly a miner at the South Leicestershire Colliery) was killed, and his brother was wounded. Both were members of the 8th Battalion. William Maddocks, of Margaret Street, Coalville, had received a card stating that his son Wilfred Maddocks was in hospital but recovering, as had the mother of Private Herbert Fern, also of Margaret Street. However, on the same road, the family of Lance Corporal E.Batho, 7th Battalion, and another former collier, was not so fortunate, receiving news that he had been killed on 14 July. *The Leicester Evening Mail* was forced to conclude that:

> Probably no street in another town of its size in the midlands has given more of its sons in this war than Margaret Street, Coalville.[29]

15343 Pte Charles Ernest Beaver, 9th Battalion, of Ashwell, Rutland. Killed on 14 July.

15331 Pte Horace Lefevre Phillips, 8th Battalion, of Uppingham, killed on 14 July. He was a close friend of Dick Read.

Pte George Porter, 9th Battalion, wounded on 14 July.

The morning of 15 July dawned clear and bright, but distinctly cool at first, as early mornings at that time of year, whether in England or in France, are wont to be. After a breakfast of toast and cheese, cooked over an open fire on the end of a bayonet, Dick and Jackie of the 8th were detailed by their RSM to assist two padres who had appeared on the edge of the battlefield:

> We departed with them to a huge shell hole, about two hundred yards away, in which several of our pioneers were working with shovels to lengthen and deepen it. Here one of the padres told us to relieve two of the men. About ten minutes after we had started digging the grim purpose of the hole became evident from the approach of a party carrying bodies on stretchers, which they deposited in the excavation, departing afterwards for more. The padres then knelt and carefully removed the identity discs from a score or more of dead...[30]

The blood-stained identity disc of 12874 L/Cpl Horace Chesham, 8th Battalion, returned to his next-of-kin after he was killed on 15 July at Bazentin. Chesham was born at West Bridgford, Nottinghamshire, and was part of a large Nottingham contingent which joined the 110th Brigade. After the war his grave was not located, and he is commemorated on the Memorial to the Missing at Thiepval.

Some of the bodies were of members of the 38th (Welsh) Division, killed over a week previously in the attack which had cleared Mametz Wood, and Dick observed that,

> many uniforms still bore the flash of the Red Dragon of Wales. Another layer was added and then the padres motioned to us to stop

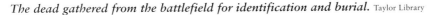

The dead gathered from the battlefield for identification and burial. Taylor Library

diging. One of them read reverently a short service as we stood with our shovels, watching, in spite of ourselves, the motions of his colleague, who, we concluded subsequently, must have been a Roman Catholic padre. At the time he made a certain impression on us, and somehow brought us face to face with the fact of death and the hereafter in a way that we could not remember considering before. But there was no time for reflection then.[31]

Later that day, an extraordinary event took place which, were it not for quick thinking on the part of a staff officer, might have resulted in disaster - and ignominy - for the entire 110th Brigade. Around midday, men from all four battalions suddenly began to appear from Mametz Wood. Apparently rumours that the brigade were about to be relieved had, in the presence of scarcely any officers, developed into 'fact'. The situation may also have arisen due to the presence of a large working party from the East Yorkshire Regiment which moved into position in front of one of the battalions, giving the impression to its exhausted members that relief had indeed arrived. Whatever the reason, men began to leave their trenches and stream back in the direction they had advanced two nights previously. Only the Brigade-Major, grabbing the horse of a nearby artillery driver and riding headlong towards them, yelling for all he was worth, had averted disaster. David Kelly, who was accompanying him, assisted, and

> *got together about eighty men, and joined them on to the returning battalions, then wandering round Bazentin Wood [I] found the Brigadier sitting in a shell-hole, meditating over the risk which had been incurred.*[32]

10135 Pte Robert Wagstaff, 6th Battalion, wounded on 14 July. He was born at Higham Ferrers, Northamptonshire.

20077 Pte Leonard Evans of Leicester, 8th Battalion, killed on 15 July.

Courtesy of Leicestershire Record Office

'Leicesters of 21st Div...', Lieut. B.U.S.Cripps, intelligence officer of the 2nd Battalion Welsh Regt (on the left of 110th Brigade) records the near disastrous event of 15 July in his diary.

B.U.S.Cripps, Liddle Collection

2nd Lieutenant Arthur Howard Smith, 9th Battalion, killed in action on 14 July – 'he was always considerate to his men, and a favourite with everybody'. Smith had served prior to the war in the ranks of the London Rifle Brigade, before being commissioned into the Leicestershire Regiment.

15228 Pte Albert Preston, 8th Battalion, killed on 15 July.

Nevertheless, the men were back in the front line, before the Germans had time to realise that for a stretch of several hundred yards in front of them there were no opposing troops.

Fighting continued for some of the day in the north western corner of Bazentin Wood, the Germans using rifle grenades and other projectiles to help them re-establish a foothold, but by nightfall they had retired again.

On the evening of 16 July, the 7th and 8th Battalions trooped wearily out of the line, down through Mametz Wood to Fricourt, where they set up bivouacs. The next day they were followed by the 6th and 9th Battalions.[33] On 16 July, Cave noted in his diary:

> Battalion came out of the line, and bivouacked at Mametz. I had to call the roll of the Company, and this was a heartbreaking business. The answer to most of the names was 'killed'. All men who were not definitely known to have been killed were posted as missing. For this we had to rely on the knowledge of the few survivors of course.[34]

On the night of 17 July, Dick Read and the survivors of the 8th marched away from Fricourt to Mericourt. Fresh straw in a barn and hot soup were waiting for them, as was mail from home, which they had not received for over a week. Dick recalled:

> It was a fine night and we made a ring around Sergeant Chesterton as, with the aid of the [hurricane] lamp, he called out the names on the letters and parcels. More than two thirds of them lay unclaimed afterwards; in response to his call 'Private So-and-so' a voice would shout 'killed' or 'Blighty', or two or more would confuse the issue by shouting both...the [next] afternoon we paraded with the rest of the brigade for inspection by our 21st Division commander, General Campbell, who thanked us 'for our splendid effort on July 14th'; but this parade demonstrated more clearly than anything had done previously, the terrible losses sustained. We were a mere handful.[35]

CSM Stafford, after having had time to reflect on matters at some length, chose to focus not just on the casualties but also on the achievements of the Brigade, when writing to Captain Ward:

A modern photograph of the entrance to the courtyard at Mericourt, where Dick Read and the survivors of the 8th Battalion crowded around Sergeant Chesterton, as he issued the mail after Bazentin. Richard Lane

14623 Pte William Arthur Haines, 6th Battalion, killed on 15 July. He was born at Mountsorrel.

I think, Sir, you have every reason to be a proud man (I hope you will pardon me for saying so). Only well trained and well disciplined troops could have faced the Hell we faced. It was your training, Sir, and I'm a proud man to have served under such an Officer. The 'Boys' did wonderfully well, Sir, and I'm proud to be Com Sgt Major over the 'Remnants'. We have always prided ourselves on being the BEST Company in the Battalion and I think Bazentin-le-Petit proved it.[36]

In this statement lies some clue as to the strength of the bonds between officers and men, and the sense of loyalty which existed both between comrades, and in the men for their battalions. It was these strengths, perhaps more than anything else, which allowed the survivors, not just of the Leicestershire Brigade but in other Kitchener's Army formations as well, to accept the losses and to continue fighting in the name of their cause on the Somme that summer.

For those wounded who had been able to extricate themselves from the battle zone (or who, like Signaller Hillyard, were carried out on a stretcher, often by a party of German PoWs) the treatment they now received was on the whole fast and efficient. Private Harry Wileman of the 6th Battalion took four days from battlefield to Blighty, passing from Field Dressing Station to Casualty Clearing Station, then via Base Hospital on the French coast and hospital ship to the 2nd Southern General Hospital at Bristol, arriving on 18 July. Jack Horner was treated at an overcrowded ADS - Advanced Dressing Station - bandaged, given an injection, and labelled 'walking wounded'. Shipped to England, he was driven by motor ambulance

14705 Pte Charles Lowe, 9th Battalion, killed on 14 July. He enlisted at Oakham.

15020 Sgt Ernest Knott, 9th Battalion, killed on 14 July. He too enlisted at Oakham.

German PoWs were often used to carry British wounded from the battle zone. Taylor Library

16014 Pte David Nutt, 7th Battalion. He died of wounds at No 13 General Hospital, Boulogne, on 31 July, after being hit at Bazentin.

17469 Pte James Tookey, 7th Battalion, of Coalville. This photograph was taken in Stockport where he was a hospital patient, in the summer of 1916. Tookey was wounded in Mametz Wood, as he put it 'by a careless German', on 15 July, during the Bazentin Ridge battle. His brother 18121 Pte Percy Tookey, 8th Battalion was killed in action on 19 September 1916.

to a Naval hospital outside Plymouth:

We were shown our wards, and my first request to the Ward Sister was: 'Could I have a bath?' We were still lousy, and in the same uniform which we were in when we went into battle.

The sister had a look at my arm, and said I could have a bath, and gave me slippers, pyjamas, and a dressing gown. (What a luxury! We had to sleep with our trousers on, especially in the Line - there was no other way) and to leave all our dirty clothes, uniform as well, except boots and hat with badge...I don't know what they did with them, but I hope they burnt the bloody lot and killed all the little bastards which had given me and others so much discomfort. And so to the bathroom - lashings of hot water, soap, a big bath towel. It was rather difficult to scrub down with the left arm, but I managed. It was so wonderful to feel free from lice after all these months...After breakfast we were kitted out with Hospital Blue, blue jacket with white facings, blue trousers, white shirt, red tie - quite smart.[37]

Many of the wounded, including James Tookey of Whitwick, and Fred Tilley of Smeeton Westerby, found themselves at the Pendlebury Red Cross Hospital, a voluntary hospital at Stockport. It was formerly the Sir Ralph Pendlebury Orphanage, which had been converted for the duration of the war and which was run with assistance from a number of VAD nurses. Some of the wounded had made it back across the channel, only to succumb to their injuries in Britain, as the War Graves headstones in so many village cemeteries will testify. Others had been delighted at first at receiving a 'blighty one' (ie a wound serious enough to require evacuation to Britain, but not life-threatening) such as Dick Read's fellow apprentice, Taylor, with whom he had enlisted:

[he] had been hit in the lower forearm. As he came towards us, holding it and his useless dangling left hand with his right, he extended it to us,

The name and address of another Leicestershire Brigade survivor, in the same album; Pte Fred Tilley, of Smeeton Westerby, served with 'B' Company, 8th Battalion. D.M.Clarke, Liddle Collection

Tookey's name and address, in a nurse's autograph album. D.M.Clarke, Liddle Collection

137

Circled in this photo is 20596 Pte Harry Wileman of Leicester (6th Battalion), convalescing at the Southern General Hospital, Bristol, after being wounded at Bazentin. His journey across the channel to England began on 18 July - it took four days from treatment at an advanced dressing station on the battlefield, through a casualty clearing station (CCS) to a base hospital on the French coast, until coming home by hospital ship. Harry was killed with the 6th Battalion in October 1918. Mr Norman Hastings

shouting 'put it there, Dick, better born lucky than rich!' and on he went.[38]

But Taylor was not as lucky as he might at first have seemed, for like so many others, his wound would trouble him for the rest of his life:

Nearly 23 years after the battle, the body of one of those killed, 11788 Pte William Tite, was discovered by a farmer ploughing his land near Bazentin. Tite was from Wigston, and an ex-Regular soldier who had previously served in the Boer War. Having taken his final discharge from the army around 1911, he had immediately volunteered for the 6th Battalion when it was raised in 1914.

Dianne Thier/Dennis Tite

TEL.: SLOANE 8121.

Ref. SL/39504.

IMPERIAL WAR GRAVES COMMISSION,

32, GROSVENOR GARDENS,

LONDON, S.W.I.

5th January 1939.

Dear Madam,

I am writing to inform you that it has now been possible to identify the burial place of Private William Tite.

The body of an Unknown British Soldier was found in the vicinity of Bazentin-le-Petit, in France, and in order to secure the proper maintenance of the grave in perpetuity the remains were carefully moved and reverently reburied in Grave 17, Row J, Plot 8 of London Cemetery Extension, High Wood, Longueval.

When this was done a portion of your husband's identity disc was found, and from this and the Commission's records, it was possible to prove definitely that this is his grave. The Commission will, in due course, erect a headstone on the grave on which his name and regimental particulars will be engraved, and in this connection I am enclosing a form which I shall be glad if you will kindly complete and return to this office.

If you wish to claim the portion of disc, written application should be made to the Under-Secretary of State, War Office, (F.8.Effects), Hobart House, Grosvenor Place, S.W.1., quoting the late soldier's number, name and regiment (which are 11788 Private William Tite, 6th Battalion, Leicester Regiment).

Yours faithfully,

SECRETARY.

Mrs. A.L. Tite,
110, Bull's Head Street,
Wigston Magna,
Leicester.

LOCAL CASUALTIES.

Heavy List of Wounded.

The following casualties are announced by the official Press Bureau, the men being privates unless otherwise stated. All are registered in Leicester except where the address is given:—

KILLED.

Cameronians (Scottish Rifles).
17550 F. Dalby.

Sherwood Foresters.
15025 F. Barnes (Hinckley).

DIED OF WOUNDS.

Leicestershire Regiment.

13301 Cpl. F. Buckley (Burton-on-Trent).	12947 L-Cpl. Rodgers (Derby).
18000 G. H. Matthews (Loughborough).	16106 A. Thirdborough.
15066 J. Noon (Coalville).	14010 Sgt. J. C. Whitlock.

WOUNDED.

Leicestershire Regiment.

25068 P. Allen (Market Harborough).	15776 A. P. Bicken (Whitwick).
10406 L. Alsory (Hinckley).	23964 A. J. Hill.
24097 J. W. Annis (Sutton Bridge).	3507 G. Hodgett (Stamford).
11065 G. Archer (Ashby).	21411 W. J. Homes (Market Harborough).
16799 I. Armstrong.	21091 G. L. Holmes (Shirebrook).
12007 R. Baker (Hinckley).	14541 Sgt. T. Hopewell.
25362 D. J. Ball.	17070 A. H. Houghton (Ibstock).
12128 W. Bayles (Cotverton Hall).	11417 E. B. Johnson (Enderby).
19218 Cpl. H. Buckle (Leeds).	19544 A. Kebby (Romsey).
18283 A. Belfield.	10109 Sgt. W. Lawrence (Llanelly).
18062 W. H. Benfield.	10471 A. Lewis (Leytonstone, N.E.).
12291 W. Beeton (Loughborough).	15401 A. Lewis (Altham).
14167 J. J. Bollandk (Chesterfield).	10889 T. Lord (Hugglescote).
15471 W. H. Boor.	11731 J. Matthews.
15336 J. Bradford (Coalville).	13737 J. Melkers (Mansfield).
13605 G. Bridgen (Brampton).	13202 H. Needham (Langley Mill).
10765 Sgt. W. Burden (Darlaston).	15015 E. Ogden (Widnes).
11486 J. Buck (Hugglescote).	15783 J. Oldham.
21284 G. Burditt.	17214 B. E. Parsons (Sudbetone).
12865 Sgt. W. E. Burton (West Bridgford).	11856 W. Penfold (Bermondsey, S.E.).
16901 H. Carrington.	15226 A. L. Pettit (Kegworth).
12639 G. Carter (K. Kirby).	20548 J. A. Iveston (Thornmaston).
15503 L-Cpl. F. W. Cave (Shirebrook).	2498 E. Powell.
16000 A. Chamberlain.	20466 E. Price (Ibstock).
10924 T. Clarke (Shirebrook).	13989 T. Price (Islip).
13429 C. Cinley.	10394 A. Pritchard (Market Harborough).
24805 H. Cockerill (Earl Shilton).	16071 J. C. Rawsons (Oakham).
18735 J. Cooper (Melton Mowbray).	13272 J. Roberts (Stretton).
5419 R. H. Cooper (Market Harborough).	21748 R. Rowe (Hinds Ashford).
22916 T. Crofts.	20070 L. Seal.
18428 R. Crooks.	13167 L. J. Sharpe (Swadlincote).
18015 W. Daykin (Derby).	13171 Co-Sgt-Major W. Sharpe (Hugglescote).
10184 J. Dean (Loughborough).	14185 J. J. Shepherds (Sheepbridge).
21917 G. Essex (Market Harborough).	16162 A. Sisson (Melton Mowbray).
12495 S. Fellows.	9484 L-Cpl. A. W. Skeet.
23821 A. Fox (Nott'ngh'm).	10439 L-Cpl. C. Skerritt (Melton Mowbray).
20417 J. Fox (Hinckley).	12054 G. Smith.
15480 G. Fuller (Loughbro).	19188 W. Speck (Llamberlais).
16694 R. Garner.	21173 W. Spence (Whetstone).
20982 S. A. Gell.	12743 W. Toobey.
11965 A. Glover.	14093 J. Unmey (Chesterfield).
13157 W. H. Goddard (Stamford).	12216 T. Walters (Chesterfield).
13686 G. Godfrey (Shirebrook).	13352 F. G. Wardle (Burton-on-Trent).
14414 G. S. Goodwin.	15885 L-Cpl. G. H. Watson (Anstey).
22013 J. B. Goodwin.	21286 N. H. Wells (Blaby).
22179 H. Hall (Blaby).	19297 A. Weecott (Sturminster).
15853 J. Hancock (Burton-on-Trent).	11240 J. T. Wilbraham (Hartshill).
11928 W. Hares (Thornton).	12610 G. Wilkinson (Huthwaite).
50204 L-Cpl. S. W. Harper (Kettering).	10420 T. R. Wright (Newark).
10919 F. C. Heath (Worksop).	
12806 Co-Sgt-Maj. T. W. Henson (Salford).	
18630 J. F. Hester (Salford).	
12071 H. Hatterley (Sileby).	
12926 L-Cpl. A. V. Hewitt (Sutton-in-Ashfield).	
18221 A. Hewins (Birmingham).	

Northumberland Fusiliers.

13795 F. Greeves.

One of the many casualty rolls published in the Leicester Evening Mail in July and August 1916. Despite the heading, this was in fact one of the shorter lists. Included here is the name of 17411 Pte 'Jack' Horner, hit in the arm by German bullet.

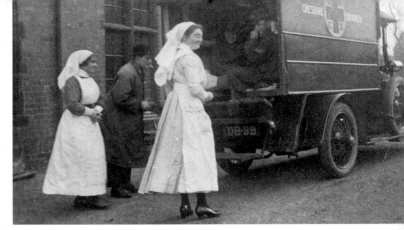

Above: Wounded arriving at the Pendlebury Hospital.
Below: Both Tookey and Tilley were treated at the Sir Ralph Pendlebury Orphanage in Stockport, which had been temporarily converted into a War Hospital.

'I met him in Leicester after the war. He couldn't grip anything with that hand. Years of special treatment and several operations were partially successful and he got a job as a handyman carpenter. Finally he took a pub in Syston. His hand continued to give him hell.'[39]

Unlike Taylor many other wounded men, such as Jack Horner, after a period of convalescence were deemed fit for active service once more. Later that same year Jack found himself again on a troopship heading back across the channel, bound for France and the front line.

1 War Diary, 7th Bn Leicestershire Regt, LRO 29.6.16.
2 I.L.Read, 'Of Those We Loved' (Pentland Press, 1994) p129
3 Read, op cit p131
4 Read, op cit p132
5 Read, op cit p133
6 D.V.Kelly, 39 Months With the Tigers (Ernest Benn, 1930) p28
7 Kelly, op cit p29
8 War Diary, 7th Bn Leicestershire Regt, LRO 14.7.16
9 Read, op cit p149
10 D.A.Bacon, unpublished typescript account, LRO p60

11 Bacon, *op cit* p60
12 CSM B.Stafford 8th bn Leic. Regt, original letter 20.8.16. Imperial War Museum Department of Documents. Also published in 'The Imperial War Museum Book of the Somme'
13 Stafford, *op cit*
14 *Leicester Evening Mail* 12.8.16
15 *Leicester Evening Mail* 25.7.16
16 *Leicester Evening Mail* 12.8.16
17 Report on 6th Bn Leicestershire Regt attack. Public Record Office WO95 2164
18 J.W.Horner, unpublished typescript account. Author's Collection
19 Read, *op cit* pp154-155
20 Lieut.A.C.N.M.-P. De Lisle, unpublished contemporary account, 'The Story of a Leicestershire Company in the Great Push'
21 De Lisle, *op cit*
22 War Diary, 7th bn Leicestershire Regt, LRO 14.7.16
23 Read, *op cit* p159
24 Kelly, *op cit* p32
25 Stafford, *op cit*
26 Leicester Evening Mail 2.8.16
27 Market Harborough Advertiser 1.8.16
28 Market Harborough Advertiser 1.8.16
29 Leicester Evening Mail 19.7.16
30 Read, *op cit* p160
31 Read, *op cit* p161
32 Kelly, *op cit* p31
33 The 6th Battalion left the line in the early hours of 17 July. Unlike the other three battalions, large numbers of its casualties for the Bazentin battle including some known to have been killed on 14/15 July, are listed as killed on 17 July. This is perhaps best explained by the theory that the exact date for the death of every man could not be ascertained, and so the date on which the casualty return was complied was used instead.
34 A.C.Cave, unpublished typescript diary 16.7.16
35 Read, *op cit* p169
36 Stafford, *op cit*
37 Horner, *op cit*
38 Read, *op cit* p151
39 Read, *op cit* pp151-152

14934 Pte Alf Sturman, 9th Battalion, (seated centre) with fellow patients at Long Eaton Red Cross Hospital. They wear the distinctive hospital uniform of blue jacket with red tie. Pete & Sue Sturman

Alf Sturman (back row, left) at the Northern Command Depot, Ripon. Like many other soldiers, he was awaiting a posting abroad, after recovering from his wounds and being passed medically fit for active service once more. Pete & Sue Sturman

140

Chapter Six

Gueudecourt

The Somme once more

After the Bazentin Ridge battle, the four battalions, sadly depleted, bivouacked at Mametz for a night, and then marched away from the Somme before entraining in the familiar cattle trucks for the country to the north once more. Having detrained, they completed the last stages of the journey by foot and by motor lorry. In his diary for 20 July 1916, Quartermaster-Sergeant Cave recorded their arrival in one of the villages which had been used for billeting prior to 14 July:

Men of the 6th Battalion Leicestershire Regiment at rest. This illustration, reproduced from one of the Daily Mail's series of 'War Pictures', shows the Battalion bivouacked after the Bazentin action. A remarkable amount of detail is visible, particularly in the men's faces, and items of insignia such as the cloth 'Tiger' badges sewn onto the helmet covers of some individuals. The Short Magazine Lee-Enfield rifles have been stacked together, while the men eat a meal prepared in the field cookers visible behind them. Fergus Read

Marched to Hangest. The inhabitants were horrified at the number who did not return of those who had left the village only a few days before.[1]

David Kelly also recalled that in Hangest the landlady of an inn wept at the news that an officer of the 6th of whom she was especially fond was dead. Over the following days the battalions were reorganised, new equipment was indented for to replace that which had been lost and reinforcements were absorbed. Major Unwin of the 9th Battalion took over command of the leaderless 7th Battalion, in the place of the wounded Lieutenant-Colonel Drysdale, and the Battalion War Diary records the arrival of three drafts totalling 300 men and 20 new officers posted from the South Staffordshire Regiment and Sherwood Foresters. Captain Beardsley remained in command of the 8th, in place of Colonel Mignon, until the arrival of Lieutenant-Colonel G.C.I. Hervey in August.

The destination of the 110th Brigade was Agnez les Duisans, near Arras. Here on 6 August they took over a section of battered trenches, known as the 'I' Sector, facing three large mine craters in No Man's Land, called Claude, Clarence, and Cuthbert (named after characters in a song from a popular wartime revue). The 'I' sector was so called because the front in this region was divided into lettered segments. To the north lay 'H' sector held

A photograph dated 19 August 1916 captioned 'after the attack' shows men of the 9th Leicestershire at rest in their billet in a French farmhouse. Pte 'Jack' Holyoak stands back row, extreme right. The expression on his face perhaps betrays something of his recent experiences at Bazentin-le-Petit. Rose Holyoak

by 64th Brigade, and to the south 'J' Sector held by 62nd Brigade. Here they remained for the next four weeks, the only other significant landmark was a large and rather damaged candle factory at the entrance to the communication trench, which provided billets for companies coming out of the front line. Dick Read recalled that to reach the forward trenches:

> we filed...down into a communication trench labelled September Avenue, now assailed by the smell of putrefying grease or fat, which worsened as, in the moonlight above the trench, we saw the gaunt outline of a battered, roofless factory building, and through gaping holes, or thrust into the sky, the twisted shafting and rusting machinery. Between it and our communication trench the ground was strewn with great barrels and other debris protruding through the two-foot high weeds – the source of the stink. We hurried on to get away from it, our feet ringing on what seemed to be an iron trench bottom. Later we found that these were a kind of tray originally used in the factory, and that, when wet, they became very slippery.[2]

An outstanding portrait taken around 18 August 1916, of Captain J.T.S.Nobbs, 6th Battalion. This photo was taken while the battalion was in the Arras area resting between the two Somme attacks in which it participated. Clearly visible are both the yellow circle insignia at the top of Nobbs' sleeve, and the cloth version of the 'Tiger' badge, sewn onto the helmet cover.
Margaret Nobbs

Here the brigade remained, through the burning hot days of August, resting even when in the line, as rats gambolled amid the weeds and wild flowers which grew along the parapet and parados of the trenches. Here again the skeletons of French soldiers dating from the offensives of 1915 could be discerned among the grass, brightly coloured rags of uniforms flapping in the breeze. Germans were rarely seen, and military activity was slight except for the occasional shell and the ever-present danger of mines. The Germans were engaged in tunnelling under the British lines in the hope of blowing an explosive charge beneath them. The New Zealand Tunnelling Company was also in the area; its purpose was to try to achieve the same objective beneath the German lines, and to destroy any German mines which were detected with a counter charge known as a camouflet.

One of the reinforcements who joined here was a private from Leicester named Charles Garlick. He had joined the 12th (Reserve) Battalion of the Leicestershire Regiment in England in April 1916, and had undergone some rudimentary training on the Leicester Tigers Rugby ground. However, Garlick had served with the Territorial Force 4th Battalion Leicestershire Regiment around 1912, and in consequence had a considerable knowledge of soldiering already. As a result of this he was quickly drafted to France, where reserves were urgently needed. On 3 August he was posted to the 6th Battalion, reaching them the next day. His fragile diary survives and records some of his experiences, providing a fascinating 'worm's-eye view' picture of the life of the average soldier in the line at this time:

27141 Pte Charles Garlick, 6th Battalion. In this photograph taken in 1912 he wears the red full dress tunic of his unit at that time, 4th Battalion Leicestershire Regiment-TF.

John Taylor

Aug 5 *Had gas lectures And inspected by CO rather a quiet day.*

Aug 6 *Paraded at 4am, trench order & shovel for laying trench boards & sand bagging. First time in trenches & got wind up.*

Aug 7 *Same orders as 6th, had a few shells drop very close & put wind up us. Had a walk round Arras at night. Very big place & plenty of ruins.*

Aug 8 *Had orders to go into the trenches to relieve the 8th and 9th Leicesters on the 9th.*

Aug 9 *Left billets at 8pm & proceeded to trenches & arrived at about 9.30 at Nicholls Redoubt, got in a dugout called Albert Hall, took packs off & loaded rifles, fixed bayonets & had orders to stand to & then had gas alert. Fairly got the W.P.*

Aug 10 *Started to carry rations for A B & C Companys [sic] from the Candle Factory & continued until the 19th. Damned hard work & very little rest wet nearly all the time.*

Aug 19 *Was relieved by the 7th Leicesters & went into billet 1/4 mile from the Candle Factory.*

Aug 21 *Paraded at 7 o'clock to carry Trench Mortar (Stoats* [nb Stokes] *Shells) to first line 3 kilos from Arras...*

Aug 29 *Left billets at 8.30 pm & proceeded to Foresters Redoubt to relieve the 9th Leicesters. Good deep dugouts.*

Aug 30 *Stand to 4.30am Laying trench boards & wiring every night...*

Aug 31 *Was relieved by the Notts & Jocks Bantons [sic] from the Somme. Left redoubt at 7.30pm, had a rest in barracks at Arras & then marched to Anguse [?] 12 kilos not allowed to smoke, got to sleep 2 o'clock.*[3]

For officers of course there was less physical hardship, as they were not required to undertake the manual labour on carrying parties or work details. However the danger to which they were exposed was the same or often greater than that endured by the men, and Kelly recalled that at Arras they had some chance to relax:

The trenches were not often shelled, and the general holiday atmosphere was only disturbed by occasional bursts of trench mortar fire on the front line and, at four in the afternoon, with comic regularity, by a few shells on Arras cathedral. We were usually having tea at that time...and the shells flew straight overhead to the Cathedral a few hundred yards away, but we had complete confidence that the efficiency of the German artillery would prevent any shells falling short and hitting our headquarters by mistake.

He continued:

'*Somewhere in the "Doing's Ruins"*' is the humorous caption to this photograph of 9th Battalion NCOs in the ruins of Arras. Someone (presumably one of the group) has written on the reverse '*Good Old Tigers – Never Say Die*'. John Taylor

From:- Adjutant, No.33 Infantry Base Depot.

To:- 2nd Lieut. S. W. Clarke.

Please note that you will proceed to join the *9th Leicester Regt.* *21st Division, 5 Army* by the train leaving *New Siding* at 8.20 pm 9.9.16.

You will report to the R.T.O. there at *7.40 pm* for further instructions.

You must be in possession of Anti-Gas Goggles, Helmets, Iron Ration and Armature Iodine.

Please see that your baggage is outside the GUARD TENT at *7 pm* punctually, also that your Mess a/c is settled ~~satisfactory~~ *before leaving the Depot.*

In the Field,
9th Sept. '16

H. Cardinal Harford CAPT & ADJT.
No.33 Infantry Base Depot.

---

battery for a bit. will also let you know about this. I speaks Wyp is quite close to me. there is a Lewis gun school not very far away. I wonder if I shall run across him? He will be able to get plenty of steps down here I don't think I have any more news tonight so will stop. if I've time I'll add more to this tomorrow. if not, I shall send it as it is. Well cherio. Lots of love to everyone

Sid.

Second Lieutenant Sid Clarke, West Yorkshire Regiment, and his orders to report to the 9th Battalion Leicestershire Regiment. Clarke described the 9th as 'some mouldy crowd'!
Liddle Collection

What's happened to my old flue? Has Carver put it right or is it still layed out. 'praps I'll want it before very long, if the war doesn't last too long.

Later now.

I have just received my orders to go up the line. I go at 7.40 tonight to the 9th Leicesters. (some mouldy crowd I 'spose) so address my letters in future. 14 W. Yorks. attd 9 Leicesters. 21st Div. Now please don't worry as I'm sure to be alright. I don't know were I'm going to. havn't the vaguest in fact.

An army boxing contest in France, circa 1917.

*Lieutenant
J.W.Dixie-Smith
8th Battalion.*

there was a general atmosphere of cheerfulness. Especially do I remember - with a slight watering of the mouth - an 8th Battalion mess graced by the presence of [Lieutenant] *Dixie-Smith, whose whereabouts could usually be divined when one heard a gramophone grinding out 'Let the great big world keep turning.'*[4]

Lieutenant J.W. Dixie-Smith was a well-known Leicester businessman and sportsman, and was well liked by both officers and rank and file. One evening in the trenches about this time, Dick Read encountered him whilst on sentry duty, and Dixie-Smith (having earlier observed him drawing) presented Read with a sketch book which he had obtained whilst on a day's leave in a nearby town.

At length, the brigade left the front line, and retired some miles back to the back-area villages around Avesnes-le-Comte. Here they were joined by more large drafts of reinforcements, including some of the lightly wounded from Bazentin, who had returned to duty. On 11 September, the entire brigade was addressed by Major-General Donald Campbell, GOC 21st Division. Campbell started his speech by addressing the assembled Tommies with the word 'gentlemen', which was a gesture well received by most, but he concluded with the news that they were once more to take part in the battle of the Somme.

That afternoon, there was a brigade boxing tournament nearby, in which Sergeant Brotherhood, the heavyweight hope of the 8th Battalion, received a broken jaw in the second round, from 'Cock' Howard of the 6th Battalion. Brotherhood was carried off on a stretcher, destined to take no part in the coming attack. That night, the estaminets in the villages around Avesnes were full of Leicesters, having perhaps a final drink, for they knew now what they could expect. Dick Read, in the village of Lignereuil, was among them:

Then the Regimental Police cleared the estaminets and we went

147

down the village street arm-in-arm singing 'Oh...the old red flannel drawers ...'

The only people who were quite sober appeared to be the orderly sergeants and orderly corporals of the day, who flitted about in the dusk, busy with returns and messages to and from the orderly rooms. From all the barns we passed issued sounds of harmony, choruses with mouth-organ accompaniments. No sooner had we reached our billet, however, than we had to parade in the farmyard for an inspection of respirators, steel helmets, iron rations and field dressings. In vain C.S.M. 'Tiny' Gamble and C.Q.M.S. Peach, helped by Sergeant Killingley, tried to maintain a proper semblance of order; the ranks swayed up and down amid snatches of song and outbursts of alcoholic elation. During the inspection of respirators, which we had to put on, one unfortunate was sick in his, which evoked much merriment.'[5]

25092 Pte Aubrey Skinner, 6th Battalion, he was killed whilst digging a trench on 17 September 1916, by a shell which killed or wounded several other men.

Heads were heavy the following morning as the 110th Brigade marched to the railway station at Frevent to entrain for the Somme once more. Upon arrival near Albert, they detrained and went into bivouacs to the south-east of that city. The weather now had started to deteriorate, and it was raining on the night of 16 September when David Kelly led the Brigade, by compass bearing alone, through the pitch blackness, to the north eastern edge of

Shattered tree stumps in Delville Wood, 1916.

Bernafay Wood. Here they were to bivouac for several days. Slightly to the north lay the shattered remains of Delville Wood, into which a number of Leicestershire Brigade men were to make forays during the coming week, as part of carrying parties for troops in the front line. Delville Wood had been fought over, captured, lost, and recaptured again several times over by September. It had witnessed particularly savage fighting in July of 1916, when the South African Brigade had hung on in the centre for six long days. Now it was a stinking wilderness of smashed tree stumps, between which lay stagnant pools of water whose rims were lined with green scum. Corpses, which had often been buried and then disinterred by shellfire, lay twisted among the tree roots.

24 September 1916, found the Lewis gunners of the 8th Battalion cleaning weapons and equipment following the incessant rain of the previous days. They were bivouacked in shell-holes covered by waterproof ground sheets on the edge of Bernafay Wood. Word went around from the battalion officers that they would be advancing shortly, and a padre arrived to announce a short voluntary service at about 4pm, on the battlefield amid the shell holes. The service was well attended, both by those of a religious conviction and also by a number of those less so inclined. Dick Read explained:

> I believe this service benefited those who took part in it. Most of us went and sang and listened because, I think, we felt that it was a chance to make a peace – to compose ourselves for the ordeal ahead. In my own case, the padre's text from the 121st Psalm recurred to me many times in those next days, and has done at times over the years: 'I will lift up mine eyes unto the hills, from whence cometh my help.' Just then, with some previous experience to give me a fairly good idea of 'what we were about to receive', I found a wealth of cheer in those words. Indeed, where else, or from whom, in these frightful surroundings, could a man obtain the wherewithal to move and act calmly ?[6]

The next day's actions were to be part of the much wider Battle of Morval, the aim of which was to push the Germans off the ridges on to which they had withdrawn following the Allied successes on 15 September. On the night of 24 September the brigade moved forward into action, to a low ridge, before which lay the as yet untaken village of Gueudecourt. It was protected by two heavily wired belts of trenches, known as Gird Trench and Gird Support. Between these trenches and the British positions, lay Goat Trench, also heavily defended by the Germans. The attack unusually was to be made in the middle of the day, at 12.35pm, instead of in the early morning, by the 8th and 9th Battalions together. The 6th Battalion was in reserve, and the 7th was detailed to follow up the attack. As soon as the attacking troops left their positions, the men of the 7th were assigned to occupy these and thenceforth to follow up the advance of the 8th and 9th. It was a clear day, and visibility was good. Waiting for 'zero' hour, David

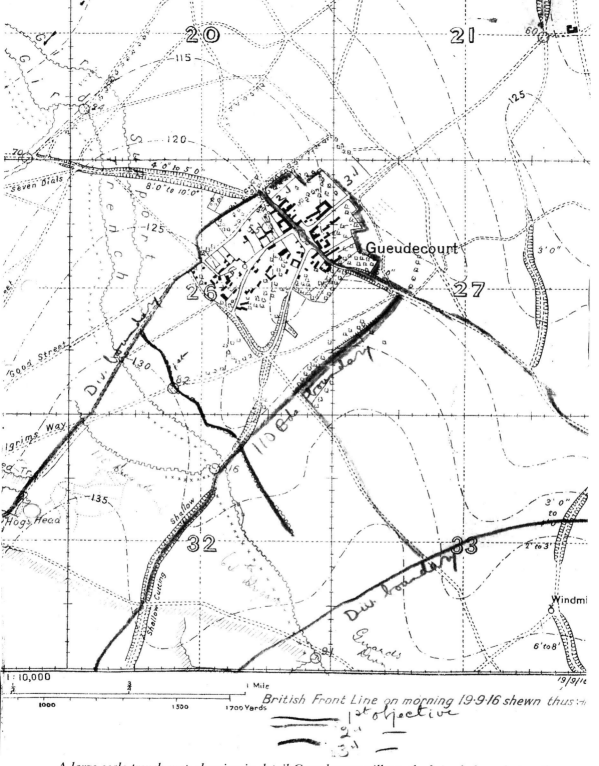

A large-scale trench map showing in detail Gueudecourt village, the brigade boundaries of the 110th Brigade's advance, and the first, second and third objectives of the 25 September attack. W.Batcheldor, Liddle Collection

Kelly made a rough sketch of the scene before him on the back of a captured German map:

> Straight in front lay Gueudecourt – a cluster of broken trees with the debris of a church in the centre, a road with two solitary trees leading from our ridge to the left edge of this village. To the left lay the village of Flers, to the right Lesboeufs, with a gaunt broken tower in the centre. Away beyond these three the skyline was broken, from left to right, by a line of poplars, the relatively extensive ruins of Bapaume, then Riencourt and Beaulencourt, and finally halfway between Lesboeufs and the skyline, the trees of Le Transloy.[7]

Flers had been the target of the first ever attack launched using tanks, ten days previously. Tanks were to be included in the forthcoming attack, and some of those knocked out on the previous outing were still visible. The attacking troops had, under the cover of darkness, moved forward to positions beyond the British front line, to foxholes scraped out by the divisional pioneers. Before the light of dawn revealed too clearly their position, the men hastened to deepen these shallow trenches with spades, entrenching tools and even bare hands, to provide as much cover as possible. Perhaps with a slight lack of imagination, this line was named 'New Trench' on British maps. As the morning dragged by, nervous tension increased among the attackers. Dick Read recalled:

> As much for the sake of something to do, I remember that Fatty Briggs handed me a drum which I placed on the magazine post of the [Lewis] gun. His hand had trembled. Mine had. Instead of putting it on in 'one-two' fashion, smartly, I bungled it and had to thump and coax the drum down into position. I kept trying to swallow, and was conscious of a feeling of cramp in the pit of the stomach.[8]

At zero hour the British artillery barrage fell with a deafening roar all along the enemy's front, and the two attacking battalions rose out of their trenches to advance. Suddenly, all feelings of nervousness were banished: -

> As though by magic, I felt calm again, [and] saw that my mates were the same...I pulled back the cocking handle of the gun. We grinned at one another and wished each other the best of luck...[9]

As whistles blew, the men began to move forward at the double, tricky as it was with a full load of kit across the heavily shell-turned ground. Two or three minutes later, the German counter-barrage began to fall all around, with great spouts of black earth leaping into the air. Soon Gueudecourt, Les Boeufs, and Morval, as well as the advancing Leicesters, were obscured by clouds of dust and flying earth.

Rushing forward into the attack, some parties of the 8th Battalion were temporarily checked by heavy German machine gun fire emanating from Gird Trench. At this moment, Captain Frank Breacher, commanding 'A' Company, 8th Battalion, spotted an abandoned bugle on the battlefield. He at once picked it up, and used it to blow the Quorn Hunt 'Tally Ho'. This had the effect of rallying the men around him, who had started to waver, but

Captain Frank Breacher, after recovering from his wounds. Also shown are his identity disc, with lucky silver sixpence, the bugle which Breacher picked up, and two notifications from the local press.

Mrs S. Chatham

at the same moment Captain Breacher was hit several times by machine gun fire. He fell backward, seriously wounded. As he was carried away by stretcher bearers, however, Breacher was still clutching the bugle, which he was to keep as a souvenir for the next forty years. Another 8th Battalion man who was wounded whilst advancing towards Gueudecourt was Sergeant George Sleath, the school master from Rothley. With shrapnel wounds to the lower part of the right leg, he made his own way back to the advanced dressing station, partly crawling and partly using his rifle as a crutch. He refused an offer of assistance from stretcher bearers, telling them to make for those wounded men who were unable to move at all. Arriving at a dressing station he was greeted with the words 'You've got a Blighty one there, Sergeant.' Later at a Base Hospital, doctors decided that the wound was more serious than that, and wanted to amputate Sleath's leg. He protested vigorously, however, and nurses worked through the night with poultices to clean and dress the wound. The following morning there was sufficient improvement in his condition for the surgeons to change their

Glen Parva.
nr. Leicester.
8.10.16.

Dear Mrs Breacher,

    I was very sorry indeed to hear that your son had been wounded and hope he is making satisfactory progress.

He was most kind in giving me information when I had the news about my husband who wishes me to say that he has every hope of your son's recovery, as we hear he has been moved from the Clearing Station to a hospital. My husband was not moved from the Casualty Station to hospital for some days, and was in France for nearly three weeks before being brought to England.

I did not receive particulars from the War Office as to the nature of his wounds for some days.

I know what an anxious time this is for you, and sincerely sympathise. I hope it will not be long before you receive re-assuring news.

With best wishes. Believe me
    Yours very sincerely
    Elsie Kent.

Elsie Kent, the wife of one of Breacher's men, wrote to his mother to express her sympathy after he was wounded.

Mrs S.Chatham

14895 Pte James Woodward, 9th Battalion, of Morcott, killed on 25 September.

minds, and Sleath maintained from that day onward that the actions of the nurses had saved his leg.

The Leicesters managed to capture Goat Trench, but many were shot down in the middle ground before Gird Trench, which was still strongly held by the enemy, as they struggled across the uneven and shell scarred terrain. The first line position had largely been cleared of Germans, and prisoners were already streaming back, but snipers who had taken cover in shell holes were also beginning their deadly work from the rear of the advancing British soldiers.

At 2.35pm the War Diary of the 9th Battalion summed up the situation on the right-hand portion of the battlefield thus:

Advance hung up on account of MG fire and rifle fire. Enemy still occupying Gird Trench on right of Sunken Road. Lieut Col Haig and Lieut Tooth advanced to New Trench and finding it empty crossed over to Goat Trench. Only dead and wounded were found in Goat Trench, accordingly Lieut Col Haig, in anticipation that the front two companies had reached Gird Trench, advanced to Pilgrim's Way where 40 OR of 8th Leic Regt were found without any officer. Lieut Col Haig decided to remain and hold on with 40 until reinforcements arrived to clear Gird Trench on right.[10]

Haig and Tooth had gone over the top with the fourth wave of their battalion. Sometime after reaching Pilgrim's Way, Haig was hit in the hand, but elected to remain with the men until the following day, when he was relieved by Captain P. E. Bent.

Further over to the left, Dick Read, finding himself and his comrades fired upon from behind, took cover in a shell hole; very quickly, they realised that they were pinned down by a singularly determined enemy soldier:

Then I had an idea. It seemed to me that one man, particularly, had us spotted, and our first job was to find him. Fatty [Briggs] agreed so, shoving the [Lewis] gun up quickly, I fired several short bursts in the general direction of the Germans in the trench while Fatty took a hurried look around. Two bullets all but struck the gun as I got it going, but after that there were no more. Fatty, shouting gleefully, 'That's made the b... get down,' rose to his knees. Suddenly he pointed. 'Hi - give it to him Dick. There the b... is, behind that barrel...back of the trench!' Raising myself, I got the butt of the gun properly into my

153

shoulder, peering through the sights and firing short bursts as I endeavoured to spot the barrel. As I saw it, to my disgust the drum came to an end. In the same instant I saw the German appear from behind the barrel, raise his rifle and steady it against the side to fire at me, but Fatty, bless him, was too quick for him. Unknown to me, he had taken careful aim with his rifle at the barrel and, almost as the German appeared, he fired. I remember well, still looking along the sights, seeing the puff of dust spout from the German's chest as he fell over backwards.[11]

David Kelly reconnoitred to establish the situation at around 4pm. What he discovered was that Gird Trench was now being shared between Leicesters and the partially expelled German garrison, who were throwing bombs for all they were worth. In the trench,

where a hasty block had been made - I found Captain Tooth, Adjutant of the 9th Battalion, who greeted me with the words, 'Thank God, here you are'. I discovered later this address was not so flattering as it sounded; it was due to the fact that I was 'wearing wash-leather gloves and carrying a malacca cane as though in Piccadilly', and consequently conveyed the impression that things must after all be

24873 Pte Cecil Allett, 8th Battalion, of Oakham, killed on 25 September.

18371 Pte Herbert Berridge, 8th Battalion, killed on 25 September. He was from Morcott, Rutland.

11745 Pte Wellesley George Carter, 7th Battalion, killed on 25 September. He was a plumber by trade, and lived at Wing.

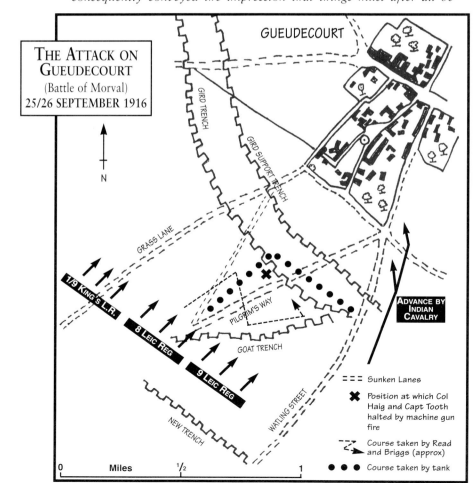

THE ATTACK ON GUEUDECOURT
(Battle of Morval)
25/26 SEPTEMBER 1916

GUEUDECOURT

N

GIRD TRENCH

GIRD SUPPORT TRENCH

GRASS LANE

ADVANCE BY INDIAN CAVALRY

1/9 KING'S L.R.

8 LEIC REG

9 LEIC REG

PILGRIM'S WAY

GOAT TRENCH

WATLING STREET

NEW TRENCH

= = = Sunken Lanes

✕ Position at which Col Haig and Capt Tooth halted by machine gun fire

Course taken by Read and Briggs (approx)

● ● ● Course taken by tank

0   Miles   ½   1

25892 Pte William Killips, 9th Battalion, killed on 25 September. He was born at Carrickfergus, Co Antrim, and was a railway booking clerk. He was killed one month after arriving in France.

25908 Pte Frederick Goodwin, 6th Battalion, of Ayston. Frederick was wounded on 26 September and died of wounds in hospital on 12 October.

26159 Pte John Goodwin, brother of the above, 9th Battalion. He was killed on 25 September, the day before Frederick was mortally wounded.

normal. He informed me that his Colonel was wounded and in a dugout in a sunken road leading to the second trench that was being shared with Germans. Leaving him I found Major Beardsley, second-in-command of the 8th Leicesters, and together we made a dash across the open to the Colonel's dugout. Though the distance was short, Beardsley's orderly was hit by a sniper on the way, and I learned then that every orderly who had been sent back with messages to brigade headquarters had been knocked out on the way.[12]

Lying in No Man's Land, Read and Fatty Briggs could see the bombing battle taking place between Germans and British in Gird Trench. On one occasion they observed a party of Germans, heavily armed with grenades, leave their portion of the trench and crawl along the open ground in an attempt to get behind the British. Read and Briggs opened fire on them with the Lewis gun, to devastating effect. At this point, the two Tommies decided that they had better rejoin the main body of their battalion, which was in Goat Trench. In fact, when they arrived, they discovered that it was a mixed group of Leicesters and King's Liverpool Regiment, who had attacked on the left of the 8th Leicesters, with no officers and commanded only by NCOs. Sergeants Kirk and Chesterton of 'C' Company had taken command of the Leicester contingent, and having heard from Read of their comrades in the bombing fight up ahead, Chesterton ordered his men to work forward along Goat Trench (which their trench maps showed them led into Gird Trench) to support them:

Just here was a German strong point in the trench which had been blown in by a big British shell. We had noticed the timbers protruding at all angles when we were firing from the shell hole. Our bombers started to clamber over, and I remember well Fatty and I following behind them when there was a 'crack' and the back of the leading man's head seemed to fall way as he pitched forward. Another 'crack' and another fell, shot through the chest, apparently at point blank range. The rest of us stopped still until Sergeant Chesterton, grabbing a couple of Mills grenades, set an example by hurling them well and truly, for the explosions were followed by screams. At this we made a concerted dash, sometimes firing from the hip and progressing about thirty yards, picking our way over a mass of dead and wounded Germans. Many were terribly hit by our Lewis fire from the shell hole. One sat in the trench bottom, literally trying to put back his insides. Seeing Sergeant Chesterton he stopped and reaching for a nearby Mauser automatic, intended to take a shot at him, but couldn't, and fell back, unconscious with the effort.[13]

Eventually increasing German opposition and the continuous rain of stick bombs forced Chesterton and his party to halt. They could get no further towards Gueudecourt - which apparently now lay abandoned - and so built a hasty bomb-block across the trench from whatever debris of wire and empty ammunition boxes they could find. Grimly, they resolved to hang on. By 4.30pm, things were quietening down, and both sides by now were

A typical trench scene which confronted soldiers of both armies, as they fought to capture and re-capture ground. Taylor Library

tiring. In the lull in the fighting, Dick Read decided to have a smoke of his pipe. In the confusion of the afternoon's battle, he had not noticed the breast pocket of his tunic literally ripped away by a bullet or shell shard:

> *On taking my pipe from my pocket,* [I] *found that half the bowl was missing...The pocket was a ruin and the remains of the pipe and the packet of Chairman tobacco had somehow hung in it.*[14]

At dusk, Chesterton and Read of the 8th Battalion, and the thirty more men with them, received an unexpected visit from Major Beardsley. He had apparently been searching for hours for isolated pockets such as this, and when after taking stock of the situation and noting the men's location, he returned to battalion headquarters, it was with the promise that rations and water would be there soon.

As darkness fell, the isolated parties in the trenches, including that of Dick Read, strained eyes and ears for any sign of creeping German attackers. At length, they posted sentries, and took turns to rest - many falling instantly asleep after the exertions and strains of the day. It had been typical of the confused nature of much of the fighting on the Somme, indeed on the western front as a whole. In the labyrinthine systems of trenches constructed by the Germans, attacking waves of infantry were quickly broken up and dispersed into small groups, while parties of defenders who had been overlooked sniped at them. Neither side could really be certain of the location of the enemy, or of that of the remainder of their own formation.

The early light of dawn, at about 6.30am on 26 September, brought an amazing sight, which few prior to this would have seen. A tank, one of those detailed to assist the attack the previous day, was now on the scene, accompanied by a large bombing party of the 7th Battalion under Captain A.W.H. Tyler and Second-Lieutenant H.J.Walsh. It was finally about to break German resistance around Gueudecourt. The tank rumbled along Gird

Trench which had been shared between the Germans and the party of the 8th Battalion under Sergeant Chesterton, and Read, who had been asleep, awoke to the commotion that its presence had aroused. He remembered:

> *I heard strange sounds amid the general shouting and 'rat-tat-tat' of machine guns. Looking where Fatty and Hughes were pointing excitedly I saw, for the first time, a tank in action. It was a Mark I (Male), halfway up the slope, parallel with the trench, and strings of German soldiers were standing with their hands up, being shepherded by Sergeants Chesterton and Kirk and their exultant men. The roar of the tank's exhausts were accentuated as its snout rose in the air, taking the protruding beams of a strong-point in its stride, to fall with crushing frightfulness on the next obstacle. More Germans rose from the trench beyond with arms held high, as, at length, we saw it disappear beyond the crest of the rise - going strong.*[15]

The War Diary of the 7th Battalion for this day reported that:

> *Tank moving along the trench from PILGRIM WAY eastwards, followed closely by the battalion bombers, who were kept supplied with bombs by C & D Coys. The attack was entirely successful. Many of the enemy were killed in the trench, all dug-outs were bombed with great effect, phosphorous bombs proving very useful for this purpose. In about 30 minutes the trench was cleared as far as WATLING ST. Here a break in the trench caused by the SUNKEN Road caused a temporary check, but 2/Lt WALSH rushed his men across the gap in sections & continued the advance without loss. Our men entirely outthrew the German bombers & when 200 yards beyond WATLING ST. the Tank left the trench and proceeded towards the village the bombers were able to carry on without a check. At this point a large number of the enemy left their trench and surrendered to the troops holding the trench to their front.*[16]

As the afternoon drew on, a new spectacle attracted the attention of the

Tanks rolling forwards, behind British lines on the Somme, September 1916. This photograph is believed to have been taken between the 15 and 25 September attacks.

Leicestershire men. A party of Indian cavalry from 'A' Squadron of the 19th Lancers – the Hotchkiss machine-gun section with their guns and ammunition mounted on the saddles of the horses, perhaps twenty all told – were advancing at a trot up the sunken lane which led ultimately to Gird Support Trench. Several Leicestershire men attempted to warn them of their imminent danger, but their mission was to reconnoitre Gueudecourt, and they would not be dissuaded from this. Upon reaching the ruins at the edge of the village (the Germans had apparently allowed them to advance this far unmolested) they tied up their horses, and attempted to enter the village on foot. At that moment they came under sustained machine-gun fire, with several men and horses hit, and the others scattering. The surviving horses wandered aimlessly around No Man's Land for several days after this incident.

During the previous night, parties of the 6th Battalion had begun to move up into position on the western edge of Gueudecourt. Now that the Germans had abandoned any claim to the village and positions around it, the men of the 6th moved forward on the morning of the 26 September to occupy it. Lost to their possession, the Germans began to shell Gueudecourt savagely, and by the evening the 6th Battalion had prudently decided to evacuate it and had taken up position in shell holes nearby. This however

German prisoners of war entering a holding compound, at Bray-sur-Somme behind the British lines, in September 1916.

20149 Pte Thomas Bottomley, 6th Battalion, of Exton, killed on 29 September.

40048 Pte William Jarvis, 7th Battalion. He was killed on 1 October, the day his Battalion marched out of the line at the close of its part in the Somme battles. He was from Billericay, Essex.

was not before a number of casualties were sustained by the 6th, one of whom was Lieutenant George Gillet. A friend of David Kelly, he was killed in a trench by a chance shell, at the moment a mess orderly had been sent by Lieutenant-Colonel Challenor to inform him that he had been relieved and could return to the Officers' Mess dugout for tea.

That same evening, the 8th and 9th Battalions left the front line, marching back about half a mile to positions slightly less exposed to enemy fire. Soon the men had small fires going in the bottoms of the trenches, heating tins of American pork and beans which they ate with army biscuits. Blackened mess tins of hot tea, liberally laced with rum were also passed around, and the men slept the sleep of the just under heavy German groundsheets, purloined from the enemy trenches for the purpose. The next morning, sunlight filtering through the late September mist had the men astir early, and Dick Read took his first opportunity to absorb the view in daylight:

> The trench commanded a fine view of the landscape in front, to the left and right of the country beyond Gueudecourt, which from here lay in a shallow valley, now just another collection of tree stumps and rubble, whence issued reports of desultory rifle and machine-gun fire. Occasionally several fresh spouts of red and grey rubble would rise over it, as the enemy artillery searched for our 6th Battalion men there. Behind it and to the right stretched away a long gentle slope of cultivated fields, culminating in a low ridge upon which nestled the village of Beaulencourt. To the right of it and beyond, we could discern the trees and buildings of Le Transloy, both villages as yet still standing. Along the ridge to our left, our view was bounded by the villages of Ligny-Thilloy and Le Barque, with a wooded mound before them which a map showed as the Butte de Warlencourt.[17]

Later, on the morning of 29 September, the 7th Battalion was detailed to move forward to relieve the 6th. Lieutenant-Colonel William Drysdale, wounded at Bazentin and only recently back in command of the 7th, was on a preliminary tour of the trenches. He was being shown around some of the positions his men were to take over later that day, when he was hit by a sniper and killed. Arthur Cave recorded in his diary for that day:

> Today passing the regimental aid post on my way to the line with rations etc. when I saw a stretcher on the ground with a body on it

Indian cavalrymen, tending their animals, on the Somme in 1916.

The villages of Les Boeufs, Ligny Thilloy, and Le Barque, as they appeared at the end of the summer of 1916. Liddle Collection

covered with a blanket. I lifted up the blanket to see who it was and found it was the Commanding Officer, Lieut-Colonel Drysdale, who had just been brought in, shot through the head by a sniper.[18]

For the rest of the day, small groups of 7th Battalion men gathered by the stretcher to pay their respects to Drysdale, and many men, among them Corporal Charles Monk, lifted the blanket on the stretcher, and saluted their dead colonel. Major R. B.Unwin again took command, but was wounded himself later that night.

The 110th Brigade remained in the vicinity of Gueudecourt until the beginning of October 1916, when the battalions came out of the line, and began to march away from the Somme, via Delville Wood and Bernafay Wood, then by way of Montauban and Carnoy to Meaulte. At this last place a curious encounter took place, between the old hands of the 8th Battalion, and some of their former opponents:

> *we halted for ten minutes or so in the street, where a gang of German prisoners were re-metalling the road. As we stood there, the driver of the steam roller stopped his charge and called upon some of his mates to observe our badges and shoulder brasses. All stopped work and crowded round us, asking if we were the same Leicesters who used to be in front of them at Monchy au Bois and Bienvillers. When we replied in the affirmative, we chatted as with old friends until we fell in again. They were of the 73rd Infantry Regiment, and when I mentioned 'Charlie', who sang the English songs, several laughed excitedly with many 'ja! ja!'s, but said that he had been sniped through the head one morning, just before the regiment left the sector for the Somme. 'Boum...Charlie kaput!' As we fell in again they said they had been captured at Ginchy and grinned as they made us understand that for them the war was finished. They certainly had got something there, and looked well fed and contented. Just then we would have changed places with them gladly!*[19]

On 4 October the Leicestershire Brigade entrained once more for the north and the Pas de Calais. After several stops and billets for the night in villages along the route, they detrained at Bethune. From here they marched along the Sailly-la-Bourse road, into the countryside of Loos. Here in this grim coal mining district of France, small communities of low brick-built terraced cottages huddled around pit heads (the so-called Fosses), and although each village had its own name – Noeux-les-Mines, Bully-les-

The paybook of 12544 Pte Albert Smith reads like a roll call of 7th Battalion officers on the Somme in 1916, the signatures of Capt. J. T. Mitchell, Lieut. G. Smith, Capt. C.Hewitt, 2nd Lieut. J. Curtis and 2nd Lieut. W. Norton are all discernible among others. Mr S.Smith

This photograph of the Quartermaster's section, 7th Battalion, was taken probably at Bethune in the autumn of 1916. Those in the back row are all men from the village of Mowsley, left: Charles Monk, centre: 'Butch' the Battalion butcher. In the front row from the left are: an officer's servant, the Armourer sergeant and seated on the right Sergeant Dangerfield. Sonny Monk

Another 7th Battalion photograph, taken around the same time. Seated in the centre is Sergeant Dangerfield, whilst standing behind him on the right is Corporal Ernest Durrant. Durrant had recently rejoined the Battalion, after being hit in the arm by a bullet whilst in No Man's Land on a night wiring party at Arras, the previous August. Fergus Durrant

Mines, Philosophe, Loos-en-Gohelle, and Vermelles – in reality the places sprawled into one another, forming a conurbation, and it was often difficult to tell where one ended and another began.

The Brigade took over positions in the Northampton Trench sector, opposite the infamous Hohenzollern Redoubt. Here, in October 1915 during the Battle of Loos, the 1/4th Battalion of the Leicestershire Regiment was to all intents and purposes destroyed in an attack on the redoubt. The Leicestershire men of the 110th Brigade were not only aware of its grim reputation - a number of them would undoubtedly also have had brothers or other relations who had been killed or wounded here.

The most novel feature for us of this sector was an uninterrupted series of mine craters stretching right along the front line and making an attack or even at most places a large raid, impossible for either side...Behind us lay the ruined village of Vermelles, occasionally swept by machine gun fire and to the right lay the old Loos battlefield. The second main feature of this line was the enemy's highly organised system of trench-mortar bombardment. This was greatly facilitated by his possession of a colossal slag heap...called Fosse 8, which in that flat, devastated country dominated the local situation,[20] remembered David Kelly. The trench mortars used by the Germans were of a larger calibre than anything available to the British at this time. They resembled oil drums when in flight, and the Tommies nicknamed them 'rum jars' (hence the verse in a popular wartime song: *'There's a Rum Jar coming, I can hear the bugger humming, there's Rum Jar coming over there'*). The devastation caused to a stretch of trench by one of these devices was considerable, and they were greatly feared. Having no adequate reply to them, the policy adopted in this part of the line was one of 'live and let live', in the hope of not provoking the Germans to reply, a state of affairs which did not contribute greatly to the morale of the men. Another unfortunate factor was the grim state of the trenches in this area. Having been constantly bombarded and blasted by 'rum-jars', they were in a poor condition. As autumn rains poured down, they deteriorated in places into a sticky morass, and the only comfort to be found when in the line was in a few extremely deep dug-outs. Even in these, the air was damp and fetid, and the occupants lived in fear of a 'rum-jar' blowing in the entrance steps. Dick Read, in the front line, remembered it as a sector without any redeeming features:

> When, shortly after arrival, we peered in the dusk through a slit in the bags of the Northampton Trench parapet, we saw, some hundreds of yards behind the reverse rim of the crater, the vast and overpowering bulk of a colliery slag heap – to wit, Fosse 8 – which we had first seen in the distance when leaving Sailly-la-Bourse. It dominated the British positions here completely, and, I recall, did not exactly help us to become reconciled to our lot. Back in the support trenches, we could see away to our right two damaged high latticed steel towers, presumably the German line near Loos. They went by the name of 'Tower Bridge'. We soon found that it was courting death to look over the parapet, except under exceptionally favourable circumstances. The enemy snipers were amazingly alert and were excellent shots. To raise a trench periscope meant that in a few seconds it would be smashed.[21]

The four battalions now began to receive fresh drafts of reinforcements. Some more of those wounded at Bazentin were back, and there were a few

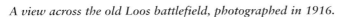

A view across the old Loos battlefield, photographed in 1916.

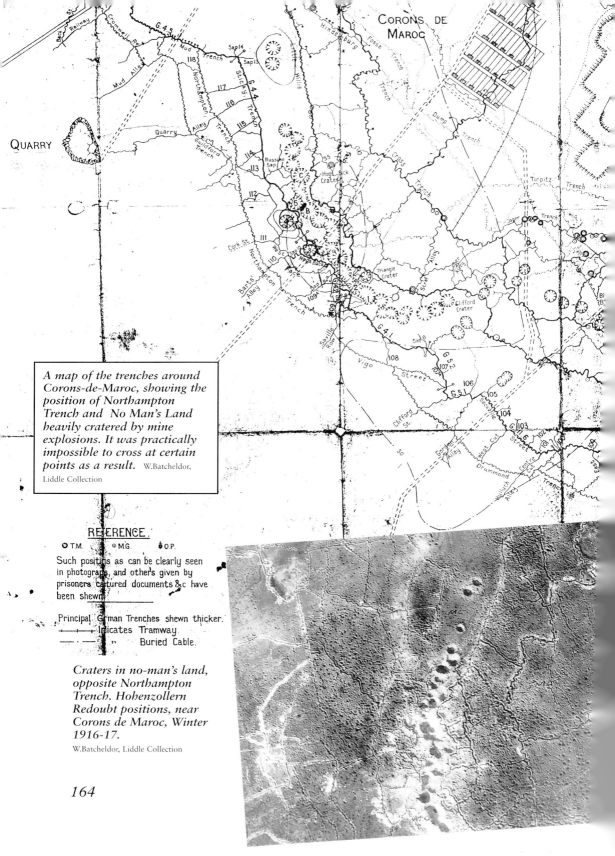

A map of the trenches around Corons-de-Maroc, showing the position of Northampton Trench and No Man's Land heavily cratered by mine explosions. It was practically impossible to cross at certain points as a result. W.Batcheldor, Liddle Collection

REFERENCE

⊙ T.M.   ⊙ M.G.   ⊙ O.P.

Such positions as can be clearly seen in photographs, and others given by prisoners captured documents &c have been shewn

Principal German Trenches shewn thicker.

———|——— Indicates Tramway.

— · — · — Buried Cable.

Craters in no-man's land, opposite Northampton Trench. Hohenzollern Redoubt positions, near Corons de Maroc, Winter 1916-17.

W.Batcheldor, Liddle Collection

The 'Tower Bridge' pit-head winding gear at Loos – the most distinctive landmark in the area.

new faces as well. Major A.A. Aldworth MC had assumed command of the 7th Battalion in the wake of the loss of two commanding officers in two days at Gueudecourt, with the rank of Temporary Lieutenant-Colonel. In periods of his absence, Major T.C. Hewitt was in command. Major Beardsley, also as Temporary Lieutenant-Colonel, remained as commanding officer of the 8th Battalion for the rest of that year of 1916. Having assumed charge both in the wake of the Bazentin Ridge casualties, and after Gueudecourt, his record was second to none. He was popular with officers and rank and file alike. On 11 October, Second-Lieutenant Frank Pitts, newly posted to the battalion from the 3rd, wrote to his sister

I have been transferred to the 8th, a Battalion of the new army, which came out last year. Bertie Beardsley is in command ! You see, there is no 3rd Batt. at the front; it is always in England, and reinforcements are taken from that. The 8th is not a Territorial affair!![22]

Pitts was from Loughborough, the son of Canon Pitts, a well-known local clergyman, and he seems to have known Beardsley socially before the war. However, it was unlikely that a Second Lieutenant would have addressed his commanding officer by his first name to his face, whatever their connections outside the army. On 27 December Pitts wrote again to his sister to tell her that Colonel Beardsley had been very kind to the battalion. In the tradition of the British Army, the men had had Christmas dinner of roast beef, pork, plum puddings, fruit and cigarettes, whilst the officers and sergeants waited upon them. They had been allowed a good rest, and had visited a concert party almost every evening over Christmas. The 8th Battalion had left the front line towards the end of December, and was billeted in the village of Auchel. A period of complete rest and recuperation followed, in which the men drilled, exercised, and played football, and other games. The change of scenery was undoubtedly beneficial, and morale was quickly restored. The other battalions in the brigade did likewise, coming out of the line to billets in nearby villages, and undertaking a similar period of rest and training. Worn-out boots and items of uniform were replaced, and more of the lightly wounded rejoined. The battalions were still below strength, but had the advantage that by now, almost every member was an experienced veteran of the Battle of the Somme. However, at the beginning of 1917, Beardsley

Christmas, 1916. A 21st Division card sent home by Sgt 'Dick' Read, lists the positions attacked or occupied by the division the previous summer. Chester Read

165

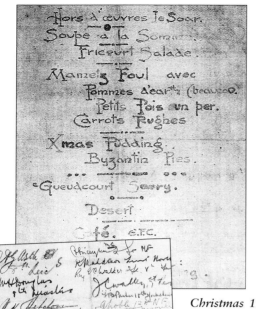

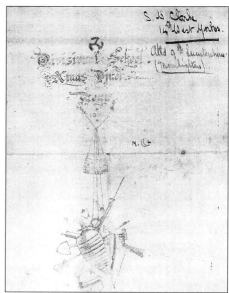

Christmas 1916. A menu signed by officers attending the 21st Divisional school at the time, including several from the Leicestershire Brigade. This copy belonged to Sid Clarke, of the 9th Battalion who were apparently known as 'the Moonlighters'. The reason for this is not clear. S.W.Clarke, Liddle Collection

reverted to his rank of Major, and Lieutenant-Colonel Gerald Hervey returned to take command. He was not well liked, and Pitts wrote again to his sister, on 22 January 1917:

> I'm sorry to say our new Colonel, who is a Regular, is a dreadful 'snot'. He used to be in command of the 8th before I came to it, while Bertie Beardsley was still a captain. Colonel Hervey got wounded on the Somme, and Beardsley leapt into his place. Nobody ever had a good word for Hervey, and I can quite see it. I'm awfully sorry. He never gets to know his subalterns for the simple reason that he won't mix up with them, as they are so beneath him![23]

It seems that Hervey was equally unpopular amid the rank and file. As Read commented pointedly, he suffered in comparison with his predecessor, the much respected Colonel Mignon. To be fair to him, Hervey represented the distinction between the 'Old' and 'New' Armies. In the latter, men and officers alike were very much civilians in uniform, and a much greater atmosphere of 'openness' existed throughout. Hervey came from an old pre-war Regular Army background, in which second-lieutenants, at least until such time as they acquired a second pip, should be seen and not heard. About this same time, Lieutenant-Colonel Heathcote DSO arrived to take command of the 7th Battalion. There is no record of his reception or the reaction of the other officers in the Battalion but, like Hervey, he too was a regular soldier.

Pte William James Clarke, who arrived with the 8th Battalion as a reinforcement in January 1917.

Lieutenant Colonel G.C.I.Hervey. 8th Battalion.

In the New Year of 1917, the Brigade suddenly left the comfortable billets in which it had spent Christmas, and headed north to Belgium - for the first time since landing in the summer of 1915. Bacon recalled the journey, in the by now-familiar draughty cattle trucks used to transport men on the railways of France:

> *The 9th Battalion marched...for Lillers and there entrained with the rest of the Brigade about 6.30pm. The night was bitterly cold; the trucks neither heated nor air tight, and a miserable journey ensued, during which the water in the service bottles froze solid. No advance party had been sent forward owing to ignorance of the impending move, and consequently no billets had been secured for the troops; after a cross country march of some 5 miles from the detraining station (Poperinghe) to Houtkerque, a small and straggling village on the border of France and Belgium, the men were tired and low spirited. It was a bitter night - the coldest spent during the war I should say, and one had to shiver and walk about till daylight, at what time strenuous efforts were made to wake the inhabitants and secure accommodation.[24]*

It was rumoured that with Flanders in the grip of one of the sharpest frosts that winter, and the Yser Canal frozen quite solid, the enemy might take advantage of the situation to attack across it. Consequently, reinforcements were being gathered in the area as a precaution. The War Diary of the 7th Battalion records that:

> *In order to create an impression on the enemy that we were concentrating troops towards the North of the YPRES salient, route marches were carried out from the 3rd to the 5th inclusive. The Battn. with pack animals etc ... commenced marching early each afternoon and continued until it was dusk. It then turned about & marched back to billets. Route taken: - roads EAST of HOUTKERQUE. Through WATTAU to St JAN der BIEZEN.[25]*

The Winter of 1916/17 was the coldest in living memory in northern France and Belgium. Taylor Library

Whatever the truth of the matter, the Brigade spent a chilly couple of weeks in barns and other billets, shivering under blankets, with fields around them caked with thick frost. There had been difficulties in finding enough suitable accommodation, and billeting officers had been forced to scour villages a considerable distance apart to find what they were seeking. Bacon described his own circumstances, attached as he was to the headquarters of the 9th Battalion, and in doing so painted a remarkably vivid picture of the domestic life of the Belgian peasantry with whom the men were billeted :

Captain J.T.S. Nobbs, photographed in January 1917.
Margaret Nobbs

'[the billets] *of the battalion, and in fact of the whole brigade, were very scattered: the 9th Leic. Regt was housed partly in Houtkerque, partly in Watteau and partly in Winezeal, some 2 or 3 miles separating the companies, 3 of which were in France and 1 in Belgium. Probably the most motley assortment was at Battn Headquarters which was housed in a small moated Farm House which lay astride the Frontier. In this house were all the officers, who occupied bedrooms and a living room, while in the great kitchen some 35 men – Orderly Room Staff and Office, Orderlies, Officers' Servants, Signallers and the like were crowded together in addition to the portly matron who ran the show, and who hugged closely the one fireplace in the room. In order apparently to prove that the capacity of the room was not taxed to its limits, some dozen or so farm hands frequented the kitchen for meals, so there was neither room to work properly or enjoy life. The one redeeming feature of this mass billeting was the fact that it was warm, which was far from the case with the officers' portion of the house, where the thermometer averaged 31 and where greatcoats were worn by day and thrown over the bed by night.*[26]

No attack ever materialised across the frozen Yser, but an unpleasant few days were spent by the Leicestershire Brigade in the area, before February when they entrained once more and headed south.

1 A.C.Cave, unpublished typescript diary 20.7.16
2 I.L.Read, *Of Those We Loved* (Pentland Press, 1994) p170
3 C.E.Garlick, manuscript diary. J.Taylor collection.
4 D.V.Kelly, *39 Months With the Tigers* (Ernest Benn Ltd 1930) p38
5 Read, *op cit* pp176-177
6 Read, *op cit* p188
7 Kelly, *op cit* p45
8 Read, *op cit* p194
9 Read, *op cit* p194
10 War Diary, 9th bn Leicestershire Regt, LRO. 25.9.16
11 Read, *op cit* p199
12 Kelly, *op cit* pp46-47
13 Read, *op cit* pp201-202
14 Read, *op cit* p203
15 Read, *op cit* p206
16 War Diary, 7th bn Leicestershire Regt, LRO. 26.9.16
17 Read, *op cit* p207
18 Cave, *op cit* 29.9.16
19 Read, *op cit* p210
20 Kelly, *op cit* p51
21 Read, *op cit* p215
22 2/Lt F.B.Pitts, typescript letter 11.10.16. Liddle Collection, University of Leeds (LC)
23 2/Lt F.B.Pitts, typescript letter 22.1.17 LC
24 D.A.Bacon, unpublished typescript memoir, LRO, p70
25 War Diary, 7th bn Leicestershire Regt, LRO. 3.2.17
26 Bacon, *op cit* p70

Chapter Seven

Force of Arms
Fontaine and the Hindenburg Line

36582 Pte John Cecil Ashworth, of Colne, Lancashire, 9th Battalion. He died of wounds on 6 March 1917.

In February of 1917 the trains from the Franco-Belgian border brought the 110th Brigade back to familiar, but not exactly pleasant, countryside, this being the grim and unremitting desert of slagheaps and pithead winding machinery around Loos. This time however, they were in a sector of the line somewhat to the north of that which they had held before Christmas. Here they were billeted near Noyelles, and alternate battalions held positions (approached via a tunnel lit by electricity) around the lip of an enormous crater. The front line ran from a position known as Post 8, down through Cordon Alley trench. As was the case at Northampton Trench, the men were well and truly under the cudgel of the German 'rum-jars' which came over in response to any form of activity. British trench mortars were of too small a calibre to reply effectively, and their reliability could sometimes be deeply suspect, especially the two inch 'toffee apple' mortar. On 15 March, the 7th battalion had two officers wounded by the accidental explosion of a bomb. Second-Lieutenant K.C.Stiven survived, but Captain J.T.Mitchell died of his injuries the following day.

Nevertheless, the sojourn of the Leicestershire Brigade in this less than healthy environment was to be rather unexpectedly curtailed. In February 1917 the Germans withdrew to the Hindenburg Line – a series of positions which they had begun to prepare the previous autumn and winter, partly as a consequence of the Battle of the Somme, and partly due to the losses which they had sustained at Verdun before that. By falling back on a shorter line, the German army reduced the pressure on its manpower. In response to this retirement, a number of British units were quickly relieved from the front line to follow up the Germans, one of these being the 21st Division.

Accordingly, at the end of March 1917, the 110th Brigade left the trenches for Bethune, where for a couple of days uniforms and kit were inspected, before the Brigade for the first time 'embussed' in a motley selection of London Omnibus Company buses, which had been painted khaki for the duration of the war, and which were driven by members of the Army Service Corps. Dick Read remembered that:

> *All had boarded up windows and solid tyres, so that on the sadly deteriorated pave of the French roads the journey was not exactly pleasurable from our point of view. One and all however, we envied the drivers – for two very good reasons: they didn't have to go into the trenches; and whereas an infantryman's pay was 1s. 3d. per day (with proficiency pay), theirs was 6s.0d., with all sorts of extras.*

25890 Pte H.E.Findley, 6th Battalion. He died on 24 March 1917, and was buried in Vermelles British Cemetery.

John Taylor

169

In our bus we could see little or nothing, but apparently our convoy skirted Arras, leaving it well to the east, and the afternoon saw us trundling along once more over roads already familiar to those of us who relieved our French allies at Berles-au-Bois in September 1915 – Saulty, Mondicourt, Humbercamps, La Couchie, Gaudiempre and Pommier.[1]

The news of the extent of the German retirement was now beginning to reach the rank and file, and the fact that the enemy had abandoned their front line positions from Arras in the north to St Quentin in the south seemed amazing. In some places the Germans had fallen back over twenty kilometres, and when the buses dropped off the men of the Leicestershire Brigade at Humbercamps, they were intrigued to find that the former front-line villages of Berles-au Bois and Bienvillers, had been left high and dry by the tide of war. They were

The ruins of Monchy-au-Bois, perhaps as the Leicesters would have seen them in the spring of 1917. Annie Damiens

now many miles behind the British front. The curiosity of both officers and men was aroused by the now vacant enemy positions:

I visited Monchy-au-Bois, the village which then [in 1915] had lain in the German lines, and examined the German headquarter dugouts, and the little cemetery where several English officers, including poor Champneys, lay buried, inspected three great concrete barriers across the Berles-Monchy road, and watched some French territorials burying the Frenchmen who had lain out so long in No Mans Land [sic] on the same Berles-Monchy road[2],

recalled David Kelly.

The ruins of Monchy church. Annie Damiens

In early April the brigade began the advance to follow up the German retreat, along the Berles-Monchy road, and then via Adinfer Wood. Dick Read noted:

> Little did we know then what lay in store for us there [in Monchy] as, on the following morning, in drizzling rain, loaded to the limit with extra rations, ammunition, shovels and bombs, we tramped through Bienvillers...Everything looked deserted, sodden and derelict, our impression heightened by the rain, now changed to a driving wet mist. Little had we thought that the 110th Leicestershire Brigade would enter Monchy-au-Bois in this fashion.[3]

They found Monchy to have been heavily fortified, with many concrete installations, and bunkers, and liberally scattered with machine gun posts – now all abandoned. Those men who had been eager for an opportunity to attack the village and show the Huns 'what they were made of' back in 1915, were, observed D.A.Bacon, now largely thankful that such an opportunity had not been presented to them. Dick Read continued his narrative:

12819 Sgt 'Dick' Read, 8th Battalion, photographed in the spring of 1917. Shortly after this he was accepted for officer training and a commission.

Chester Read

> We splashed on in silence, enveloped in our dripping ground sheets, our thoughts of other days: of the winter of 1915, and of pals now gone. Ahead lay the dark mass of Adinfer Wood, and beyond, the ruins of Adinfer village, where we halted, looking upon another vista of desolation and noticing that the fruit trees in the gardens had been ringed by having a complete strip of bark removed at the base. They would die. It was a few yards from the road to a well serving a destroyed farm-house. We looked down it, but the appalling stench drove us away – it had been fouled with excreta. I think at these moments we felt more bitter about the enemy than at any other time before or after.[4]

What Dick and his comrades were to discover was that the Germans in their retirement had operated a 'scorched earth' policy. Nothing which could conceivably be of use either to the British Army or to French civilians was left intact. Wells were fouled and trees chopped down. Roads were destroyed by having the pave ripped from them, or rendered impassable by trees felled across them. Nearly every crossroads had been reduced to a smoking crater by an explosive charge detonated at the centre. David Kelly marvelled at the efficiency in the devastation left by the Germans, and the fact that it was far from random or sporadic:

> Boiry St Martin [was] the first village where we were able to observe the thorough destruction left by the Germans in their wake.
>
> Right across the belt of land stretching back from the old trench-line to the new Hindenburg line it was the same story: every crossroads had become a great mine-crater, every house was blown up so scientifically that the roofs encumbered the floors, even cellars were hard to find, trees wherever possible had been cut down, wells had been everywhere destroyed. As we advanced across this wilderness the

The village of Boiry-St-Martin, before it was systematically destroyed in the German retreat.

horses had to be sent on ever longer journeys to be watered.[5]

Second-Lieutenant Frank Pitts, serving still with the 8th Battalion, wrote to his father Canon Pitts of Loughborough at the beginning of April to tell him of the conditions which he had experienced during the follow up to the German withdrawal:

> *Of course we are taking ground, but what does the Boche leave behind him in his retreat? Nothing, absolutely nothing. Every village we pass is just a mass of bricks and wood, blown to atoms. Wells have been poisoned – of course we are most careful – not a civilian anywhere, but instead dead British and Germans! Oh, the piteous sights there are about. As we follow up, we have to make our own shelters, as there are no such things as any barns or houses standing. So you can see how fearfully difficult it is to keep up the proper supply of food and water.[6]*

Pitts also took the opportunity to ask his father to send out some vermin repellent, purchased from Boots. In these circumstances, an enforced lack of cleanliness meant that officers just as much as other ranks, were susceptible to lice.

Another, even more sinister aspect of the enemy retreat was about to be encountered. Most of those buildings or other features left intact had been booby-trapped, with the intention of causing maximum casualties among unwary Tommies. Reaching Hamelincourt, the 8th Battalion prepared to bivouac for the night, until Dick Read and some comrades discovered a small house which was nearly intact save for doors and windows:

> *after careful examination of the gaping doorway we went in, gingerly, step by step, fearful of booby traps. Nothing happened, and shortly after our C.S.M. and C.Q.M.S., having heard our news,*

21301 Pte William Henry Cox, 6th Battalion, killed on 11 April 1917. He was formerly a conductor on the Leicester Corporation Tramways. George C

The village of Hamelincourt, as it was circa 1916.

40904 Pte Fred Snow, 8th Battalion, of Loughborough. Killed on 11 April 1917.

Malcolm Smith

13268 Pte John Thomas Day, 6th Battalion, killed in action on 10 April 1917. He was born at Redmile, Leicestershire, and lived at Uppingham.

promptly appropriated it for themselves and their minions, foresaking barely completed shelters. The C.S.M.'s batman was in the act of laying a fire in the grate of one of the two ground-floor rooms when two of us, exploring the cellar with my torch, spotted a cluster of gun cotton slabs in blue cardboard containers, smothered with printed instructions and diagrams in German, hanging from a cord about two feet from the floor. What looked like a slow burning fuse was wound loosely round the cord, and as we traced it upwards, we head the batman chopping wood directly above it.

We rushed up the cellar steps and raked out the wood and paper – sure enough, the end of the fuse terminated in a coil under the grate.[7]

What the men of the Leicestershire Brigade were now discovering was that the Germans had not retreated – they had withdrawn, to a position infinitely stronger and better equipped to withstand attack than those they had left. Furthermore, it would be months before the British would have the full infrastructure of roads, billets and communications fully restored in the area which had been conceded. The situation was as obvious to Dick Read and his comrades footslogging through the waterlogged fields as it was to anyone else. For every mile east that they advanced into this wilderness, they were logistically at a greater disadvantage, against an enemy who was tactically in a far stronger position than they were.

Moyenneville was reached on 3 April, and St Leger the following day. Here, marching in the dark across muddy fields, explosions, firing and Very Lights up ahead told the Brigade that they were nearing the front line, and the limit of the enemy retirement. Daybreak the next day saw the 8th Battalion moving up to the Hindenburg Line itself:

on reaching a road our officers checked on their maps, and as they

appeared satisfied, we crossed it at right-angles, making our way in a clearing mist up a long gradual slope, culminating in a definite ridge. Here we extended and were ordered to get down in the wet grass until our officers, having again checked our position, waved us forward again. Rising to our feet, we saw at the bottom of the long slope of fields perhaps a thousand yards distant, a dark brown band many yards in depth, threading its way as far as we could see it on either side of the front. Three hundred yards or so in the rear of this, we could see another band of staggering thickness, running approximately parallel with it...'[8]

The village of Moyenville.

remembered Dick Read. He and his comrades were ordered to get as close to the Line as possible, before getting under cover:

> *As we slowly picked our way forward, we made out the brown bands to be belts of rusty wire defences of terrific strength, and hoped fervently that we would not be called upon to surmount these obstacles that morning. Between the belts of wire we could make out the piles of sandbags and turned up earth of a trench system, and we were expecting to be fired on when a single machine gun opened up, the bullets whistling high over our heads*[9]

This then was the mighty Hindenburg Line. It was built during the summer and autumn of 1916, using the labour of thousands of Russian prisoners of war. These men had been transported from the east specifically for the task, and worked under the direction of the finest military engineers in the German Army. With the belts of barbed wire constructed in such a way as to channel attacking troops into the path of machine guns, elaborately

10944 Pte Benjamin Nutt, 6th Battalion, of Uppingham. He was killed in action in the trenches by a shell on 1 May 1917.

Belts of barbed wire in the Hindenburg Line system. Liddle Collection

9974 A/Cpl
Alfred Ball, 6th
Battalion, died of
wounds on 10
April 1917. He
was born at
Shenton,
Leicestershire,
and lived at
Thurlaston.

Steve Law

constructed traverses at intervals to minimise the effect of blast, and concrete fortifications for extra strength, Kelly had assessed it accurately when he concluded that it incorporated all the lessons of trench warfare learned by the Germans up to that point. It was not constructed as one trench but in fact as several lines, each with its own wire and fortifications. Moving up in March, the Leicestershire battalions took over the front line near Henin sur Cojeul. Croisilles village lay inside the British line, and was taken over by the 7th Battalion, Kelly commenting on this village:

'I remember a crucifix in the Northern Quarter standing significantly amid the debris, but we blew it up for fear it had been left as a calibration point for the German artillery[10].

The nearby village of Fontaine les Croisilles lay in the German front line itself.

The attacks of March 1917 had gained a toe-hold in the labyrinths of the Hindenburg system, but nothing much more. The British front line in the Leicestershire Brigade sector was in fact a portion of the old front line trench of the Hindenburg system, which had been captured in earlier fighting, and which further to the south was still held by the enemy. Likewise, the old support trench east of this one, known as Tunnel Trench was also still partially in German hands, partly in British. It was called Tunnel Trench because the elaborately planned and dug trench contained for the protection of its occupants not a series of dugouts, but instead a continuous tunnel which had been bored out beneath the trench, and which was reached by descending steep sets of stairs at various intervals. The ownership of the tunnel and the trench above it were in dispute, and both were blocked at about the same point, with rubble and debris, from behind which the belligerents glowered at each other.

The writer and poet Siegfried Sassoon in his autobiographical novel, *Memoirs of an Infantry Officer*, has left a graphic description of what life was like in the tunnel:

'There were fifty steps down the shaft [to] the earthy smell of that

10135 Pte Robert
Wagstaff, 9th
Battalion, killed
on 3 May 1917.
He had
previously served
with the 6th
Battalion, until
wounded in
1916.

The village of Croisilles.

An aerial photograph dating from the spring of 1917, looking east towards the Hindenburg Line (foreground).

triumph of Teutonic military engineering...along the Tunnel the air blew cold and seasoned with mephitic odours... All I knew about the tactical situation was that if one went along the Tunnel one arrived at a point where a block had been made by blowing it in. On the other side one bumped into the Germans. Above ground there was a barrier and the situation was similar...The Tunnel was a few inches higher than a tall man walking upright; it was fitted with bunks and recessed rooms; in places it was crowded with men of various units...Prying my way along with an electric torch, I glimpsed an assortment of vague shapes, boxes, tins, fragments of broken furniture and frowsy mattresses.[11]

Sassoon also described the situation above ground:

The Outpost Trench was about 200 yards from the main trench, which was now our front line. It had been solidly made, ten feet deep, with timbered firesteps, splayed sides, and timbered steps at intervals to front and rear and to machine gun emplacements. Now it was wrecked as though by an earthquake and eruption. Concrete strong-posts were smashed and tilted sideways; everywhere the chalky soil was pocked and pitted with huge shell holes; and wherever we looked the mangled effigies of the dead were our memento mori.[12]

On 3 May 1917, the Leicestershire Brigade took part in a major assault on

16071 Pte John Charles Rawlings, 7th battalion, of Braunston, Rutland. Killed on 3 May 1917.

British dead around a fortified stronghold.

the Hindenburg Line positions. The plan was for the 64th Brigade to attack down the Tunnel Trench in a southerly direction, attempting to clear the bomb blocks and the Germans behind them, and thus gaining possession of Tunnel Trench in its entirety. Meanwhile, the scheme called for the Leicestershire battalions to attack eastwards, towards the portion of the old German front line which was still in enemy hands. The night before, ammunition dumps were formed close to the assembly trenches, but received heavy and sustained shelling from the Germans. The Leicestershire Brigade bombing officer, Lieutenant P.Hinckley, was seriously wounded by a shell fragment in the village of Heninel whilst supervising the unloading of boxes of Mills bombs from transport wagons and their dispatch to the front line companies. He had only returned to duty a short time previously, having sustained a wound at Bazentin the previous summer.

David Kelly, the Leicestershire Brigade Intelligence Officer, received some new aerial photographs of the enemy dispositions a few hours before the leading waves were scheduled to go over the top, and took these up to the front line. His intention was to pass this new information to the headquarters of the battalions which were to attack:

> *The 9th Battalion headquarters were in an unfinished dugout shaft, just beyond the sunken road* [from Heninel to Fontaine], *and in the forward assembly trench. Hundreds of men were sitting in the trench trying to sleep, in too many cases for the last time. As always the officers seemed to accept such encouragement about the general situation as I could give, while the old hands among the Tommies were sceptical yet quaintly cheerful, in a way characteristic of them.*[13]

The Leicestershire attack was part of the wider Battle

PTE. A. H. SMITH MISSING.

Mr. and Mrs. W. Smith, of 30, Medway Street, Leicester, have received official news that their only son, Private A. H. Smith, 27065, Leicestershire Regiment, has been missing since May 3rd. They will be grateful for any news of him. He formerly worked for four years as apprentice at the Co-operative Printing Works, Church Gate, Leicester, and joined up on April 3rd, 1916. Going to the front he was wounded, but recovered, and returned into action. He was 20 years old last March.

of Bullecourt. The village of that name, which had been built into the heart of the Hindenburg Line further south, was the objective of the Australians and the 2nd West Riding Division on 3 May. The assault was one of the biggest affairs since the Battle of the Somme, being launched as it was on a ten divisional frontage, but curiously it received little or no coverage in the newspapers at the time. Perhaps this was because the attack was not successful, Arthur Cave calling it in his diary, 'our grand failure'.[14]

He continued:

The 8th and 9th [Battalions] attacked the Hindenburg Line, with the 6th and 7th in reserve. After the attacking battalions had captured Fontaine Wood and Cherisy, they had to retire, the 7th Battalion attacking to cover their withdrawal. The attack was carried out in complete darkness, and the enemy seemed to be well aware of our intentions. A heavy barrage came down simultaneously with our own and owing to darkness units rapidly lost touch with those on their flanks. Over a thousand yards of No Man's Land had

25620 Pte Sidney Chambers, 8th Battalion, of Glenfield. He was killed in action on 3 May 1917. A talented musician, he had played in the band of one of the Leicestershire Regiment reserve battalions in England before being posted to France. In this photograph he wears a musician's badge on the sleeve of his tunic.

Mr W.Chambers

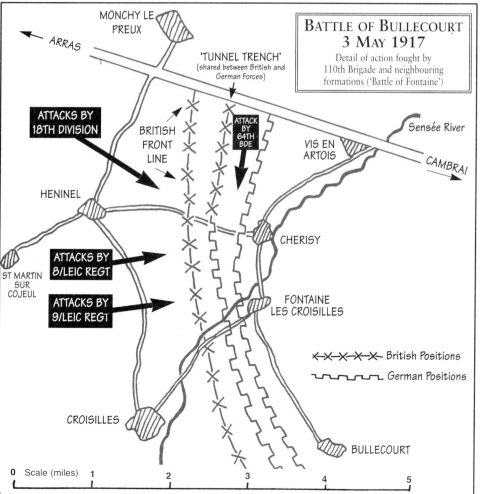

32375 Pte William Edward Webster, 7th Battalion, wounded on 3 May 1917.

to be covered before the enemy was reached. Large numbers of the 8th and 9th Battalions were taken prisoner.[15]

The attack had suffered from a number of fatal flaws in its planning and conception. The leading battalions, the 8th and 9th, were ordered to form up in an area known to be covered by the enemy defensive barrage. In the event, when this did fall it was lighter than expected due to the effective counter battery work carried out by the British artillery. None the less the damage had already been done; the anticipation of it had a bad effect on the morale of the men, they were unnerved and the start of the battle was a hurried and disorganised affair as they struggled to get clear of the German shell fire. Both the 8th and the 9th Battalions wandered too far to the right, influenced by the actions of other troops on their left who had already lost their bearings and who were drifting to their right. Today this may seem to be an odd mistake to make, but in the featureless landscape of the Hindenburg Line, and in the half-light, landmarks and points of reference were difficult to locate, and attacks frequently had to be conducted on a compass bearing. The War Diary of the 8th Battalion records under the date 3/5/17:

> *The battalion was disposed in two waves of two lines each, with a wave of moppers up behind. From right to left 'A' Coy (Lt.F.R.Oliver), 'B' Coy (Capt A.G.Astle), 'C' Coy (Major T.L.Warner) formed the line of attack, each company having a two platoon frontage. 'D' Coy (2/Lt J.W.Corbett) was drawn up in two lines, 60 yards in rear. The formation was two waves, each of two lines, 10 yds between lines and 60 yds between waves, with 'D'Coy as 'moppers up'.*[16]

The main German resistance came from the position known as York Trench. On the right, about a hundred men of the 9th Battalion Leicestershire Regiment actually broke through York Trench, however, and reached the Fontaine-Cherisy road.

A 21st Division gallantry card, presented to Pte John 'Jack' Holyoak, 9th Battalion for his part in the fighting of 3 May 1917 in the Hindenburg Line. The presentation of cards such as these by the higher command was a recognition of the fact that a soldier had performed a deed which under different circumstances might have earned an MM or a DCM.

Rose Holyoak

In Loving Memory of

MY DEAR BROTHER

ERNEST GARRETT,

8th Leicesters.

Killed in Action in France.

3rd MAY, 1917.

He passed like a shadow away,
We could not believe he was dead,
Until he was missed from among us
Then we knew that his spirit had fled.

I think of him in silence
No eyes can see me weep;
But ever in my aching heart
His memory I shall keep.

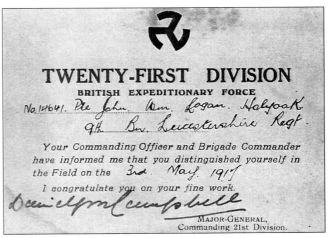

TWENTY-FIRST DIVISION

BRITISH EXPEDITIONARY FORCE

No. 14641 Pte John Wm. Logan Holyoak

9th Bn. Leicestershire Regt.

Your Commanding Officer and Brigade Commander have informed me that you distinguished yourself in the Field on the 3rd. May 1917

I congratulate you on your fine work.

MAJOR-GENERAL,
Commanding 21st Division.

D.A.Bacon was with 9th Battalion Headquarters that morning, and remembered that after the ranks had moved off for the attack:

> *nothing could be gleaned as to the results or positions – one thing alone was consistent, and that [was] the infernal and devastating fire of the enemy. By that time parties of our men were reported as being in the Wood, and even in the village [of Fontaine] but as the troops on either flank had been held up no further advance was possible and indeed the positions gained were precarious and could not be consolidated. From either flank large numbers of the enemy continually harassed our men and being well supplied with bombs effected a deadly slaughter; some little time later a decided counter attack was hurled against the left flank, the weight of which pressed back the seemingly disordered ranks of the Bedfords of the 18th Division.* [17]

A couple of tanks had been allotted to the 110th Brigade for the attack, but were of little use. Indeed, many of the tanks used at this point in the war were in fact Mark II training tanks, pressed into front line service. Their armour was of inferior quality, and they were extremely vulnerable:

> *One tank, which had advanced towards the Wood was forced to retire owing to the extremely heavy shell fire directed upon it, while the other, as far as could be ascertained, had broken down shortly after leaving the assembly positions.* [18]

Even Bacon's Headquarters were not immune to the hammering the British lines were now receiving courtesy of the German artillery:

> *Shortly after the attack was first launched, our own trenches were practically levelled and during the early morning some bags of surplus grenades at the top of the Headquarter sap were hit and contributed to the general firework display. For over an hour none of the Headquarters [personnel] could either get out of the sap and neither could anyone enter – luckily few of the grenades burst downwards, but the position was unpleasant to a degree. Further to the top of the sap, affording scarcely no protection from shell fire, it was expected that this would be blown in and the entrance choked up at any moment, but here again the Headquarters were lucky.*[19]

Brigadier-General Hessey, the officer commanding the Leicestershire Brigade, now

Officers of A coy, 8th Battalion, photographed in France, early 1917. Seated on the right is 2nd Lieutenant F.B.Pitts, who died as a result of the Hindenburg Line battle in May 1917. At first reported missing in action, he was in fact captured mortally wounded by the Germans, who later buried his body. F.B.Pitts, Liddle Collection

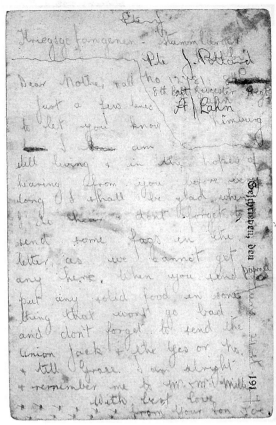

12781 Pte J.Pollard, 8th Battalion (seated centre) in a German PoW camp. He was captured along with numbers of other 8th Battalion men, on 3 May. However, his family at 95 Bismark Street, Leicester, did not learn that he was safe until the late summer of 1917, when they received the postcards (seen here) which he had posted via the Red Cross. John Taylor

ordered the 6th Battalion to attack Fontaine Wood in order to protect the left flank of the exposed troops who had already gone over the top. Before this could be done, however, the Germans launched a counter attack which effectively cut off the men involved in the battle for York Trench, and of course those men who had gone beyond it.

At 7.15pm the 7th Battalion had attacked along the sunken road between Heninel and Fontaine, and a trench which ran parallel to it, but even though this action had made some progress, by 10pm the attack had been abandoned and Hessey ordered everyone still holding out in scattered posts on the battlefield to make their way back – if they could. Some men took four hours to cover the 1000 yards distance, crawling from shell hole to shell hole to avoid enemy fire.

Arthur Cave continued rather despondently:

> the attack attracted little attention, the official communiqué merely saying – 'Great resistance at Bullecourt, Fontaine, and Cherisy, and our troops had to fall back from advanced positions captured by them'. Another way of saying that the attack failed completely, and we were back on our original positions from where we started.[20]

The 9th Battalion had suffered particularly heavily, and Lieutenant Sid Clarke reported in a letter to his mother that he was safe, but was only one of four officers out of sixteen to emerge unscathed from that battalion's attack.[21] In the 8th Battalion, Second-Lieutenant Frank Pitts of 'A' Company had been wounded and left behind in his battalion's withdrawal. On 11 May his father, a well-known Loughborough clergyman named Canon Pitts, received a telegram from the War Office telling him that his son was missing, believed wounded.

On 24 May, Lieutenant Raymond Sennett, also of the 8th Battalion who had been wounded in the attack, wrote to Canon Pitts from his bed at 1st Eastern Military Hospital, Cambridge, in response to the clergyman's enquiry, but was unable to help:

> I regret that I can add nothing to the official news of your son. I caught a glimpse of him half an hour after the commencement of the attack,

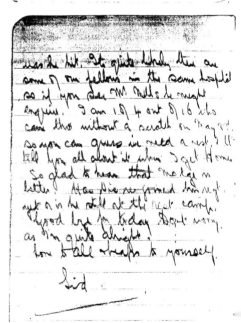

2nd Lieutenant S.W.Clarke writes to his mother to reassure her after the Fontaine action – 'I am 1 of 4 out of 16 who came thro' without a scratch on May 3rd'.

S.W.Clarke, Liddle Collection

27141 Pte Charles Garlick, now with the 8th Battalion, was killed on 3 May 1917. His home was at 91 Oxford Street, Leicester.

John Taylor

and he was then alright. I was lucky enough to get slight flesh wounds a few minutes after.

The operations of the 3rd May were a strong attack on Fontaine-les-Croisilles. The defence was too strong for us, the attack on our right was held up, and the 8th and 9th had to withdraw and leave their wounded. I met Major Warner of ours at a Dressing Station, and he told me Pitts was badly wounded, but he spoke from hearsay only.

The other two A Company officers are also wounded and missing. The company lost nearly all four officers and 75% other ranks.[22]

The next day, Mr Alfred T. Harris of Market Harborough, wrote to Canon Pitts enclosing some letters which he had received from Second-Lieutenant Clifford A. Payne, officer now commanding 'A' Company, 8th Battalion, and survivor of the 3 May attack, in an effort to reassure him about his son. One read:

I am writing with reference to your son 2nd Lieut. Wm. Harris, who at present is posted as 'missing' since our show on the morning of May 3rd. No doubt by this time you have had official notification from the War Office and I can tell you the following, which has come from a most reliable source, viz. A sergeant of our company who was out in a shell hole for four days after the show and eventually got back to our lines. He tells me that he actually saw your son, with another of our officers taken prisoners and at that time were quite fit, i.e. they had not been hit. Unfortunately some of our men met with the same misfortune. I don't know any further news altho' I have put out endless enquiries. I was the only one who got out of the fearful battle (officer) in our company and I consider myself a lucky fellow...The other officer missing with him is 2nd Lieut.F.B.Pitts whose father is Canon Pitts of Loughboro.[23]

British prisoners leaving the combat zone under a German escort.

Further information supplied later by this officer indicated that Pitts was captured after leading his platoon forward into an enemy position.

Throughout June of 1917 Canon Pitts heard little more news of his son, receiving only two enquiries from anxious mothers in respect of their own sons who were missing. One lady, Mrs Emma Hancox Soden, of 69, Hawkesbury Road, Leicester, was desperate for information about her son. Reading in her newspaper that Lieutenant Pitts was a prisoner, she wrote politely to ask if he might be able to enquire after her boy whom she believed was also a prisoner:

> I can assure you Sir there is getting a great unrest amongst the people its just on the balance of a revolt it's the cruel way in which our boys are treated when Prisoners. Theres plenty of money being collected and we feel something ought to be done to get us news of our boys in Germany they have committed no crime but we give them willingly for the Country but this cruelty we cannot bear. Something will have to be done I am no revolutionary only a quiet woman of 67 but cannot help hearing the murmur amongst the people we only want justice for the boys and may God in his mercy protect them all.[24]

She also enclosed a card, bearing the words:

> Private F. J. Hancox 25574 9th Battalion Lestershire [sic] Rgt – if your dear son could make enquiries for this poor Mothers Boy – No letters have been received since 29th April. May 3rd went into attack in Bullecourt not been heard of since.[25]

From 61, Merridale Road, Leicester, came a similar letter from a Mrs Tutty, who wrote:

> I hope you will excuse me writing to you but i saw in the paper that your son is a prisoner of war in Germany and my Son has been missing ever since the 9th of May and he was my sons officer wich [sic] he was servant to and i have not heard any thing of him only that he was reported missing and i am a widow mother and i am anxious to know tidings of him Sir would you be kind enough to wright [sic] and ask your Son if he knew anything about him as i shall be pleased to know[26]

Her son was 20888 Private Frederick Tutty of No 3 platoon, 'A' Company, 8th Leicesters. Sadly however, both he and Hancox, along with many of their comrades had been killed on 3 May.

Quite unexpectedly, on 25 July 1917, Canon Pitts received via the good offices of the Red Cross a letter in a shaky and unfamiliar hand, but apparently from his son, which related with startling immediacy the circumstances under which Second Lieutenant Pitts was obliged to surrender his small band. Part of it read:

> My incident was a misfortune, our rifle band drifted away, and were soon giving their hands up to the enemy. A few stuck it out, but they got mauled terribly, so I stopped any more giving away their lives (and God knows) I thought I was doing for the best.[27]

However, a few days later, Pitts Senior received the tragic news that his son

10050 Pte Harold C. Partridge, 6th Battalion, of Loughborough. He died of wounds on 4 May 1917.

Martin Moore

Oh, my darlings at home,
                            I once that I should never write to you
again ! I suppose you heard about the dreadful Week's doings in
France. Well, I wonder if anyone thought he would pass through
it in any kind of dilapidated condition ! My incident was a
misfortune, our rifle band drifted away, and were soon giving
their hands up to the enemy. A few stuck out, but they got
mauled about terribly, so I stopped any more giving away their
lives (and God knows) I thought I was doing for the best. The
Red Cross Germans certainly were very good, and helped all they
could to our injured men and officers - I had not been touched
up to this ! More dirty work was going on around us, and our
bombardment never died a second. Well, it was decided that our
party was to move away at once, myself and 3 men, under a
German, waiting to arrange about a stretcher case which did not
look like getting away, and finally which did not, poor fellow.
Well, off we started, we last four (of course, the British were
close too now !). We Tried one way - no; snipers; we tried
another - 'ping' (too close that one).All I then knew was that I
had been hit and was writhing at the bottom of a shell, the
others vanished ! What is the use of explaining the detail ? I
didn't waver, I came to one awful conclusion - I was in that
same German trench within an hour - how was it done ? Ah, God
must have helped me as he never did before. A red cross was
binding me up, giving me water. Well,this about 7 or 8 days ago,
and this is the 3rd hospital I have been to. Of course, I am
still in bed and very weak, but the worst is now over. I wonder
what it will be like to be properly on ones feet again ! Does
this now mean that I may not see dear dear darling England for
goodness knows how long ? Also, I am an officer, that might -
probably will - in a short time, help me, and yes, the war may
end, and prove this a blessing disguise ! Now, let my dear loved
ones know all this, they can write to me (I think the Germans
will let you know what address to put for a short time). This
has quite tired me out, and there's not a breath of air in the
room either. I wonder if that green card reached you 2 or 3 days
ago !
        Good bye. I expect Plee wee will see me just about the
same sometime.

                    Frazz

*A typed transcript of the letter, which the Pitts family received
from Frank, who was in German hands. The original was in a
shaky and unfamiliar hand, with some words crossed through,
and others missed out. Possibly it was written by a fellow
patient or a medical orderly.*

had died of his wounds not long after his capture. He was buried by the Germans in Bouchain Military Cemetery, but in 1924 the Imperial War Graves Commission removed all those British soldiers whose bodies lay in this cemetery. Pitts' remains were reinterred in Cabaret-Rouge British Cemetery at Souchez, where his grave can still be seen (XVI-G-7).

The assault on 3 May had claimed a number of lives in addition to those of Tutty, Hancox and Pitts. In the 9th Battalion Captain F.P.Cox had also been killed, and Captain H.E. Milburn was a prisoner. In the 8th Battalion, Captain A.G.Astle had been killed. A number of decorations had also been awarded. Acting Captain James Charles Vanner, 7th Battalion, was awarded the Military Cross for his part in the attack in the evening which in part relieved the pressure on the 8th and 9th and allowed them to withdraw. In the vicinity of Fontaine Wood he had shown conspicuous gallantry:

> *when leading and controlling the front line of an attack, and in
> making a daring reconnaissance under heavy fire to clear up a critical
> situation. He then consolidated the line taken and repulsed a strong
> counter-attack.*[28]

Another Military Cross was awarded to the Medical Officer of the 7th Battalion, Captain Robert Bruce Wallace MB RAMC, for his actions on this day near Fontaine les Croisilles, when, even though wounded himself,

> *he not only continued to dress wounded but went out with stretcher
> bearers and brought in men unable to move.*[29]

In the 6th Battalion, which had played a supporting role, Company Quartermaster-Sergeant James O'Gorman had been killed. He was the son of a regular soldier, and had been born at Secunderabad, India, where his father had been stationed. Total casualties in the rank and file for the 3 May attack, excluding those who later died of wounds, were 24 killed in the 6th Battalion, 17 killed in the 7th, while the 8th lost 97 men and the 9th Battalion 67.

On 8 May, Lieutenant-Colonel G. C. I. Hervey had returned to take over command of the 8th Battalion from Major Beardsley. They were still in the front line, and were relieved on 11 May to return to Berles-au-Bois to rest and absorb reinforcements. From 13 to 23 May the battalion was engaged on a course of musketry which included a competition organised by Lieutenant-Colonel Hervey, 'in which great interest was shown'[30], according to the Battalion War Diary. On 24 May, 110th Infantry Brigade sports took place, on an open piece of ground north of the Bienvillers-Monchy road, the War Diary of the 8th Battalion again recording that 'fine weather prevailed and an excellent programme was successfully carried through.'[31] On 1 June

A map of positions occupied around Croisilles, June 1917, by the 6th Battalion. Carried by Lieut J.H.Harratt. John Storey

Lieutenant J.H. Harratt, 6th Battalion. Harratt was a schoolmaster from Ibstock. When granted a commision, he chose the Leicestershire Regiment as he wanted to serve with the local men.
John Storey

26159 Pte Thomas William Lewin, 9th Battalion, killed on 15 June 1917.

32977 Pte George Everett Jackson, 6th Battalion, of Ketton, Rutland, who died of wounds on 24 June 1917.

the 8th Battalion left Berles after a three week rest, and returned once more to the vicinity of Croisilles, where they were in reserve. On the night of 15 June the Battalion moved up to Lincoln Trench, to assist in a renewed assault on the Hindenburg Line. The 9th Battalion moved up with them, and came under heavy and sustained shellfire. Particularly accurate shooting was observed from a high velocity naval gun behind the enemy lines. As well as ammunition dumps being hit, the 9th suffered around forty casualties.

The plan was essentially the same as that which had been tried on 3 May. This time it was the 58th Division which was to attack down the Hindenburg Line to bring in the portion still in enemy hands. They were to be supported by the 12th and 13th Battalions of the Northumberland Fusiliers and the 8th and 9th Battalions of the Leicestershire Regiment, who were once more to make a simultaneous frontal assault.

At 2.30am the Fusiliers went over the top, with one company of the 8th Battalion. The battalion War Diary states that:

> When 'C' Company arrived in Burg Trench to take up the position of counter attacking company, they received instructions to go forward at once and go over the top with the three companies, 13th Northumberland Fusiliers who were already in position, one company having been...delayed.
>
> Owing to the congestion of the very narrow trenches, Capt. Matthews experienced great difficulty in getting 'C' Company into Humber Trench (front line) and finally led them from Burg Trench over the top to Humber Trench in time for the front platoon under Lieut. F.Haines to go forward with the remainder of the line. The second platoon under 2/Lt Gregory was eventually able to go forward with the 2nd wave.[32]

Around this time the companies of the 9th Battalion, under the command of Lieutenant-Colonel P.E.Bent began to move up the communication trenches called Factory Avenue and Nelly Avenue. They were heading for the front line positions in Burg Trench and Lincoln Trench, vacated by the Northumberland Fusiliers and the 8th Leicesters who had gone over the top, although the 9th Battalion does not appear to have followed them into the attack. On their way up, they had passed through a furious enemy counter barrage which had been enough to claim a significant number of casualties. D.A.Bacon who was probably close to Lieutenant-Colonel Bent with 9th Battalion Headquarters, remembered:

> Almost immediately after our barrage opened, the enemy's counter fire became intense and many casualties were caused both among the attacking troops and those in support. For some time the attack appeared to succeed on the Right front, but on the left the assault was held up by the very thick enemy wire defences and machine gun fire. Despite these obstacles and the enemy's stout defence, our men, or at least some of them, eventually got into the hostile works and hung on for several hours; and desperate hand to hand fighting took place, in

A German machine gun team prepares for the British attack.

which the enemy had any numerical advantage.[33]

The 8th Battalion War Diary essentially confirms what Bacon saw, but implies that none of the Leicesters managed to penetrate the enemy front line:

> *The whole attack was held up at the enemy wire by an intense Machine Gun barrage, the wire had also not been cut and it is estimated that there were hostile machine guns placed at intervals of only about twenty or thirty yards in Tunnel Trench... At 3.30am the attacking force was compelled to withdraw, this being twenty minutes after the Zero hour, 3.10am. In connection with the engagement, the following awards were made for gallantry- MILITARY MEDAL: Cpl J.W.Briggs and Pte G.Dyer, both of 'C' Company.*[34]

The attacks of 15 and 16 June by the Leicestershire Brigade had been attended once more by a complete lack of success. On this occasion those who lost their lives included Private Harry Holyoak, aged 24, who with his cousins had enlisted for the 9th Battalion in September 1914. In the

14642 Pte John Harry Holyoak
Rose Holyoak

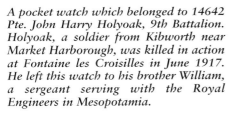

A pocket watch which belonged to 14642 Pte. John Harry Holyoak, 9th Battalion. Holyoak, a soldier from Kibworth near Market Harborough, was killed in action at Fontaine les Croisilles in June 1917. He left this watch to his brother William, a sergeant serving with the Royal Engineers in Mesopotamia.

intervening period, he had returned home to be married. His leave had passed all too quickly, and before there was an opportunity for his wife Violet and himself to visit a photographer's studio to record the event, he had left for France to rejoin his unit. His wife was not to see him again.

Lieutenant F.P. Haines, mentioned in the 8th Battalion War Diary, was killed on 16 June, as was the Medical Officer of the battalion, Captain S.Pool RAMC. His grave along with that of Holyoak and a number of other men killed around this time from the 110th Brigade lie in Croisilles British Cemetery. In July 1917 the Brigade went into divisional reserve, but remained in the Tunnel Sector, battalions taking turns in the front line until the beginning of September. Time out of the line was spent in training. No major attacks were carried out, but casualties continued to be sustained, mainly due to shellfire.

1 I.L.Read, *Of Those We Loved* (Pentland Press, 1994) p249
2 D.V.Kelly, *39 Months With the Tigers* (Ernest Benn, 1930) p58
3 Read, *op cit* p250
4 Read, *op cit* p250
5 Kelly, *op cit* p60
6 2/Lt F.B. Pitts, typescript letter 10.4.17 Liddle Collection, University of Leeds (LC)
7 Read, *op cit* p252
8 Read, *op cit* p254
9 Read, *op cit* p254
10 Kelly, *op cit* p60
11 S.Sassoon, *Memoirs of an Infantry Officer* (1930) p225
12 Sassoon, *op cit*, pp221-222
13 Kelly, *op cit* p66
14 A.C.Cave, unpublished typescript diary 3.5.17
15 Cave, *op cit* 3.5.17
16 War Diary, 8th bn Leicestershire Regt, LRO. 3.5.17
17 D.A.Bacon, unpublished typescript account, LRO pp75-76
18 Bacon, *op cit* p77
19 Bacon, *op cit* p77
20 Cave, *op cit* 3.5.17
21 S.W.Clarke papers, LC.
22 Lieut R.Sennett, typescript letter 24.5.17, held with F.B.Pitts papers LC.
23 2/Lt C.A.Payne, typescript letter 17.5.17, held with F.B.Pitts papers LC
24 Mrs E.H.Soden, typescript letter undated, held with F.B.Pitts papers LC
25 Card enclosed with above letter
26 Mrs Tutty, typescript letter undated, held with F.B.Pitts papers LC
27 2/Lt F.B.Pitts, typescript letter undated (rec'd 25.7.17) Pitts papers LC
28 Capt J.C.Vanner, citation for Military Cross, London Gazette.
29 Capt R.B.Wallace, citation for Military Cross, London Gazette
30 War Diary, 8th bn Leicestershire Regt, LRO 23.5.17
31 War Diary, 8th bn Leicestershire Regt, LRO 24.5.17
32 War Diary, 8th bn Leicestershire Regt, LRO 15.6.17
33 Bacon, *op cit* pp80-81
34 War Diary, 8th bn Leicestershire Regt, LRO 15.6.17

32806 Pte Frederick Stacey, 6th Battalion, killed in action on 17 August 1917. He was from Leicester.
Eric Kellaway

Chapter Eight

'Go On, Tigers!'
The fighting at Polygon Wood

Early in September 1917, the 21st Division entrained for the north. Shortly before leaving Artois, a football tournament had been held at Hauteville, with the 7th Battalion emerging as clear champions. Their prowess on the pitch must have been remarkable to watch, for their team beat the 8th Battalion side 4 – 1 in the first round, won the second round with a 3 – 1 win over the 6th Battalion, and beat the 9th Battalion by the same score in the Final. The cup was presented to them by the brigade commander, Brigadier-General Lord Loch CMG MVO DSO. At the same time the 7th Battalion also won two events at the final of the Brigade boxing competition at Avesnes le Comte. However, the talents of the Battalion for Rugby left something to be desired, for in this they were beaten 8 – 0 by the 6th Battalion.

Now for the Leicestershire Brigade, it was back to Belgium for the third time since their arrival on active service. They waited at Caestre, just inside France, for a fortnight. Here they were joined by reinforcement drafts, and the War Diary of the 7th Battalion records that between 17 and 22 September:

> A draft of 69 O.R. joined the Bn. They were all men who had been out before and a fair portion had been in the 110th Inf. Bde.[1]

One of the reinforcement drafts which arrived there contained Jack Horner. After recovering from his wound received at Bazentin, he had been posted for a spell to the 1st Battalion Leicestershire Regiment, before being invalided home again with a condition known as Trench Fever. Now he was back in France for the third time, and was posted to the 6th Battalion, where he met up with Billy Hill, an old pal he lived next door to back home in Leicester and with whom he had enlisted in March 1915. Here at Caestre, Horner recorded in his memoir, the Battalion had a competition for the best turned-out guard – 'the Colonel and his officers were always on the look-out for ideas that would keep the troops occupied...'. The prize on offer being a fortnight's leave in England:

> A brilliant idea! This was put on Daily Orders,

15493 Pte Frank Wileman, 6th Battalion, of Measham, Leicestershire. He wears both the old collar insignia and the more recent yellow sleeve patches of the 6th.
Below: A silk card which Frank sent home to his mother.
Mrs Eileen Springthorpe

190

One of the officers who served with the 9th Battalion in 1917 was Second Lieutenant Arthur Newberry-Choyce. That year a book of his war poetry 'Crimson Stains' was published. It was followed in 1920 by a novel 'Lips At The Brim', and in 1921 by another volume of poetry, 'Glinting Dandelions'. After the war Newberry-Choyce toured the United States, styled as 'the Leicestershire War Poet'.

Courtesy of Leicester City Museums

then there was a scurry of activity throughout the Battalion, all in off-duty time, as each Company had to provide a Guard of ten men, Sergeant and Corporal, for inspection in seven day's time[2]

All hands were turned to the competition, with a variety of tricks and ruses in evidence:

there was no Khaki blanco for the web equipment, so it was well scrubbed to bring out what there was of it, for it had been blancoed many times before. Trousers could be pressed if one knew how (and you didn't tell others how to do it...simply rub some soap down the original seam, and press with any handy brick. No hot irons available.)

There was no Brasso for the buttons and the brass tips of the webbing, so a bit of mortar [worked instead] – ...simply scrape some mortar off a brick wall with a jack knife, crush in the top of your mess tin, add a little spit or water – a good substitute for cleaning buttons, mess tin etc, and give them a shine you could see your face in...

Then there was the question of how to get a square pack. Its not possible to do it, with ordinary filling – boots, shirt, underwear, socks etc; some used pieces of stick, criss-crossed at the back of the pack to hold it square. Others, more ingenious, got hold of some cardboard from the Quartermasters Stores, and one lad acquired a piece of plywood, and no one asked him where he

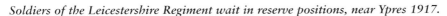

Soldiers of the Leicestershire Regiment wait in reserve positions, near Ypres 1917.

got it from. One didn't ask questions like that. You would be told to mind your own B----- business.[3]

The four teams of guards that were mounted included men from each company mixed up together. The competition was judged by the Colonel, and the party who were smartest duly received their leave in Blighty. The competition was light hearted, but it had a serious side. By encouraging the men to pay attention to detail in this way they became more competent and (and it was to be hoped) more thorough soldiers, and investing soldiers with a pride in their appearance is part of the process by which pride in one's unit – esprit de corps – and therefore improved morale is created. For the same purpose of fostering an identity with one's unit, the Brigade sports competitions were actively encouraged by the officers, and it must be said, keenly followed by the men in the ranks. Other than this, the battalions undertook company training at Caestre, including bombing and bayonet work.

Later that month the Leicestershire Brigade moved to occupy a desolate group of huts in a rear area of the Ypres Salient, in the region of Scottish Wood. The low lying countryside of this part of Belgium had seen bitter fighting almost continually since the earliest days of the war. There was little to break up the long skylines, and the high water table was apt to make it marshy. The attentions of the artillery of both sides had done little to improve either of these characteristics. By the end of September, the Third Battle of Ypres had been underway for two months. Millions of rounds of artillery ammunition had been expended, anything which might conceivably be used as an observation post had been pounded to oblivion, and the fields had become a waterlogged cratered lunar landscape of shell-holes. David

Kelly commented:

> As the infantry line was pushed forward, each advance at great sacrifice, huge masses of artillery followed behind, the guns bunching together wherever a piece of relatively dry and unbroken ground could be found, and to the guns came, often twice a day, melancholy trains of pack mules and horses, their bodies caked with mud and loaded with ammunition, the weary drivers on foot urging them on amid shells crashing right and left, and shrapnel bursting overhead.[4]

As if to add to the terrible reputation of the battle after the war, it was here in the summer of 1917 that the Germans first introduced Mustard Gas:

> The 'mustard' variety of gas-shell...was difficult to distinguish from the more harmless kinds unless the stuff splashed one, when it caused severe blisters, but had two unpleasant characteristics – it lingered some hours and rose in vapour under the sun if there was any, and it contaminated clothes, so that persons thus affected could infect a whole dugout. The other types in fashion were lachrymatory ('green-cross'), chiefly intended to make the gunners wear masks, and the 'blue cross', which...affected the heart and lungs, causing coughing and hoarseness.[5]

In this description, Kelly had neglected to mention also that amid the wasteland of flooded shell-holes, mustard gas was apt to saturate and dissolve in pools of water, so that anyone tempted to use shell-hole water for washing or drinking, even if he boiled it in a mess tin beforehand, was likely to poison both himself and any comrades.

Arthur Cave summed up the situation in one sentence: 'Foulest place we have yet struck.'[6]

But what was the rationale for launching an offensive in such a location?

An aerial photograph looking obliquely at Zonnebeke Lake at the end of September 1917 clearly shows the ground conditions faced by the troops during the Third Battle of Ypres. This area was slightly to the north of the sector allotted to the 110th Brigade.
Liddle Collection

The battle called officially Third Ypres but which will forever be known as Passchendaele, was born out of a number of strategic ideas. Firstly, Field Marshal Sir Douglas Haig had always wanted to fight the Germans in Flanders. Here, the British were closest to their supply ports of Le Havre and Calais. Secondly, the plan was inextricably linked to the U-Boat threat to British shipping. The Admiralty believed that Britain's lifeline was about to be severed by the U-Boats, if the bases from which they operated on the Belgian coast were not captured. Haig believed that the Germans had 'avoided the issue' on the Somme by conceding ground which was of no use

This photograph is believed to show a French army 'soldiers' council', meeting in Amiens. It was the French army mutinies and its parlous state in the Summer of 1917 which in part at least forced Haig's decision to launch the Third Ypres offensive. Ruth Broadhurst

to the Allies. Here, in Belgium, they would have to fight for every yard – and be bled white in the process – or give up a large tract of land which would hand the Allies the U-Boat bases. The question was decided finally by the French army mutinies in the spring of 1917. Some 60 French divisions had refused to attack. If the Germans discovered this, and attacked the French, the war would probably be lost. Hence, it fell to the British army to keep the Germans occupied until order could be restored in the French army, and the need to launch the offensive took on a renewed urgency.

The Leicestershire Brigade joined the battle on the night of 30 September 1917, when they marched up to Polygon Wood along duck board tracks which were the only means of crossing the battlefield. To leave the track was to invite disaster, as the ground on either side had become a treacherous swamp of glutinous mud which could easily suck under a soldier who was heavily laden with equipment, rifle, and frequently sandbags full of bombs or trench stores such as barbed wire or wire supports.

Polygon Wood had been captured by Australian units in the days previously, and that night the Leicestershire men took over the newly-won positions in the right half of the Polygon sector, just outside the wood and facing roughly south east, from the Aussies. These included a number of former German pillboxes, in the parlance of 1917 known as 'Mebus' after the abbreviation of the German word for concrete shelter, which was often marked on captured enemy maps. The 8th Battalion occupied the left hand

A fatigue party pauses while carrying duck boards across the battlefield during the Third Battle of Ypres.

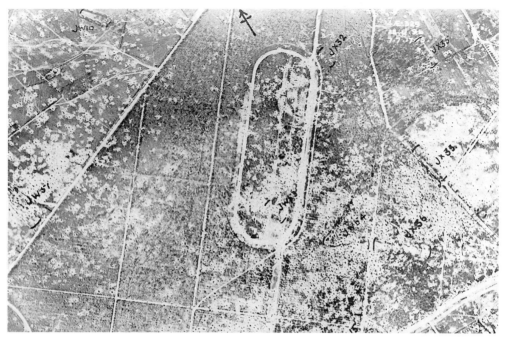

An aerial photo of Polygon Wood, looking vertically downwards, taken in late September 1917. The craters made by shells are clearly visible. The oval shape is the trotting track of a Belgian army riding school, which was located in the wood prior to the war. It remained a prominent feature when viewed from the air, even after considerable fighting and much destruction on the ground. C.E.Townley, Liddle Collection

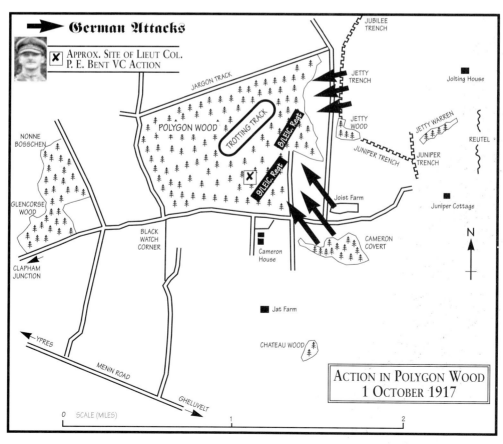

German Attacks

☒ Approx. Site of Lieut Col. P. E. Bent VC Action

JUBILEE TRENCH

JARGON TRACK

JETTY TRENCH

Jolting House

POLYGON WOOD

TROTTING TRACK

8/LEIC. Regt.

JETTY WOOD

JETTY WARREN

REUTEL

NONNE BOSSCHEN

JUNIPER TRENCH

JUNIPER TRENCH

9/LEIC. Regt.

Joist Farm

Juniper Cottage

GLENCORSE WOOD

CAMERON COVERT

N

BLACK WATCH CORNER

Cameron House

CLAPHAM JUNCTION

YPRES

Jat Farm

MENIN ROAD

CHATEAU WOOD

GHELUVELT

ACTION IN POLYGON WOOD
1 OCTOBER 1917

0   SCALE (MILES)   1   2

Looking across Polygon Wood. Few trees have survived the almost continuous bombardment.
G.D.Fairley, Liddle Collection

portion of the brigade frontage, with the 9th Battalion holding the right hand half. D.A.Bacon of the 9th remembered:

> *Though we had fully prepared for a rough night, the first hours passed quietly enough and we began to hope that after all, the Ypres bark might be worse than its bite. The ordinary precautions of a battle front were observed; patrols were pushed out to reconnoitre the ground and to give alarm in case of sudden attack. At headquarters, as soon as the relief was reported complete and the Australians had cleared, and orders as to dispositions and instructions in case of alarm had been given, it was decided to try to obtain a nights rest. I use the word 'try' because we were mud-wallowing in the open air, it was bitterly cold and no blankets could have been brought, and we were on the edge of a volcano that might and as a matter of fact did, belch forth at any moment. Firstly, we dug ourselves in as well as possible, in front of the headquarter Mebus, and with the aid of some old wood planks lying about, contrived to make a little shelter and firing position. At midnight, we lay down in the mud with the idea of sleeping, each one taking turn at sentry.* [7]

Behind them, in support, was the 7th Battalion, with the 6th Battalion in reserve, well back in the wood. The men of this Battalion had the opportunity to have something of a look around, and Horner recalled:

> *We were very near [a] road...where there had been some very heavy fighting, and we could see the result of that all around us, the terrain pockmarked with shell-holes, mud ankle deep. A tank lying at a grotesque angle near the...road, and underneath the road, the Germans had excavated it, and made it into a very good Dug out with bunks, and plenty of space, and easy quick ways to get out in a hurry,*

197

A German blockhouse in the heart of Polygon Wood, after its capture. Note the destruction caused by British – and German – large calibre shells. G.D.Fairley, Liddle Collection

and they must have done that when the tanks came charging along. We were allowed to go inside the dug-outs and have a look, with very strict orders not to touch anything. There might be booby traps. I must say they were very good indeed, much better than anything we'd done.[8]

Shortly after the relief was complete, in the early morning of 1 October 1917, the Germans launched a counter-attack in strength with fresh troops from the direction of Cameron Covert and Cameron Copse to the south and east, to recover the ground lost to them. A terrific artillery barrage began at about 4.40am, with the German gunners laying down smoke to obscure their infantry who were forming up. About forty minutes later they launched an attack the brunt of which fell upon the 8th Battalion, which in turn suffered heavy casualties and began to fall back. The situation on the right, with the 9th Battalion, was no less critical, and Bacon remembered:

At 5.30am, the enemy launched a determined infantry assault

Blockhouses on the eastern edge of Polygon Wood, after capture. Such shelters could accommodate a platoon or sometimes even a battalion of German infantry. Later of course they would be used to accommodate similar numbers of British soldiers. G.D.Fairley, Liddle Collection

Tanks wrecked and abandoned on the Ypres battlefield. These photographs were taken after the end of hostilities, in 1918. Although the ground has visibly dried out, the depth to which the machines have sunk can be appreciated. R.J.R. Tanner

Captain A.A.D.Lee MC, 9th Battalion. Arriving in France in October 1915, Lee was awarded the Military Cross for his work during the Bazentin Ridge battle in July 1916. He was killed at Polygon Wood on 1 October 1917, leading his men forward.

against our positions, through the smoke screen. The first wave of attackers was beaten off by 'A' Company using Lewis Gun and Rifle fire. The second wave was also successfully driven off on the [battalion] Front, but penetrated somewhat into the lines of the battalion on our left flank [8th Leicesters]. By this time the SOS was being sent up all along the Front – several were discharged at Head Qrs, both night and daylight rockets – and the situation looked threatening; Brigade Headquarters was called upon for immediate help. Under the determined pressure of the enemy 'A' Company commenced and continued to fall back. Lieut Col P.E.Bent DSO commanding the 9th Leicesters, decided to make a counter-attack, with such forces as were available, as no help could be expected from the troops in support for some hours, owing to the conditions of approach and the heavy and deep enemy barrage.[9]

The 7th Battalion began to arrive at about 9am but it had been fearfully cut up by shell fire on the way, and had been reduced to scattered groups. It was in any case too late, as the worst of the fighting was now over. It began to push platoons forward to reinforce the front and to drive out any Germans who had got into the British lines. The shell fire was intense, and in the process the battalion lost Captain A. A. Clarke MC killed, and Second-Lieutenants P. E. Agar and C. G. Scarfe wounded. The Battalion War Diary further records:

2/Lieut R. T. W. Miles who had gone forward to reconnoitre assisted by 1 platoon of 'D' Coy joined in the counter attacks was killed and then Sergt MOSS who was wounded in the leg still led the platoon forward until practically all became casualties under hostile machine gun fire and Sergt MOSS was again wounded in the face. There was a gap of 250 yards to the East of CAMERON HOUSE and from our Bde boundary due S[outh][10]

Further gallantry had been displayed by Temporary Lieutenant-Colonel Philip Eric Bent, who had come to England from Canada to join the army on the outbreak of war, and who was in command of the 9th Battalion. He

36531 Pte Charles Poole, 9th Battalion, was killed in action on 1 October 1917. He was from Colne, Lancashire, and a member of a large reinforcement draft from the East Lancashire Regiment which arrived with the 8th and 9th battalions in early 1917. Above: Pte Poole's memorial scroll and plaque, mounted in a wooden frame, which hung on the wall of his parents' home in Colne. Inset: A portrait photo of Poole.

2nd Lieut R.T.W.Miles, 7th Battalion, killed in action in Polygon Wood on 1 October 1917. Aged 34 when he died, Miles had been a farmer in South Africa prior to the outbreak of war. He fought with the Kimberley Regiment in German South-West Africa in 1915 and then as a trooper with the 8th Hussars, before being commissioned into the Leicestershire Regiment.

Lieutenant Colonel P.E.Bent VC DSO, 9th Battalion. Bent won the supreme award for his heroism in Polygon Wood on 1 October 1917, when in the face of a German counter attack he rallied Battalion HQ details and led them forward

was awarded the only Victoria Cross gained by the Leicestershire Brigade for his bravery in leading the counter-attack to recover the positions lost by his battalion. Kelly relates how Bent,

was in a 'pillbox' on the west side of [Polygon] Wood when a runner came in saying 'SOS gone up from (the reserve) company'. 'Then we'd better get on', said the Colonel, and went forward with his headquarter personnel. Collecting the reserve company and everyone available, the Colonel led a counter-attack, and, struck down in the moment of victory was last seen – for his body, doubtless blown to pieces, was not found – waving his pipe and calling, 'Go on, Tigers!' This very gallant officer was, I think only twenty-four at the time and was a civilian [before the war], but was so devoted to his work as a soldier that when granted ten days leave he was back in less than a week with his battalion.[11]

Bent had been shot through the temple and died instantly. His body being lost to the muddy ground was never recovered, and today he is commemorated on the walls of the Memorial to the Missing at Tyne Cot, Passchendaele. Bent also had connections with Ashby de la Zouch, having been educated there, and a further memorial to him in the form of his sword may be found in Ashby de la Zouch parish church.

During the early part of the morning the 9th Battalion had also lost one of the most colourful characters to serve in its ranks, Private Sidney 'Togo' Bolesworth. He and a fellow soldier, Private Joe Paul, were designated battalion snipers, and had crawled out to a shell-hole in front of the British lines in order to give them a better view over the German positions. They had taken a few shots at the enemy when the German counter-attack erupted before them. Paul was hit in the leg, but managed to escape, while Bolesworth was shot dead, his body last seen in the muddy shell-hole. His

7832 Pte Sidney 'Togo' Bolesworth DCM, 9th Battalion. Mrs K.Best

Togo Bolesworth (left) during his boxing days, around 1908.

Greg Drozdz

remains were not recovered, and he too is named on the Tyne Cot Memorial.[12]

'Togo' Bolesworth was born in a cottage in Spring Gardens, Hinckley in 1889, the third of four brothers. Aged 13 he had started work as a half timer in a hosiery factory. A 'well set up lad' who could 'give a good account of himself', young Togo liked to box in his spare time. When, three years later he tired of life at the factory and decided to join the army, he discovered that soldiering and boxing went well together. He was posted with his Battalion of the Leicestershire Regiment to India, and in 1908 won the All-India title at welter weight. He later won the title again, at Poona in India, this time as a middle weight. He returned home from the army in 1912, and boxed in numbers of contests across the midlands. He was reckoned to be the hardest hitter at his weight in the country at that time, and the biggest fight of his career came at the Olympia Skating Rink on Trinity Lane in Hinckley, in May 1914, when he fought Billy Sherwood of Walsall for a purse of over £100. Sherwood was knocked out by Togo in front of an enormous crowd who had travelled by train from Leicester, Birmingham and elsewhere to see the spectacle.

With the outbreak of war, Bolesworth was recalled to the Colours, where he would experience the highest of peaks and the lowest of troughs in the coming years. In 1915 with the 1st Battalion Leicestershire Regiment he was awarded the Distinguished Conduct Medal and Croix de Guerre for his undisputed bravery in the field – even though wounded he had remained at his post until he was relieved, and had the presence of mind to deliver a report on the situation to his commanding officer before receiving medical help. Returning to England to recover from his wounds, he was posted to the 3rd Battalion at Patrington near Hull. Whilst there, he became involved in an altercation with another soldier, whom he struck. The soldier died during the night, ostensibly of concussion, and Togo found himself charged with manslaughter at York Assizes. He was imprisoned for two months whilst awaiting trial, but it is a remarkable testimony to his stature within the Leicestershire Regiment that a group of officers paid for a Barrister to conduct his defence. Togo was acquitted after two doctors testified that the fatal injuries could not have been inflicted during the fight, and the judge apologised to him for the fact that a man of his good service should have been detained. He hoped that it would be some consolation that he could return to his regiment without a stain on his character.

In the event, Togo did return to France, but this time to the 9th Battalion. He arrived in the summer of 1917, and quickly re-established himself once more as a man whom his officers could rely upon in any situation. As with the 1st Battalion, he refused the offer of a stripe or stripes, despite the positions of responsibility which he often held. When he died, he was still only a private soldier. After his death, his officer Lieutenant Griffiths wrote to tell his mother that Bolesworth was

> well liked and respected by not only all in the sniping section but in the Battalion and many officers thought he was the best soldier in the regiment.[13]

The situation remained tense throughout the day, the War Diary of the 8th Battalion for 1 October 1917, recording that,

> At 10.15am, Captain J.B. Matthews with the left support company (D) moved from its position J.10.a.8.2, in order to make a counter attack against the enemy, holding the high ground in the vicinity of JOIST FARM. Unfortunately, Captain J.B.Matthews MC was killed instantly by a sniper when making a reconnaissance, preparatory to the attack.[14]

29000 Pte Reuben Kent, of Swadlincote, 7th Battalion. He was killed on 1 October 1917.
Mrs J.Davis

Shortly afterwards at 10.30am the War Diary of the 9th Battalion describes how a Corporal Outhwaite (who it must be assumed was a Lewis gunner) brought down single-handed an enemy aircraft which was attempting to shoot up British troops on the ground and had dropped to a height of only 200 feet in the process. The enemy machine crashed in No Man's Land, and Outhwaite's achievement was a remarkable one.[15]

Casualties continued to be inflicted by the Germans throughout the day, the 8th Battalion War Diary again noting that at 2pm,

> small parties of the enemy were seen moving about the S.W. edge of JETTY WARREN but were dispersed by rifle fire. Shortly afterwards a hostile MG opened traversing fire along the road in J.10.c. central, and Lt.Col. Utterson DSO was hit in the arm by a bullet.[16]

Major T.C.Howitt now took over command of the leaderless 9th Battalion as well as his own sadly depleted 7th Battalion, and the two were temporarily amalgamated as the 7th/9th Battalion. Further attacks were expected during the afternoon, but in the event, it was dusk before the enemy tried to break through again. This effort was dispersed by an accurate British barrage. That afternoon and evening, the 6th Battalion moved up into position to support the three weakened battalions in the front line. German shelling was still causing casualties, one of whom was Jack Horner, back in France for only a few weeks:

14983 Pte Charles William Greenaway, of Tickencote, 9th Battalion. Killed on 1 October 1917. Prior to the war he had been a footman, and was his company commander's batman.

> My company, 'A', were moving up in single file in support of the 9th Battalion, when from nowhere (I don't remember hearing or seeing any shelling) a piece of shrapnel hit my left forearm. I was knocked flat, and when I came round I was alone with a smashed arm. I gripped my arm above the elbow with my right hand to stop the blood flow, and somehow got my arm lying across my stomach, the blood

soaking my tunic.[17]

Horner had probably been left for dead by his comrades, and began to make his own way back for help:

> *I stumbled on, God knows where, for I don't – through the mud and slime, on this great sea of mud. I didn't know where I was going, or how long I had been stumbling around, for I saw no one, and in all this space, no one saw me. Honestly, I have no recollection whatever of these wanderings. It was dusk, maybe night time, when I saw a chink of light, some distance away, and I made for it as best I could.*
>
> *It was a German Pill Box. I went in, and again almost faded out, but, Thank Heaven! They were British, using the Pill Box as an advanced Dressing Station, by stretcher bearers and medical orderlies. I asked for water (I can still taste the petrol in that water now). They asked me where the Hell I'd come from. I couldn't tell them, I was all in, but they knew from my shoulder flashes which division I came from, and that was...miles away.*[18]

Jack Horner was lucky to have found help when he did. In the desolate wilderness of the Ypres Battlefield, many of the badly wounded could not be found by stretcher parties and were left out to their fate under the rain. Even those who could walk, like Horner, risked a similar fate unless by chance they stumbled upon a medical post.

From the aid post, it was a journey by ambulance back over uneven roads (which were often in the Ypres Salient known as 'corduroy tracks' – rows of tree trunks laid out across the mud) back to a Casualty Clearing Station:

> *I was weary, tired and wet through, covered in mud. They made me*

A German Pill Box used as a dressing station on the Ypres battlefield. Jack Horner stumbled into one of these as he made his way, wounded, across the battlefield.

and many others as comfortable as possible in the circumstances, to wait for the ambulances to come up the Line. We waited many hours, how long I don't know. I was all in, and about out; very very tired and weary, and I have not much recollection of where I was. Eventually the ambulances came. I don't remember whether they were horse-draw or motors, but it was the most painful and horrible journey I have ever made in my life; with every lurch and bump, the smashed bones were digging into the raw flesh. It was a nightmare journey.[19]

On 4 October at a Brigade conference it was decided to amalgamate the 8th and 9th Battalions for the moment at least, due to the weak state of both battalions. The joint force came under the command of Major R.R. Yalland, of the 6th Battalion, before Lieutenant-Colonel Aldworth of the 7th Battalion took it into the line once more on 7 October.

During the remaining days up to the middle of October the 110th Brigade left the front line for rest billets twice. After both occasions it returned to the front line in the Polygon Wood area to act first as a Divisional reserve and secondly as a Corps reserve in case of a British breakthrough, which never occurred. Active operations had ceased, in this area at least, and it took no further part in any major attack. This is not however to say that circumstances were pleasant or quiet. D.A. Bacon with the 8th/9th Battalion recalled:

Early on the morning of the 8th [October] *the two rear companies moved to new positions in Polygon Wood, and the Head Qrs moved*

'Corduroy tracks' enabled transport to traverse the battlefield. It was over these that the wounded travelled in horse drawn or motor ambulances.

west some 300 yards and occupied a line of 3 Mebusses, just within the Wood, and which had been used by the 8th Battalion Hd Qrs on the 1/2nd October. These Mebusses were all in a derelict condition within, being some six inches deep in water, and the entrances, partly demolished, faced the enemy, thus rendering them exceedingly vulnerable; the only alternative was to wallow in the mud and despite disadvantages, the former was preferred. Two days were spent in the new positions, no changes in disposition of any kind occurring, but the time was most unpleasantly passed and the conditions here were most demoralising for the troops. A fresh artillery duel opened up on the 8th, and continued with unabated fury until the afternoon of the 10th – at times more violent than at others; the weight of this appeared to be concentrated about Battn Hd Qrs especially, though the forward area and indeed the Support Positions further back as far as Black Watch Corner and Clapham Junction received plenty of attention. The enemy on this occasion made use of very large calibre shells, presumably ranging on the Mebusses in the hope of breaking them in and so destroying the only available cover. Around our own particular fragment, the fire was directed with deadly accuracy, and a continual shower of 8 inch missiles, containing high explosive, burst on the roof and landed all around, sending up clouds of mud and splinters. It was absolutely unsafe to go out, and constituted a death trap within; the gap serving as the door was 6 feet wide and it required but one shell to enter, to annihilate the occupants. Like rats in a trap for two days and nights, we crouched in the waterlogged hovel, and it was again miraculous that while the roof and walls were hit 40 or 50 times, no shell came in via the opening.[20]

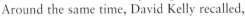

Around the same time, David Kelly recalled,

our brigade went again into the line, which as a result of the latest battle was pushed forward to about fifteen hundred yards east of Polygon Wood, to include the Reutelbeck – on the map a stream, on the ground a huge lake owing to shell-fire – and the sites of Reutel and Molenaarelsthoek villages, which it would be quite inadequate to describe as merely blown to pieces: I remember going out with two of the Battalion commanders in a joint endeavour to identify Reutel, which had figured in a divisional order as some kind of boundary mark, and that we could not agree as to the precise location! It was purely an exercise in map reading, as not even one spec of brick dust – let alone half a brick – had survived.[21]

36647 Pte Robert Ronald Tillotson, 8th Battalion, killed in action on 21 October. He was formerly number 28231 of the East Lancashire Regiment, and like Charles Poole of the 9th Battalion he also came from Colne in Lancashire.

The 8th/9th Battalion was dissolved and returned to its constituent components on 12 October, Major T.L.Warner DSO being in command of the 8th until Lieutenant-Colonel T.C.Howitt DSO arrived to take over. However, one might argue that with a step like this becoming necessary in the first place, the writing was on the wall for one of these two battalions at least.

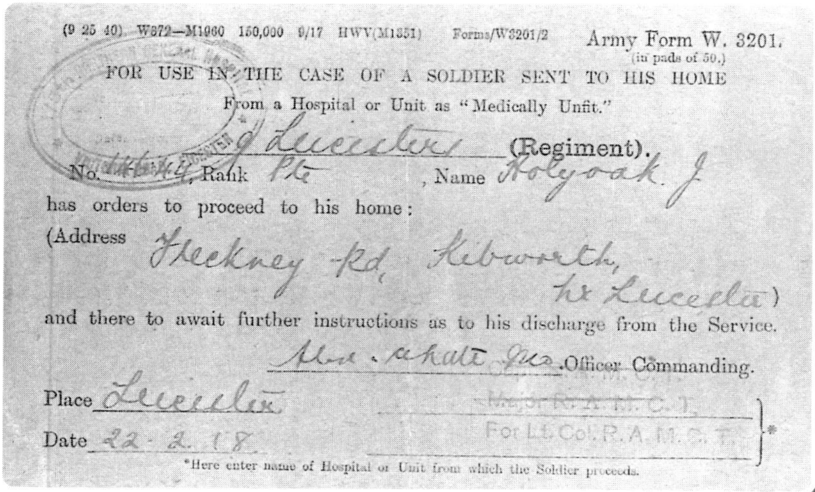

The following is handwritten form content:

(9 25 40) W872—M1960 150,000 9/17 HWV(M1351) Forms/W3201/2 **Army Form W. 3201.**
(in pads of 50.)

FOR USE IN THE CASE OF A SOLDIER SENT TO HIS HOME

From a Hospital or Unit as "Medically Unfit."

9 Leicesters (Regiment).

No. *14641* Rank *Pte* , Name *Holyoak. J*

has orders to proceed to his home:

(Address *Hackney Rd, Kibworth, nr Leicester*)

and there to await further instructions as to his discharge from the Service.

Alex. White Jus. Officer Commanding.

Place *Leicester*

Date *22·2·18*   Major R. A. M. C. 1.

                          For Lt. Col. R. A. M. S. T.

*Here enter name of Hospital or Unit from which the Soldier proceeds.

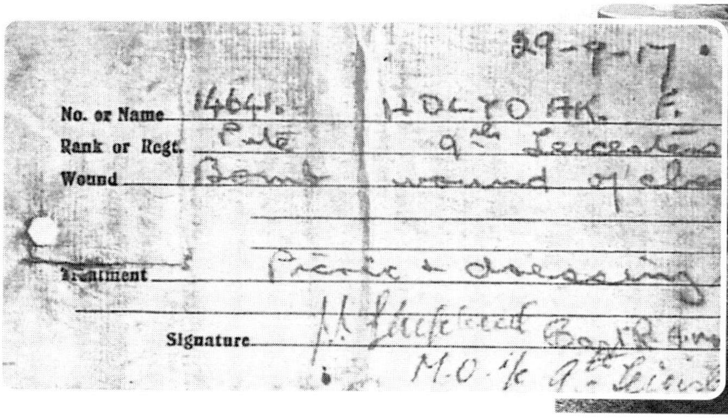

29-9-17

No. or Name *14641.*   *HOLYOAK. F.*
Rank or Regt. *Pte*   *9th Leicesters*
Wound *Bomb*   *wound of elb*

Treatment *Picric & dressing*

Signature *J. H. Lucefield Capt R.A.m*
          M.O. ⅓ 9 Leice

14641 Pte Jack Holyoak, 9th Battalion, in 1917, with the 'triage' label fixed to his tunic when he was initially treated by his battalion medical officer at a dressing station, and the document entitling him to proceed home on furlough pending his final discharge from the army. Rose Holyoak

The Leicestershire Brigade left the front line for a four or five day rest around the second week of October, entraining for billets at Sercus. On 15 October 1917, they were back in the front lines near Reutel, east of Polygon Wood, where they were to remain until 16 November, when they were relieved by New Zealand troops, and left the front line for the last time. However, the focus of the offensive had shifted somewhat to the north now, and the attention of British and German High Commands was centred upon the struggle for Passchendaele village itself and the spur of high ground upon which it sat. Around Polygon Wood, things had now fallen relatively quiet in the front line at least. However, the approaches, of which there were two, were still subject to fearsome shelling:

> one [ran] *south of Polygon Wood, past an old pill-box, called Black Watch Corner, the other north of the wood, and known as Jargon Track. This latter led through a deep hollow, always full of gas, from which nothing was visible but sky and shell holes, and through a*

12701 Regimental Sergeant Major Shearing Brownsworth, 7th Battalion, killed in action on 5 November 1917.

203279 Pte J.M.Jones, 7th Battalion, of Oadby, gassed in early November 1917, with the card sent to his next-of-kin to inform them of his arrival in the UK, and the copy of the Gospel of St. John he was given whilst he was recuperating in hospital. The photograph below shows a group of wounded recovering at Woodhall Spa, Lincolnshire. Pte Jones stands seventh from right, behind the seated man.

Mr Peter Greenhill

group of badly smashed pill-boxes – broken blocks of masonry with the steel rods sticking through the gaps – which enjoyed the sinister name of 'Dead Mule Dugouts'. The name was due to the presence of at least a dozen dead mules lying in heaps at the side of the track. There were a number of dead men as well. From this gloomy spot nothing but shell-holes could be seen, and the curious stale smell of gas, putrefaction and thrice disembowelled earth was overwhelming.[22]

25910 Pte James Pykett, 9th Battalion, who died of wounds on 23 November 1917, and was buried at Aubigny.

The stay of the Leicestershire Brigade in the Ypres Sector had been – in comparison with the experiences of some units – an uneventful one. They had taken part in no major attacks, and had experienced only two really heavy days of fighting at the beginning of October. Yet the toll in casualties had still been significant. Private J. W. L Holyoak had been seriously wounded on the way up to relieve the Australians on 29 September by a bomb fragment which had pierced his heart. He would take no further active part in the war. The commanding officer of one battalion had been killed, and that of another wounded. Hinckley had lost in Togo Bolesworth probably the greatest middle weight boxer it had ever produced. Once again, the pages of the *Leicester Evening Mail* and other local newspapers made for grim reading, as some of the most extensive casualty lists since the Somme over a year previously were published.

1 War Diary, 7th bn Leicestershire Regt, LRO 22.9.17
2 J.W.Horner, unpublished typescript memoir. Author's collection.
3 Horner, *op cit*
4 D.V.Kelly, '39 Months With the Tigers' (Ernest Benn, 1930) p77
5 Kelly, *op cit*
6 A.C.Cave, unpublished typescript diary 4.10.17
7 D.A.Bacon,unpublished typescript account, LRO p85
8 Horner, *op cit*
9 Bacon, *op cit* p86
10 War Diary, 7th bn Leicestershire Regt, LRO 1.10.17
11 Kelly, *op cit* p79
12 Much of the information here concerning 'Togo' Bolesworth comes from an article published in the Hinckley Times of 14.11.52, which was in turn based mainly on information supplied by Joe Paul of Hinckley.
13 Hinckley Times, 11.1.18
14 War Diary, 8th bn Leicestershire Regt, LRO 1.10.17
15 War Diary, 9th bn Leicestershire Regt, LRO 1.10.17
16 War Diary, 8th bn Leicestershire Regt, LRO 1.10.17
17 Horner, *op cit*
18 Horner, *op cit*
19 Horner, *op cit*
20 Bacon, *op cit* p89
21 Kelly, *op citt* p82
22 Kelly, *op cit* p83

Chapter Nine

Heroic resistance; desperate endeavour
The Spring Offensives

In November 1917, with the abandonment of the Third Ypres campaign in a terrible wasteland of mud and water and following the near collapse of the Italian Army at Caporetto, the 21st Division, including the Leicestershire Brigade, received orders to proceed forthwith to the southern Alps. The intention was to reinforce the Italians with a number of British divisions, but back on the Western Front fate intervened once more. The Cambrai offensive, launched almost as an afterthought on 20 November, brought unexpected success. The ground here was rather dry and relatively undamaged – unlike that around Ypres – and made good going for tanks. Some 300 machines were launched into the first day of the battle, which had been carefully thought out by the staff of the Tank Corps and which was attended by unprecedented gains of ground. The Hindenburg Line was penetrated for several thousand yards, many prisoners were captured, and back in Blighty the church bells were rung in many villages to herald the end of the war. Unfortunately the Germans had other ideas. The infantry who had accompanied the tanks found themselves overstretched, and with scarcely any reserve formations left after the campaigns of 1917, were desperately short of reinforcements. The Germans recovered quickly from their initial shock, and on 1 December launched a massive counter-attack on the dangerously exposed flank of the salient, which the offensive had created. Moving fast, with lightly-armed storm troops, the Germans effectively cut off a large portion of the attacking formations, some of

Lightly armed with carbines and grenades, German stormtroops move forward.

A 21st Division Christmas card, from 1917. It was sent home to his mother by Frank Wileman, of the 6th Battalion. As he pointed out to his mother in his message, the card lists every major action fought by the division up to that time.
Mrs Eileen Springthorpe

40179 Pte Jethro Harris, (right) 8th Battalion, in hospital blue, Winter 1917. Simon Jervis Photographic Archive

whom fought to the bitter end whilst many others were forced to surrender.

The move of the 21st Division to Italy was cancelled, and the 110th Brigade was thrown into the confusion of the battle. Arriving by train at Tincourt, behind the Cambrai front, they marched via Villers-Faucon to the St Emillie-Epehy sector. The weather was atrocious, and officers and men alike were forced to stand and wait in the pouring rain without top-coats (transports were many miles in the rear) for two hours as the administrative chaos was resolved and the brigade staff reconnoitred the positions they were to take over.

Everywhere were signs of the battering the brigade being relieved, which was part of the

210

Pte H. Weston, 8th Battalion. The yellow square insignia of the 8th is very clear in this photograph, as is the cloth sew-on version of the 'Leicester' shoulder title. These became increasingly common in the second half of the war, as metals like brass became scarcer. Weston's home address was 11 Bell Street, Wigston Magna.
John Taylor

55th (West Lancs) Division, had taken. David Kelly remembered:

> *somewhere near Vaucellette farm we found an artillery major lying dead in pink silk pyjamas, rifle in hand, in front of his battery headquarters, which he must have awakened to find in No-Mans-Land.*[1]

However, by the time the 110th Brigade reached the firing line to the east of Epehy village, the front had stabilised, and the German counter offensive had petered out. The British army, after such early promise, was either back on the line on which it had started or slightly behind it.

The winter was now to be spent improving the defences of the Epehy district, and digging new emplacements and trenches in front of the village. For some weeks only fire trenches existed, and the front line had to be approached overland, during the hours of darkness, until communication trenches could be dug. The Royal Engineers, were also hard at work within Epehy village, constructing concrete emplacements, blockhouses, and observation posts, some of which are still visible today. Reinforcements were absorbed whilst at Epehy, and for a young soldier just posted to France the sector could appear full of danger. One such soldier was Private F.E. Pothecary, who arrived in France in January 1918 and was posted to the 6th Battalion:

A block house at Epehy, Cullen's Post, constructed by the Royal Engineers in the winter of 1917/18. It is still standing today, a vivid testimony to the strength of its construction. Bill Mitchinson

> *The Battalion was in the line at Epehy & we was at Saulcourt and we had to go up each evening as carrying parties and go out to repair the barbed wire which was very frightening at first. Our officer said, 'Don't worry, if you are going to get it, you won't know anything about it' and that took some of the fear away...We lived in a deep dug out with two entrances (about thirty steps down). We had to pass through a gas prevention chamber half way down. The beds were wire netting racks, three tiers high, and the only light was from candles. It was always hot and stuffy. At the top of the steps there was always a gas guard who would beat on a hanging shell case when there was gas about. He would also use a spinning rattle. We had to go down to the front line every day and repair damage and do anything that wanted doing, digging latrines etc (never a dull moment). We had three days of this and then the front line. Here we lived in slits cut in the front [beneath] the parapet, and covered with a ground sheet. Food came up in big containers from the field kitchens carried on stretcher type wooden frames, 'no fires in the line'. At dusk, we had to 'Stand To' and then it was 'two hours on, four hours off' to stand on the fire step all night, which was a cold and dreary job.*

Sometimes great rats would run just in front of you and put the wind up you. At dawn everyone 'Stands To' after which we would have a foot inspection and whale oil would be issued to rub on the feet to prevent frost bite.[2]

Tsarist Russia collapsed in the Spring of 1917, and before the Kerensky Government in turn fell to the Bolsheviks that October, it had sought an armistice with Germany. Millions of German troops had been released from the Eastern Front and were now on their way to France. With the punitive treaty of Brest-Litovsk, in March 1917, Germany and Austria had extracted harsh terms from their prostrate foe, and vast quantities of grain and other supplies came under the control of the German war machine. Few could doubt that with German in a better military position in relation to Britain and France than at any time since the start of the war, she would play her hand soon. She would attempt to decide the outcome of the war before sufficient American troops could reach French soil to make a difference to the balance of power.

In February 1918, due to the casualties of 1916 and 1917, the shortages of manpower across the BEF, and the inability of the Home Front to continue to supply reinforcements at a sufficient rate, every brigade in the BEF began the process of reducing from four battalions to three. Those men who were thus released would be used to reinforce the other battalions. In the Leicestershire Brigade, it was the 9th Battalion upon which the axe fell. The 9th was a battalion with a fine fighting record, indeed it was the only battalion in the brigade to have gained a Victoria Cross, and it was not necessarily weaker in numbers than the other battalions. However, in the British Army, the system of 'last in, first out' holds good, and most men accepted this. The 9th was the last to form, and so was considered junior to the other three battalions. Hence it was selected for disbandment.

Corporal D.A.Bacon, in his recollections, records that,

this came as a severe blow to those of us who had been associated with the battalion since its formation or since its embarkation from England. On 6th February the Colonel addressed the battalion in the

203247 Pte Herbert Sutton, 6th Battalion. He joined the battalion on 1 January 1918, and served with it throughout the battles of April and May.
Mrs J.Moreton

201586 Pte James Ball. He served with the 9th battalion in 1917, but when it was disbanded in February 1918 he was posted to the 11th Battalion. He lost his life on 14 April 1918, and at the time of his death he was 42 years of age. With a reputation as a local hard man who liked his beer, for some time he had been a platelayer at Groby Granite Quarries by day, and a gamekeeper on the Earl of Stamford's estate by night. His age exempted him from conscription, but the landlady of The Plough Inn at Ratby bet him a packet of cigarettes that he would not enlist. He did so, with tragic results, and his widow never spoke to the landlady again.
Mr Jim Briggs

morning, informing them of the change and expressing the hope, that though divided, the glorious reputation of the Leicestershire Regiment would be upheld by all.[3]

Apprehension was not confined solely to those in the ranks. A junior officer, Second-Lieutenant J.C. Farmer, found himself now posted to the 8th Battalion. It was not a prospect that he relished, mainly because he regarded the colonel of the 8th as a martinet.[4]

On 9 February Bacon recorded that:

all arrangements for the disbandment of the battalion commenced ...in accordance with these instructions and those received from the Higher formations, a draft of 8 officers and 200 other ranks was dispatched to join the 11th Battalion (Pioneers) Leic Regt (6th Division). On the 10th the remainder of the battalion was dispersed as follows – 3 officers and 60 other ranks to join the 6th Leic Regt. 14 officers and 198 other ranks to the 7th Leic Regt and 10 officers and 222 other ranks to the 8th Leic Regt. The battalion was now virtually disbanded, except for the Transport Section...the Colonel, Adjutant, all Warrant Officers, Quartermaster sergeants and orderly room staff.[5]

The Orderly Room Sergeant of each disbanded battalion was ordered to proceed to General Headquarters at Rouen, with the unit's documents. This task fell to Bacon, as Orderly Room Corporal, in the absence of the sergeant, who was on leave at the time:

As I had already been assured of a position on the Brigade Head Quarters staff through the kindness of the Adjutant (Capt. A. Leake) and Capt. G.E.G. Tooth MC (a former Adjutant of the battalion and now GSO3, 21st Div) I was not at all sorry at the prospect of a little holiday away from the line.[6]

Arthur Cave recorded the disbanding of the 9th Battalion in his diary on 7 February, and noted that:

The brass band of the 9th battalion, the only one in the Brigade and the envy of [all], was transferred to us en bloc, band and bandsmen[7]

Another of the block houses still standing at Epehy, Morgan's Post. This is one of the positions defended for a considerable part of the day on 21 March 1918, by the 7th Battalion.
Bill Mitchinson

With the onset of March, enemy activity opposite Epehy increased noticeably. Kelly, positioned in one of the concrete observation towers constructed by the Royal Engineers, was a regular observer using a high powered telescope:

From my observation post on the east edge of Epehy village I commanded several long stretches of the great Cambrai-St. Quentin main road behind the enemy lines running between Aubencheul and Bantouzelle, which being several miles behind the line was freely used in day light by their transport, and from about March 10th this traffic, especially of lorries, began to grow prodigiously. Simultaneously new lines of flashing white posts became visible each day, indicating miles of overhead telegraph wires, and I was startled one morning to observe what appeared to be a prisoners of war cage under construction![8]

A map of the 6th Battalion positions in front of Epehy, carried by Lieutenant J.H.Harratt.

John Storey

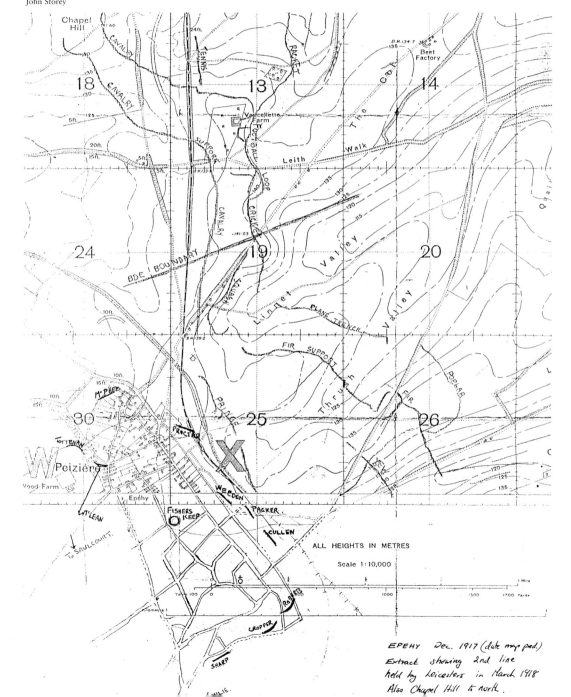

EPEHY DEc. 1917 (date map prod.)
Extract showing 2nd line
held by Leicesters in March 1918
Also Chapel Hill to north.

Kelly tried without success to have the heavy artillery behind the British lines turn its attention to a house called Rancourt Farm, which from the frequent visits of wagons was strongly suspected to be a dump. Some months later, captured German documents were found to contain the instruction that ammunition should be drawn from the main divisional dump located at Rancourt Farm.

This was very much the calm before the storm. As March progressed, winter began to release its grip on the land, and the first signs of spring began to appear. At the same time, the signals became increasingly clear that the attack was imminent, and statements from German prisoners and the occasional deserter put it on either 20 or 21 March. All the 110th Brigade could do was hurriedly to complete the defences of Epehy, and wait. All the battalions were under strength, and were holding too long a section of frontage, but everything possible had been done to prepare for the onslaught when it came. Using tactics adapted from the Germans, and the experience in the Hindenburg Line, the plan was for the front line to be quickly evacuated and for the troops to fall back on a line nearer the village. This was known as the 'Red Line' and focused on a trench called Fir Support Trench. From here the men would engage the enemy in a 'battle zone'. A new set of reserve positions (known as the 'Yellow Line') had also been dug to the west of Epehy, should the Germans prove impossible to contain in the battle zone. Telephone cables had been laid from this line to the forward positions, and had been buried at a depth of some six feet, in order that they might withstand some of the expected enemy shellfire.

On the morning of the assault itself, 21 March 1918, the left hand portion of the 110th Brigade sector (Pezieres to Epehy village) was held by the 7th Battalion, while the right hand was held by the 8th Battalion. The 6th battalion lay in reserve in the Yellow Line. Pandemonium erupted at

A German 21cm howitzer is hauled toward a forward position, ready for the Spring Offensive.

about 2.30am, and David Kelly, who had gone to bed the previous night fully dressed and equipped in the expectation of attack, awoke in his corrugated iron shelter in a sunken lane behind Epehy:

[The noise] *for a few seconds seemed to my half awake consciousness to be the propellers of a ship. It was the incessant thud of shells on every side. In another second I was in the sunken road outside of my cupola and could have no doubt that 'the day' had come. Our whole area, and all the areas to north and south, were being flooded with high explosive and shrapnel shells, the former falling in serried ranks, with concentrated fire on all roads and trenches in front of us, while an incessant stream of shells whistled over our heads to the transport routes and camps, including the ruined village of Saulcourt behind us.*[9]

10986 Pte Tom Thornton, 6th Battalion, captured on 21 March. He was a member of Lieut. Harratt's platoon, and before the war was employed at Two Steeples hosiery factory in Wigston.

As dawn began to break a fantastic sight greeted the defenders in the front line trenches. Out of the morning mist were emerging thousands of German soldiers, and across the countryside as far as one could see, lines of field grey figures were advancing. Having refined their shock tactics on the eastern front, and during the counter offensive after Cambrai, the Germans launched a new style of attack. Lightly-armed storm troops spearheaded the assault with bombers and machine-gunners to the fore. These troops swept through the avenues of least resistance, past the British strong points, making for artillery and support lines. They then left the strong points to 'wither on the vine' without support.

In the Leicestershire sector, troops in the front line retired as planned (to prevent them from being surrounded and cut off in this way) with relatively few killed or captured, and took up position in the Red Line. All day on 21 March, the battle for Epehy raged, with stout resistance being encountered

Looking east from former 110th Brigade positions in front of Epehy. Even today, the open nature of the ground is striking. On 21 March the German attack across these fields was aided by thick fog. Richard Lane

by the Germans, from Fir Support Trench and the Prince Reserve Trench. The War Diary of the 7th Battalion on this date records that,

> During the whole of the day the enemy made many futile attacks from NE of Fir Support and Red Line, attempting to bomb down the latter from new Squash Trench which he had entered early in the attack. The defence of Fir Support was conducted by 2nd Lieut. Wright with about 20 men against numerous bombing attacks in one of which flame throwers were used but these were stopped on our wire by rifle fire and the cylinders, catching alight, the enemy were burnt with their own weapons. Good work was done by the whole of this platoon and particularly by Pte Hickin who on 2 or 3 occasions walked along the parapet firing a Lewis Gun from his hip at the enemy concentrating in the trenches on the flanks. Pte Hickin was eventually killed in making one of these attacks.[10]

The orders of the 6th Battalion in the event of attack were to move forward in support of the 7th and 8th Battalions. One of the company commanders in the 6th Battalion, Lieutenant E.G.Lane-Roberts, recorded his experiences in a memoir entitled 'How I Was Captured'. His company HQ was in the

German storm troopers advance towards the British lines in the Spring Offensive.

Transcript of letter dated 5/4/18, sent to J H Harratt, probably by A H Lee, following the Kaiser's Offensive, March 1918.

Dear 'Phylis',
Was very glad to hear from you so soon and to know that you have struck lucky. As you know the batt. suffered very heavily, out of poor old D Coy, there is 1 lance corp and about 10 men of those who were up at – well, you know where. There were really few killed or wounded, the rest are missing including Twitt, Lightning, Sammy and all the sergeants except McFarlane who got away wounded in the hand.

Mac. and Dyson were killed, Smedley is missing and Lord wounded. Hoggarth is w. and m. Farmer and Bromley w. Major is missing. C.O. and West killed, Nobbs wounded, the Doc is a prisoner. We are not getting any rest, we are now up at a place you know very well and we shall soon be in the line again.

Your kit has been sent off and as it goes to Boulogne, the quickest way to get it is to write to the D.A.D.R.T., Kit Warehouse, Boulogne and ask for it to be sent on.

Jerry is due back shortly so I am just going to write to him so that he won't have too much of a shock when he gets back.

I am giving you the names of the men in your platoon who were killed or missing so that you can write if you want to.

Can't stop to write more now but shall always be glad to hear how you are going on,

Yours sincerely,
Podge

PTO
Three parcels of eatables arrived for you yesterday which we appreciated very much and I am sending the letters which were enclosed.
There was also a parcel with two books which I will send on if you desire, otherwise we shall find them very acceptable.
At present C and D are messing together and we muster 6 all told.

AHL

15 Platoon

Killed	Wounded	Missing
Sleigh	Sgt McFarlane	L/C Cort
	L/C Palmer	L/C Earp
	Dawson	Cpl Carter
		L/C Gartside
		Hall
		Shambrock
		Thornton
		Thorpe
		Wills
		Selby
		Hurd
		Taverner

Lieutenant J.H. Harratt MC, of the 6th Battalion, with the letter sent to him in hospital in April by Lieut. A.H. Lee of the same battalion, outlining events after Harratt was wounded, and detailing the fates of other 6th Battalion officers.

Mr W.J.Newman/Mr John Storey

cellar of a ruined house in Epehy High Street, and his part in the plan involved moving up to a new position behind the village cemetery:

Everyone was soon aroused and after seeing my officers on their way to their respective platoon dugouts to meet their men & guide them to their 'Battle' positions, I went off to mine accompanied by my runner, servant & 2 signallers carrying a telephone...the gas being very thick and objectionable we had to don our gas masks, but after falling down a few times and colliding with walls etc we took them off again. We all reached our

218

202600 Pte Edwin Frank Conington, of The Rosery, Ryhall, 7th Battalion, killed on 21 March. An officer wrote to his parents to inform them that he had been killed by a fragment of bomb, and added that 'Pte Conington fought exceedingly well on the 21st... and we were all sorry he was killed.'

Pte Alfred Duchemin Carpenter, 7th Battalion, of Leicester. He had originally enlisted aged 16, and served in the 9th Battalion in France until his age was discovered and he was returned home. On reaching military age he returned to the 9th, until they were disbanded. He was captured on the morning of 21 March 1918.
Steve Law

he grave of an unknown Captain, Leicestershire Regiment, in Epehy Wood Cemetery. There is a strong possibility that this is the grave of Capt. Henry Spencer-Smith, 8th battalion, the only full Captain killed in this area on 21 March. Richard
ane

position safely - in fact every man was soon in position and we got ready to try our odds with any German who chose to come our way.[11]

Lane-Roberts' plan was to hold on as long as he could, until the parties of the 8th Battalion in front of him fell back on his position, and thence to retire together to the Yellow Line where they could make a joint stand. In fact fighting continued ahead of him until the afternoon, when the Germans finally secured possession of the Red Line. It should be remembered that throughout this time the front line infantry were practically without any form of artillery support. In addition to the telephone wires which connected forward observers with the guns being cut, the batteries themselves had been smothered with high explosive and gas shells right from the beginning. Earlier in the day, the enemy had broken through the positions of the 7th Battalion in to the village of Pezieres, but had been driven out by the reserve company of that battalion, aided by two tanks. These two machines had lain for a week behind the village concealed among trees, and provided valuable assistance until they ran out of petrol and each was hit by artillery fire whilst stationary.

The battle by now had descended into a grim street fight in Epehy village. The ruined houses and lanes lined with trenches provided cover for attackers and defenders alike. Around 7pm, as darkness was falling, Kelly set off to collect information from the three battalions as to the exact situation. With the approach of night, German attacks had slackened but shellfire increased in order to prevent reinforcements and supplies coming up to the village, and Kelly had to run hard along part of the road on his final approach to 7th Battalion HQ. Having conferred with the colonel, he set off via Pezieres for the 8th Battalion. In Pezieres he was fired on from behind, indicating that the Germans had pushed back the troops of the 16th (Irish) Division on the right, and were attempting to enfilade the village. Eventually, he reached Epehy, his destination:

Arrived at 'Fisher's Keep', the headquarters of the 8th Battalion, I spent half an hour with Colonel Utterson and his adjutant Spencer-Smith. Soon after I left, the former was captured and the latter, a cheery 'good mixer', I think from the West Coast of South America, was killed. Tierens, the medical officer of the 6th Battalion came in and told us his aid-post in the south end of the village was in German hands, *and that he had been taken prisoner, but released by his captors when they saw his Red Cross arm band.* [12]

Following the capture of Lieutenant-Colonel Utterson, the remnants of the 8th Battalion were taken over by an officer of the Royal Munster Fusiliers from the 16th (Irish) Division on the right flank.

Kelly and Tierens set off together at 9.30pm to try to find the headquarters of the 6th Battalion. Across the torn ground, in pitch darkness and with heavy shells still falling, the short journey took an hour and a half. At length they reached Lieutenant-Colonel Stewart's dug out, where they received unpleasant news;

> *The whole of our right flank which had been formed by the 16th Division, appeared to be 'in the air', and the great Epehy-St-Emillie road was infested by enemy patrols. The 6th Battalion had too few men to form a defensive flank, for they had lost heavily from shell fire and the process was still going on. The dugout was full of wounded, some terribly mutilated. About midnight I took my leave of Colonel Stewart, who had always been a very good friend, for the last time. He was shot down by a sniper in front of his headquarters a few hours later.* [13]

Dawn on 22 March found the Brown Line - a last ditch line of incomplete trenches - garrisoned by headquarters men, cooks, mortar men and Royal Engineers. Having bought valuable time, the survivors of the 110th Brigade were ordered by Divisional headquarters to abandon Epehy and Pezieres. As they attempted to withdraw, a stubborn rearguard hung on to cover their retreat. Lane-Roberts was still in the village, in a dug-out in a cellar. As he emerged about 9am, he was surprised to be fired upon by a machine-gun from behind, and quickly dived into a nearby trench for cover. Realising that he had left behind his papers and kit, he tried to make his way back to the cellar:

> *As I came round the bend in the trench I saw two Germans entering the house. I fired & shot one of them & the other turned & jumped into the trench grasping me as he did so. His rifle fell and we started to struggle in the trench. He was heavily equipped & handicapped by being packed up ready for Paris. 4 times I managed to get my revolver into such a position as to shoot him but none of the bullets exploded. Finally at the 5th attempt my big burley [sic] opponent dropped with a bullet through his heart...Hearing the shots my sergeant major came along & got up to see if anyone was in view. He was immediately shot down & fell in the trench. A sergeant further along met the same fate. Some few minutes later I saw there were Germans in the cemetery in front of us & hiding behind gravestones.* [14]

Lane-Roberts and his men now attempted to retire from Epehy village but the situation was becoming critical:

> *I started off & expecting Germans to be in the trench ahead bombed my way down. Lt Thirlby, who was with me, brought up the*

220

41384 Pte Fred Sutcliffe, 6th Battalion, of Barnoldswick, killed in action on 21 March 1918. He wears the cap badge of the Yorkshire Regiment, with which he was trained in England before being transferred to the Leicesters.

31942 Pte Thomas Henry Fenn, 7th Battalion. He was initially reported missing in action, but in fact was killed on 22 March.

23914 Pte John Booth, 8th Battalion, of Oakham. He die[s] of wounds on 22 March.

41332 Pte Joseph Emmott, 6th Battalion, killed on 23 March. He was from Skipton, Yorkshire.

25698 Cpl James Sinfield, 8th Battalion, who died of wounds at Bray-sur-Somme on 23 March 1918. He lived at Ravenstone, near Coalville, and left a widow and a two-year old daughter. His widow subsequently remarried, but his daughter was brought up never to forget her father.

Mrs Mary Bentley

rear. The Germans were closing in on us now and we had not gone very far when they jumped in the trench in between us & completely surrounded us on top. Escape was hopeless now and we had to surrender – 13 out of about 35 who started...I asked to be allowed to go in search of Lt. Thirlby. I was refused but started by myself. I was threatened with the bayonet & revolver of the German officer.[15]

In fact, Second-Lieutenant Stuart Longston Thirlby was dead, killed perhaps in a last desperate fight, determined to reach his own lines and having already seen the party under his company commander forced to surrender. Lane-Roberts meanwhile was marched back to Epehy High Street where prisoners were being collected. It was apparent that the village was completely in German hands now – transport wagons were drawn up at the side of the street, reinforcements were marching through in column of fours, and German field guns were being positioned behind the village ready to support the next stage of the advance. Lane-Roberts was destined for a 36 hour forced march without any rations to Le Cateau, from where he travelled for four days in a filthy cattle truck, to Rastatt in Baden, Germany. For him, the war was most definitely over.

The survivors of the Leicestershire Brigade - those who had managed to escape from Epehy - now began a long retreat towards the old Somme battlefield of 1916. Arthur Cave recorded gloomily in his diary that not only had the baggage and transport wagons of the 7th Battalion been lost, but with them the musical instruments of the band which the Battalion had been so pleased to acquire from the 9th. That night as the weary troops slept in ditches, shellfire heralded the beginnings of another attack, but the brigade withdrew without waiting for it to develop. By midday on 23 March, the 21st Division had crossed the Peronne canal. Its three brigades (62nd, 64th and 110th) were hopelessly mixed up, and formed three columns which crossed the canal at Aizecout-le-bas, and Feuillaucourt. Drawn up on a high ridge on the left bank, they were safe - for the moment at least. David Kelly recalled,

All around stretched the old wilderness of shell-holes, mostly overgrown with grass. At our feet lay the canal, on the further side of which the German vanguards were already in view, but halted on coming under direct fire from two solitary field guns. South of us we could see the towering hill of Mount St Quentin, the ownership of which was a matter of speculation. Neither to the right nor left of us were any British troops to be seen.[16]

From here they retired once more in the direction of Clery, and the brigade took up position on a ridge to the north of the village of Hem. By now the German advance was clearly slowing, partly because the storm troops like their opponents were tiring (and of course they were by now at the limits of their supply lines), but partly also due to the distractions of well-stocked canteens. Entire regimental stores had fallen to the Germans and in some of the villages which had fallen more or less intact, German soldiers could be

Reichenbach (Schlesien), 17.7.20

Reichenbach (Schlesien), 21.9.20

Meine hochverehrte Dame!

Am 23. Maerz 1918 fand ich beim Vormarsch in der Nähe von Tincourt Bourly in der Gegend östlich Peronne in der Hand eines gefallenen englischen Kameraden

Ihr verehrte gnädige Frau!

Verzeihen Sie gütigst, wenn ich Ihnen erst heute den Eingang Ihres Schreibens vom 1. Aug. 20 bätätige Zunächst aufrichtige Versicherung meiner Mitgefühls anläßlich des...

Reichenbach (Silesia), 17th July, 1920

My highly esteemed lady!
On the 23rd of March 1918 during an advance close to Tincourt Bourly in the region east of Peronne I found the following postcard in the hand of a fallen English comrade. I hold it to be the last sign of love that the deceased intended to send to you.
As we found ourselves in an advance and had no time to spare I took the card from his hands and send it to you with the expression of my deepest regrets. God give that we shall forever by spared from such a terrifying catastrophe like this last war.

Respectfully yours

F Vogt Post Secretary

Reichenbach (Silesia), 21st September, 1920

My highly esteemed lady!
Please forgive me for not confirming the receipt of your letter of the 1st of August 20 earlier than today. First I want to express my sincere sympathy for the death of your husband.
I cannot communicate to you the exact circumstances of his death, as I was not present. I was marching with my soldiers towards Peronne. The body of your husband was lying together with those of several other English comrades on the high road.
Countless convoys, cannons and people were moving along this road. I feared that the body of your husband and those of the other poor dead comrades might be crushed (mutilated beyond recognition) by the canons and other vehicles. During a brief halt of half an hour I ordered that a grave be dug (be made), and the dead body of your husband put to rest in the ground. We said a prayer at the grave and continued on towards Peronne.
Already many troops had passed (marched by) this place and I took the envelope from his hand, presuming that it would be his last wish to send a message to you. I found no other keepsakes, otherwise I would have sent them to you. Forgive me for answering until today, but I was ill because of this sad war. My first letter was not translated clearly. With the assurance of my deepest respect I take my leave.

F. Vogt

A page of the original letter which Herr F.Vogt, a postal worker in Silesia, formerly of the German Army, wrote in 1920 to James West's widow. It describes the circumstances of her husband's death, and is shown with an English transcript. Vogt buried the bodies of West and his comrades, and found his wife's address among his effects.

Barry Summers

32975 Pte James West of Market Harborough, 6th Battalion. West was killed in action on 24 March, and his body hastily buried by advancing German forces.

Barry Summers

---

observed through field glasses, wandering around and investigating what might be purloined. Earlier in the day, the War Diary of the 7th Battalion had been destroyed by shellfire. When writing up the incident at a later date, the 7th Battalion diarist adds somewhat apologetically that the War Diary along with

> _all papers, maps etc were sent down from the Bn HQ in the trenches on the evening of March 21st and were placed on a limber which was subsequently destroyed._[17]

Fortunately for future generations, copies of the entries for every month

Lieutenant William Norton, 7th Battalion. Norton was killed on 23 March 1918. He was attending a Signalling School behind the line when the German offensive opened, and rushed to rejoin his Battalion.

200992 Pte Tom Lewin, of the 6th Battalion. Lewin, a soldier from Frederick Street, Wigston Magna, was captured at Epehy in March 1918. He died in hospital in Germany of pneumonia in October 1918.

except March 1918 had already been forwarded to the Infantry Records Office at Litchfield.

By 30 March the battle was effectively over. The Leicestershire Brigade had suffered casualties in the order of thirty-one officers and 1200 men killed, wounded and taken prisoner. One battalion commander had been killed, and another captured, but the stand in front of Epehy had been a heroic one which had slowed the German advance and perhaps helped prevent all-out disaster befalling the British Expeditionary Force. For, if the Germans had reached the channel ports, the only route by which supplies and reinforcements could reach them would have been severed. Indeed, the Germans themselves took the unusual step of mentioning by name in their communiqués the Leicestershire battalions, which had stood in their path at Epehy.

At the beginning of April 1918 the brigade entrained for the north, bound once more for the Ypres Salient. They went into rest camps in a rear area of the Salient, and then into the line in front of Dumbarton Wood, near the low rise known as Tower Hamlets. The 8th Battalion, now under the command of Lieutenant-Colonel B.W.B. Elwin, arrived at Kemmel Shelters, Dranoutre, on 4 April 1918. All was quiet, and it was anticipated that here, scarred and derelict as the landscape was after nearly four years of fighting, would be the setting in which the Leicestershire Brigade could rest and absorb reinforcements (as indeed the Second Army Commander, General Plumer, told the assembled officers upon arrival). One of those reinforcements who were posted to the 8th Battalion here was a 17 year old named R.H.Kiernan, who wrote up his experiences as *Little Brother Goes Soldiering* in 1930. Kiernan was part of a reinforcement draft of 400 men rushed out to France in the wake of the March offensive, and was posted to the Leicestershire Regiment (which in the book he refers to as *the Huntshires*) upon disembarkation. Of the men, he remarked that their talk was all of 'Epehy' and 'the 21st of March' and the events of the previous battle: 'All day long and all night in the hut they talk of the 21st of March.'[18] Shortly afterwards, moving up to the front line with his battalion for the first time, he noted:

> *Suddenly there is met a terrible stench, a stench ghastly and unutterable, pervading, sickening, horrible. The mist near the ground*

Dranoutre, as it appeared in early 1918.

is green-coloured, and one can see the mud almost moving in an ooze beside the duck boards.

It is all rises and falls and all gaping holes, large and small. A man steps off the duck boards and sinks to his knees, scrambles back and curses quietly. There is nothing but holes and mud and that terrible stench.[19]

There were still some 'originals' from the summer of 1915 left with the 8th Battalion, and Kiernan was placed with one of these men, named Jones. This man was a 'Number One' on a Lewis gun and reputedly the only man to bring his gun out of the fighting further south of a week or so previously. He showed the newcomers skills such as tying a wet cloth over the muzzle of the Lewis gun to disguise the flash when firing at night. Kiernan wrote:

All of us six carriers are 'rookies.' We carry two drums of ammunition on our chests and two on our backs. It is awkward moving quickly with it, as the connecting belt slips from the shoulders. The weight, too, is exhausting. But we are a happy team.[20]

In spite of General Plumer's assurances, however, on 9 April the second major German offensive opened just to the south, on the Lys. As the attack gained ground, the Germans threatened to work behind the entire Ypres sector, or at least to be able to take it in enfilade. Thus it was decided to leave a skeleton force in the front lines of the Ypres Salient, and withdraw the bulk of the British troops in the area to the outskirts of Ypres itself. In accordance with this plan, two battalions (8th & 7th) were withdrawn to positions along the Ypres-St Eloi road, between the Lille Gate and the village

Exhaustion, and looting from wine cellars and captured enemy supplies, combined to slow the German advance.

of Voormezeele. The 6th Battalion was left in the exposed and vulnerable position east of Torr Top, three kilometres east of Zillebeke Lake. These troops had no one behind them for nearly three miles, should an attack develop, and consequently the strain upon these men from the knowledge that should they be attacked, they almost certainly should not escape, must have been immense. Throughout this period, lack of sleep through constant enemy harassing shellfire and the need to remain alert, took its toll on officers and men alike. Even for troops back at Ypres, the pressures were intense. Kiernan recorded under the date 23 April 1918:

26266 L/Cpl George Holt, 8th Battalion. His actions in covering the withdrawal of his company with his Lewis Gun during the April 1918 fighting earned him the Distinguished Conduct Medal. Below: Holt's DCM, awarded for 'conspicuous gallantry and devotion to duty'.
Mr Ken Holt

> *We are in a 'strong point' on the left of the Ypres Canal bank. Behind us is a farm, in ruins. Every two nights we go out for a day to huts further back. We would sooner stay in. The way out is raked with machine guns and plastered like rain with gas shells. There is no explosion with these, just a sort of soft 'phut' and hiss when they hit the ground.*
>
> *Part of the way out is along a narrow pathway all slippy mud cut in the sloping bank of the Canal. Because of the strafe one has to move at top speed. The weight of the Lewis gun ammunition is terrible then, as we have to carry all of the ordinary rifleman's kit as well. We slip and fall and clutch our way along, and all the time just over the bank there is the terribly close, deafening racket of scores of machine guns, firing over the Canal, and the whizz and phut of the gas shells that fall like rain. The gas masks are choking. One's lungs almost burst, and all the time there is deafening sound.*
>
> *The Canal bank is a nightmare. It is at the back of our minds all the time we are out of the strong point. When we have cleared it there is the duck board track, and it is swept always now by the machine guns, and blue sparks fly up all along it as the bullets hit.[21]*

It must have been almost a relief when a renewed German offensive finally broke against the Ypres Salient on 25 April. The enemy were attacking along the banks of the Ypres-Comines canal, accompanied as usual by a hurricane of shelling. The position of the battalion at Torr Top was now in jeopardy, and on the afternoon of 26 April David Kelly went up to their position with orders for them to retire. That night, they safely rejoined the main body at Voormezeele.

For the next four days they held on, in strong points and concrete fortifications built into the ruined buildings in the district of Bedford House and Langhof Farm. On 27, 28 and 29 April the Leicestershire outposts on the Comines canal were strongly attacked, but held out. The conditions there were none the less desperate for the defenders. Kiernan wrote of this period:

> *There was a sudden roar, like a train coming out of a tunnel, only with a terribly steely screech. Everything went yellow and black. The walls of my chest fell in and I could not breathe. There was a great shower of black mud and water. The whole corner of the bay where I*

225

was sitting had disappeared. We are all soaked through and plastered with black mud.[22]

Next day his section was heavily attacked by German troops with machine-guns and bombs, and was forced to fall back into the next bay of their position. When they got a clear shot at the enemy, who were out in the open, they were unable to bring their Lewis gun to bear on them for fear of hitting the wounded British prisoners who were with them. The situation was perilous, and supplies could not be brought up to the men in the forward positions:

I have had no water for two days. There is a shell hole just outside the trench, but it is green, and there is a body in it...A petrol tin of water was passed down the trench this afternoon, and each man half filled his waterbottle – the corporal crawled along the top, and judged when each man had had his ration. I was the last. There was nothing in the tin.[23]

However, British artillery was now once more able to give covering fire when called upon, and the German offensive was again running out of steam. Mud, lack of shelter and above all lack of sleep were having a similar effect on the average German soldier as on the British, and this represented the last real day of fighting in the area. On the night of 30 April the 110th Brigade was relieved by the 58th Brigade of the 19th Division, and began the long march away from Ypres once more, passing on the way columns of French troops who were moving up to continue the counter-offensive. As at Epehy, the Leicestershire battalions had again barred the way to the Germans for crucial days, though once again, as at Epehy, they had paid a punishing price in terms of lives lost.

1 D.V.Kelly, '*39 Months With the Tigers*', (Ernest Benn, 1930) p87
2 F.E.Pothecary. Manuscript recollections. Liddle Collection, University of Leeds.
3 D.A.Bacon. Typescript recollections, LRO p95
4 Quoted in full in M.Middlebrook, '*The Kaiser's Battle*'
5 Bacon, *op cit* p95
6 Bacon, *op cit* p97
7 A.C.Cave. Unpublished typescript diary 7.2.18
8 Kelly, *op cit* p92
9 Kelly, *op cit* pp96-97
10 War Diary, 7th bn Leicestershire Regt, LRO 21.3.18
11 E.G.Lane-Roberts. Manuscript account, '*How I Was Captured*' LRO
12 Kelly, *op cit* p98
13 Kelly, *op cit* p99
14 Lane-Roberts, *op cit*
15 Lane-Roberts, *op cit*
16 Kelly, *op cit* p103
17 War Diary 7th Bn Leicestershire Regt LRO 23.3.18
18 R.H.Kiernan, '*Little Brother Goes Soldiering*' (Constable & Co 1930) p49
19 Kiernan, *op cit* p52
20 Kiernan, *op cit* p53
21 Kiernan, *op cit* pp58-59
22 Kiernan, *op cit* p60
23 Kiernan, *op cit* p64

Chapter Ten

No Quarter asked or given
The Battle of the Aisne

With the German offensive in Flanders checked, the 110th Brigade withdrew from the front line to lick its wounds. It had now been in the path of two major offensives, and officers and men were in urgent need of rest. Accordingly, the French government offered the opportunity for five battle weary British divisions, including the 21st, to take over a very quiet sector of the French front, away to the south on the Aisne, where they could recuperate. Their hosts were to be the French Sixth Army, and on 6 May 1918, the troop trains carrying the Tigers from Wizernes in Belgium arrived at Serzy, 20 kilometres south of Rheims. Kiernan recorded:

L/Cpl A.G.F.Meekings (right) and comrade, 7th Battalion, in France, Spring 1918. Meekings was from Leicester, and was drafted to France in the wake of the March and April offensives. However, he was only to serve with his battalion for a short time as he was captured in May 1918, and remained a prisoner until the end of hostilities. Mrs R.M.Snart

We took the train just beyond Cassel, and travelled by it for two days and nights. It was very slow, and the fellows got off at the back and ran up to the engine for shaving water, and then jumped on as their own truck passed them.[1]

They were now in the beautiful champagne country, in the valley of the River Aisne. Almost at once the relaxed atmosphere and comfort of not being under fire began to have its effect:

We have taken over French huts, big commodious huts, with wire beds. At Ypres we slept, when 'out', in an inch of dust on the floors, and wrapped our puttees round our feet for warmth. Here we lie with nothing on at night, because of the heat and fleas. All around the country is heavily forested, and there is long, lush, rich grass, and a very cold river to bathe in, near a place called Chalons-le-Vergeur, a lovely name. There is an empty town near, Hermonville, and it is fine to walk through the deserted streets. All the houses are standing, roofs on, shutters up. There is Trigny, too, where business is as usual. It is all a scream to us - you can't find a shell hole anywhere, and it is only about 10 kilometres from the Front.[2]

For the next week or more they were billeted in villages behind the front line:

The atmosphere on this front is wonderful. From a road nearby I can see the towers of Rheims Cathedral, as though it were only a hundred yards away, yet it is some kilometres. The 'feel' of the place is different from Ypres, too. Up there, on those flat, grey fields, where it is winking red and yellow stabs and flashes all night, with the unending rumble of the guns, it seemed that it always had been like that and would be so forever. It was what we expected; the British Front, frightfulness, dullness, rain, mud, dead bodies, stench, the whistle of stray bullets far behind the line, the Very lights, the hollow sound of the machine guns, never wholly quiet, ever anywhere, as though both armies could never sleep. Ypres was just what I expected of the war. It was exactly like what the papers said, that I read at school. But here it is all green and blue and bright, and Everybody is interested in us. The French soldiers grin, are friendly, and ask us questions about the underground railways in England. The give us pinard, their red wine, which they carry instead of water. There are lovely bottle-green woods with little dark streams in them.[3]

At Lagery, where an energetic French Town Major had managed to secure a mattress for every man, they stayed for several days. Here there was a small shop which sold provisions such as jam, which the men were able to buy to supplement their rations. From here, they marched to Jonchery, where a French regiment formed a guard of honour for the 8th Battalion as they marched past. Shortly afterwards, Courts Martial were convened to hear the cases of about 20 men of this Battalion, who had run away during one of the German attacks at Ypres. Ordinarily, if found guilty, these men could have expected the death penalty, but given the mitigating circumstances that all had arrived in France for the first time only days previously, and none had any previous experience of front line service, the only sentences handed down were field punishments.

The area of front taken over by the Leicestershire Brigade, on the night of 14-15 May, was on the right of the Chemin des Dames, and lay in the angle formed by the River Aisne and the Aisne canal, north east of Cormicy. About fifteen hundred yards behind the front line trenches, across a stretch of marshy ground, lay the canal. Some way behind this, visible from the front line, was the great densely-wooded ridge, the Crete St. Auboeuf. The Leicestershire battalions were the among the first British troops to enter this

Second-Lieutenant L.A.Foxon, 7th Battalion. He served with the 8th and 7th Battalion in 1918, and was badly gassed.
Mr Eric Kellaway

area since the fighting had swept briefly through here in September 1914, and French troops confirmed the fact that it was indeed a very quiet sector. Their policy again had been to fire only when fired upon, but to retaliate vigorously when challenged. Nevertheless, there were some serious shortcomings associated with the new positions, which were identified by David Kelly:

> Apart from the intense heat, the conditions seemed delightful, but there were tactical features which caused us disquiet. The [Aisne] canal with its deep two hundred metres marsh would have made an excellent front line, but as it ran so close to the front line of our neighbours on the flank, it would, so long as we remained in front of it, enable the enemy to walk along it and so surround our front line troops... Moreover the whole area was under view from the enemy heights, Hill 108, Mont Spin and the Great Fort Brimont.[4]

For the following days the Brigade tried as best it could to improve the positions which it had inherited, but although features such as parapets and parados could be strengthened, they could do little about the actual positioning of the trenches. Meanwhile, across No Man's Land, ominous signs had been observed. Prior to the attacks on the Somme and on the Lys, and at Ypres (all of which were characterised by a hurricane of shells), a mass of artillery pieces had been accumulated in each area under the command of a German colonel of artillery named Bruchmüller. Such were his skills in gathering together the lessons learned and the improved techniques developed in four years of artillery warfare, that his refined tactics quickly earned him the nickname 'Durchbruchmüller' – 'Break-through müller'. Now, Bruchmüller's battering train of heavy artillery pieces

Germans on the chalky heights overlooking the Aisne canal and Berry au Bac. These men with their signalling apparatus are observing British positions prior to the battle. Hill 108, mentioned by Kelly, is about a mile away.

had arrived behind the German lines opposite the Chemin des Dames. David Kelly on 25 May observed through his telescope enemy linesmen laying out new telephone cable, and similar warnings of increased enemy activity were being received from across the sector. Once again intelligence was leaked by German deserters, two of whom were interrogated at 110th Brigade HQ, and that same day a telegram arrived from the headquarters of the French IX Corps warning of a general attack at 1 am on the morning of 27 May. Little could now be done with this information, except to pull back from the front line into reserve positions as many men as could be spared. The 8th Battalion Leicestershire Regiment, holding trenches on the far bank of the canal, left only a skeleton force in the front line and sent the remainder of its personnel back into reserve with the other battalions.

Right on cue, the barrage opened promptly the next morning with a thunderous drum fire which could be heard for many miles. About one minute past one, a signal officer at 110th Brigade HQ tested the telephone lines to the front line trenches. There was no reply - all had been cut by the German shells which were falling directly into the trenches. From this point on, the only messages received came by runner, and many positions were never heard from again. The main infantry attack seems likely to have developed around 3.30am, but there were few survivors of the front line garrison to confirm this. As at Epehy, the Germans were initially cloaked by a blanket of thick fog. Some British positions were totally annihilated by enemy artillery, whilst others were cut off and forced to surrender. As Kelly predicted, the enemy were quickly able to reach the canal and work along it

German field gunners in open country, during the advance on Rheims, Spring 1918.
M.Bier, Liddle Collection

to get behind the Leicestershire lines, and by 7am the canal had certainly fallen. For this reason, comparatively more prisoners were taken here than at Epehy, where the Leicestershires had been able to retreat in fairly orderly stages. With the news of the attack reaching them early that morning, Quarter-Master Sergeant Arthur Cave and the battalion transports began to pack up and move out ahead of the advancing Germans. As they tried to negotiate roads crowded with refugees, some fleeing with all their possessions on a single cart, they suffered abuse from other civilians who blamed the British for letting the Germans through:

> The French inhabitants were furious with us after living in the apparent security of their own troops, and cursed us as we retired past them.[5]

In fact there was probably little anyone – French or British – could have done to stem the German attack, given the strategic shortcomings of the positions south of the Aisne. Those Leicesters who did manage to escape from the front line before being surrounded, and who got back across the Aisne canal, fought valiantly throughout the morning of 27 May in the

14106 Cpl George Herbert Draycott, 8th Battalion, captured on the Aisne.

Mrs Jean Ogle

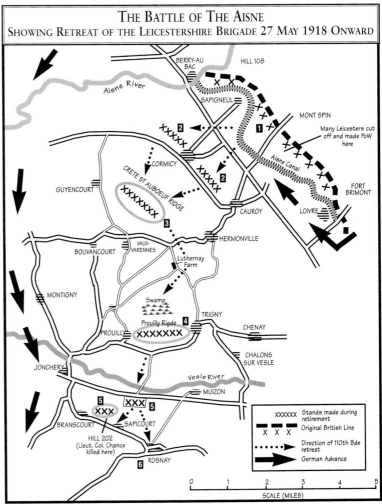

THE BATTLE OF THE AISNE
SHOWING RETREAT OF THE LEICESTERSHIRE BRIGADE 27 MAY 1918 ONWARD

Wrecked British positions on the Aisne, after the German attack of May 1918. The debacle was worse than it might have been not least because many British units filed into French trenches near the Chemin-des-Dames that were badly sited, and which they had little time to improve. Below: A German soldier pauses to examine the bodies of British soldiers, killed in the offensive on the Aisne. Personal possessions and equipment including rifles and mess tins lie scattered about. M.Bier, Liddle Collection

countryside west of the canal, near the Cormicy-Cauroy road. They were reinforced by those elements of the front line garrison which had been pulled back prior to the attack, and which were quickly moved up during the early hours of the morning.

One of these men was Private R.H.Kiernan who recounted seeing members of the front line battalions, survivors of the inferno that morning, fleeing ahead of the advancing Germans:

> I could see a big route national. There were hundreds of our fellows running along it, like a football crowd running for the trams. Jerry's machine guns were going and they were dropping, a score at a time and lying in heaps, khaki heaps.[6]

However, the general position here was rapidly becoming untenable due to the fact that the enemy had made dramatic advances further north, on the other side of the River Aisne, and was threatening to work behind this whole section of front. Accordingly, the Leicestershire Brigade received orders to fall back after nightfall to a line on the Crete St Auboeuf ridge, in front of Vaux-Varennes. Kiernan continued:

> Later that day we fell back again, not very far. It was hard to see any Jerries, but we could hear their machine guns all over the woods. Towards dusk we came to a small French strongpoint. It was surrounded with rusty wire, about a foot high, for fifty yards all round, back and front...In the strong point the riflemen gave us [Lewis gunners] all their ammunition, keeping only ten rounds, and we refilled the drums.[7]

Kiernan's party were now in danger of being enveloped by Germans moving in the gathering gloom through the woods on either side of them. They abandoned their post at the instruction of their Lieutenant, and struggling through the wire - being shot at as they did so - made for the comparative safety of the tree line behind them:

> At dusk from the copse we could see files of Germans passing at 100 yards' range on each side of us. They were dim in the mist, and they looked enormous, and the machine guns they were carrying stuck up like chimneys. They must have seen us and took us for Jerries. Just before the sky turned quite black, the officer led us across an open space from the copse into a deep forest. A straight narrow lane ran through it.[8]

The officer left behind two of the most experienced men, armed with the Lewis gun and most of the remaining ammunition, to delay the Germans for as long as possible while the rest of the party made their escape. Their firing could be heard away in the distance as Kiernan and his comrades filed through the dark woods. At length, Kiernan's group rejoined the bulk of the Leicestershire Brigade on the Crete St Auboeuf:

> On a hill in the middle of the forest there was rest of the battalion. They were lining a breast work, and peering into the dark, and shouted gladly when they saw us. From here we could see over the

black waste of tree-tops, and from them rose the yellow globes of light in a dead straight line for many miles, as though drawn with a ruler.[9]

Some time later the two men with the Lewis gun also came in. The 'Number One', named Ben, tried to hide his relief at finding his comrades again, but the stress of his task – being left to almost certain death or capture – must have been incredible, and later in the night someone heard him crying.

Just as the remainder of the 110th Brigade were arriving and beginning to take up position on this new line, reports were received that in fact enemy patrols had already been spotted behind them. Of the British 8th Division, supposedly on the left flank, there was no sign, only more German patrols. The direct route to Pevy, upon which they were ordered to fall back if threatened, was now almost certainly blocked by German troops. The only option remaining to the brigade was a withdrawal via a track running west of Hermonville, away to the south-east, which would take them to Pevy via a circuitous route, hopefully avoiding enemy patrols. Some indication of the casualties inflicted upon the brigade may be gauged from the fact that when they set off at 3.30am, they did so formed into one composite battalion.

By daybreak on 28 May, they had reached Luthernay Farm, where they halted for a rest. Here new orders – though they were already out of date, as subsequent events were to prove – were received. They were now to proceed to Pevy, as a reserve brigade in support of the 64th and 62nd Brigades, which were to take up positions near Hermonville. Unfortunately, a large party of the 6th Battalion did not receive these new orders, and remained in error with the 64th Brigade. In fact, during the hasty retreat all three brigades forming the 21st Division had become quite mixed up, and when the nominal 110th Brigade set off they took with them a large contingent of the 62nd Brigade.

The surviving elements of the 7th and 8th Battalions with their comrades of the DLI began the march towards Pevy, and by around 8am that morning

Right: Lieutenant Ronald Carnley, 5th attached 7th Battalion, killed at Cormicy on 27 May 1918. His home was on Springfield Road, Leicester, and he was the son of Mr Samuel Carnley, to whom Ronald's commanding officer Lt Col Sawyer wrote 'I cannot speak too highly of the work your son has carried out during all the fighting this battalion has been through since March 21st'. Below: Carnley's home: 'West Melton', on Springfield Road, Leicester.

Sgt Alfred Warner of Loughborough, 6th Battalion, wearing his medals, shortly after the war. As well as the 1914/15 star trio he wears the Military Medal (left) and French Croix de Guerre with bronze star (right) awarded for gallantry during his part in the fighting on the Aisne in 1918.

Yvonne White

they were in sight of the village. They were within 500 yards of it when they realised that it was in enemy hands. Rifle and machine-gun fire erupted from the high ground around the village, and had they continued much further they would almost certainly have walked into a trap from which escape would have been impossible. As it was, with fire coming from the front and right, the only prospect of escape lay across a stretch of marshland, to the prominent heights of the Prouilly-Trigny ridge. Acting quickly, the officers divided the formation up into a number of smaller columns and led them individually in single file across the swamp. Kiernan wrote:

We came to some marshes covered with thin reeds much higher than a man. We put the machine gun down, pointing towards where we thought Jerry would be. But soon we could hear his deep voice talking and shouting behind us. Ben carried the gun away a bit to the flank. I was the last in the file, and turning around there was a Jerry behind me with his rifle at the port. He was a little chap, with a drooping black moustache. I fired at him, and dodged into the reeds.[10]

David Kelly also remembered:

Wading laboriously through that swamp (where Colonel Sawyer of the 7th Battalion plunged up to his neck) we offered a splendid target to our enemies a few hundred yards away, but owing perhaps to some miscalculation due to the deceptive terrain, most of their bullets went over our heads. The two German prisoners who had given us such valuable, if disconcerting information a few hours before had been loaded by our Brigade headquarters orderlies with 'dixies' and rations, and as they staggered through the water were

A sketch map issued with operation orders to Leicestershire Brigade officers, showing the country between the Rivers Aisne and Vesle, over which the German offensive in May was launched. It is tempting to think that the water stains were caused when the map was dropped crossing the swamp!

W.Batcheldor, Liddle Collection

cursing their late comrades, some of whose bullets were splashing round them.[11]

Emerging from the swamp, they began the arduous ascent up the hillside to the top of the ridge. As they did so, the members of a French colonial infantry unit could be discerned at the summit. Joining forces with them, the Brigade formed a cordon around the top of the ridge, facing in every direction. As the day drew on, it was clear that the Germans were once more working their way around the flanks of the position, and a further withdrawal became necessary, this time in the direction of the River Vesle. Leaving the French troops and some British on the summit, Kiernan's party were brought down to the bottom and made a defensive line facing north.

> *The 'second-loot' [Second Lieutenant] and our machine gun team are on the roadside at the foot of the ridge. Some French fellows passed with a little Jerry prisoner. They're grinning and joking and seem delighted with him. He looks about sixteen, and has a little round, cropped fair head. The 'second-loot' says, 'ask him what the bloody hell its all about.' The little Jerry said, 'Prussienne compagnie - na hinten - nein Englische prisonnier'. He was very aggressive, and self-important and excited. I told the officer, 'I think he's trying to say that there's a Prussian company over the hill and that they say they'll take no English prisoners.' He said, 'That sounds bloody cheery, anyway'.*[12]

Later, Kiernan's section made ready to move off. As they were waiting to do so, they were passed by French infantry on their way up to the battle, who expressed similar sentiments to those of the civilians about the English soldiers:

> *we were taken away from the ridge in the thick black of the night. We had formed in fours in the road, waiting for the different battalions to come in, and French troops were passing us in fours on our left. They cursed us and said things of which I could only catch the drift –*

A French Regiment on their way to the front line. Taylor Library

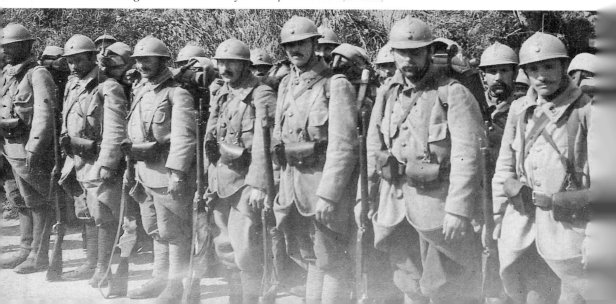

all about the English – 'Sacre's and 'Merde's and deep spitting, bitter
things. I hoped they'd find Jerry in the same mood as we'd left him.[13]

By nightfall, they were across the River Vesle, and took up position in the
tile-works west of Muizon. It is interesting to note here that lack of
awareness (or perhaps knowledge) of their surroundings which in some
respects characterised the British Tommies in the First World War. Many of
Kiernan's party and Kiernan himself believed that they were crossing the
Marne (which was many miles away) instead of the Vesle, and began to sing
a song composed by some wag:

'Forever on the march, our song so let it be,
We've crossed the Aisne, we've crossed the Marne,
We'll soon reach gay Paree,
And in this cruel strife, we live from hand to mouth,
And nightly pitch our box latrine -
A day's march further South.'[14]

Nevertheless the Germans continued their relentless drive, and having
crossed the Vesle themselves further to the west at Jonchery, once more
threatened to outflank the position of the sadly depleted Leicestershire
Brigade. A section of men under Lieutenant-Colonel Chance of the 6th
Battalion left the tile-works for a position known as Hill 202, on the ridge
west of Rosnay. From here they could hope to give early warning of the
approach of any Germans, and possibly hold them up for a time. The 6th

*A British tank captured by the Germans and used during the advance on the Aisne, May
1918. Many of the tanks like this one which were used by the German Army fell in to their
hands in the aftermath of the Cambrai battle in 1917.* Taylor Library

German troops advance through the town of La Fere, during the advance on Rheims.

M.Bier, Liddle Collection

Battalion War Diary for 29 May 1918 gives a detailed account of Chance's actions on the hill, probably written by an officer who was with him:

> Lt Col Chance's force moved from Rosnay and took up position in the wood on Hill 202. A patrol was pushed forward to get in touch with the situation at Branscourt and a reconnaissance was carried out by Lt Col Chance of situation W. of Hill 202. The enemy shelled Hill 202 heavily during the morning about 40 OR were placed in position on the forward slope of Hill 202 where they were able to bring considerable fire to bear on enemy advancing over the Branscourt Valley.
>
> The general tendency of all enemy movements after 11am was across our front to SW along the Branscourt-Savigny Road when infantry, horsed vehicles and guns were frequently seen. Fire was kept up on this road but the range was too long for rifle fire to be effective. At 1pm on the left towards Treslon troops were observed withdrawing. Col Grist of the Lincolns and the CO SW Borderers of 25th Division reported to Col Chance and after reconnaissance brought their battalions into action on the left of Hill 202 to check the enemy advance on the left. About this time 3 Coys of French Colonials took up a position with our troops in front of Hill 202 and a battalion of French Territorials took up a position on the S. of the Rosnay-Treslon Rd. 4pm enemy attacked in strength from Branscourt

32375 Pte William Edward Webster, 7th Battalion. He was taken prisoner, badly wounded, on 27 May. He subsequently died in a German field hospital on 24 June 1918.

southwards. *Excellent results were obtained by rifle & MG fire and attack brought to a standstill opposite our front.*[15]

Colonel Sawyer had remained in command at the tile-works. By the afternoon, orders were received by him to the effect that more French troops were on their way to relieve the hard-pressed Tommies, and they could withdraw as soon as officers were satisfied that the French were in position. The news came none too soon, for in spite of the upbeat tone of the 6th Battalion diarist, by late afternoon the men on Hill 202 had been forced off the high ground, Lieutenant-Colonel Chance being killed by a shell in the process. The party under Lieutenant-Colonel Sawyer had also lost the tile-works, and was now holding on just outside Rosnay.

The following day, 30 May, the remnants of the Brigade began to withdraw. That night they bivouacked in the Forest of Epernay, and the next day reached Etrechy. The battle had cost the Brigade in excess of fifty

Lieutenant Colonel E.S.Chance, commanding the 6th Battalion, who was killed in action on 29 May 1918. He had been posted from the 2nd Dragoon Guards to take over the battalion following the death of Lieutenant Colonel Stewart in March.

A Roll of Honour published in The Green Tiger after the war, listing those members of the Leicestershire Brigade who appear on the Soissons Memorial to the missing.

Eric Kellaway

SOISSONS MEMORIAL

The following is a list of the names of members of the Regiment who belonged to the Leicestershire Brigade, and who lost their lives in the Battles of the Aisne (May—June, 1918), and the Battle of the Marne (July—August, 1918), and who have no known grave. The Memorial was unveiled at Soissons by Lieut.-General Sir A. Hamilton Gordon, on July 22nd, 1928.

Battn.	Regtl. Number	Rank.	Name.	Date of Death.
6	10415	Pte.	Allen, C.	27/5/18
8	30286	Pte.	Argyle, E. F.	27/5/18
6	42240	Pte.	Armitage, V.	28/5/18
8	46967	Pte.	Ashton, C. J.	27/5/18
7	41615	Pte.	Atkin, F. W.	27/5/18
7	40245	Cpl.	Baker, H.	27/5/18
6	42247	Pte.	Barley, E.	27/5/18
4	—	Lieut.	Beeby, C. S.	27/5/18
8	41684	L./Cpl.	Beedell, B. S.	27/5/18
6	41294	Pte.	Bentley, W. A.	27/5/18
7	202794	Pte.	Bloor, B.	27/5/18
7	12200	Cpl.	Brailsford, H.	27/5/18
6	23568	Pte.	Brown, B. W.	28/5/18
8	201986	Pte.	Burton, S.	27/5/18
8	37812	Pte.	Caldicott, W. J.	27/5/18
5	—	Capt.	Carnley, R.	27/5/18
6	37983	Pte.	Carr, H.	28/5/18
6	14550	Q.M.S.	Chapman, J. L.	29/5/18
7	42686	Pte.	Clark, F. C.	27/5/18
8	41310	Pte.	Clark, J. H.	27/5/18
8	41771	Pte.	Clark, R A.	27/5/18
8	204100	Pte.	Clarke, A. C.	27/5/18
8	42486	Pte.	Clarke, L.	27/5/18
7	41617	Pte.	Coker, E. H.	27/5/18
6	42255	Pte.	Collumbell, R. H.	27/5/18
8	41866	Pte.	Cooper, J. B.	27/5/18
7	18397	Sergt.	Coulson, A., M.M.	27/5/18
6	47144	Pte.	Coulthard, W.	28/5/18
8	15558	Pte.	Cox, J.	28/5/18
8	39509	Pte.	Crawley, E. G.	27/5/18
7	36064	Pte.	Cudworth, J. I.	27/5/18
7	34010	Pte.	Curson, H.	27/5/18
8	40909	Pte.	Danvers, J. A.	27/5/18
6	235438	Pte.	Dean, W. H.	28/5/18
6	10256	L./Cpl.	Delaney, J.	27/5/18
8	41780	Pte.	Dick, J.	27/5/18
8	41779	Pte.	Dunn, E.	27/5/18
6	47093	Pte.	Edge, A. E.	29/5/18
8	30492	Pte.	Edwards, A. L., M.M.	27/5/18
8	41784	Pte.	Ellis, N. J.	27/5/18
8	41785	Pte.	Elsden, C. A.	27/5/18
7	235553	Pte.	Flanagan, C. W.	27/5/18
9	—	2/Lieut.	Flint, H. P., M.C.	27/5/18
7	36137	Pte.	Foster, F.	16/6/18
8	42503	Pte.	Fox, P.	27/5/18
8	14593	Sergt.	Freer, A.	27/5/18
6	241789	Pte.	Frith, F.	27/5/18
7	41252	Pte.	Gait, G. H. C.	27/5/18
8	235576	Pte.	Garner, A.	27/5/18
8	33111	Pte.	Gilbert, A.	27/5/18
6	12366	Sergt.	Gill, C. W.	28/5/18
8	37313	Pte.	Gill, L.	28/5/18
8	46382	Pte.	Goodwin, H.	27/5/18
3	—	2/Lieut.	Guy, N. G.	27/5/18
7	47560	Pte.	Hall. F.	27/5/18
8	42027	Pte.	Hallanby, A. W.	27/5/18
8	17336	L./Cpl.	Hazell, E. G.	27/5/18
7	11882	Pte.	Hepworth, R.	27/5/18
7	14626	Pte.	Hill, C.	27/5/18
7	235176	Pte.	Hill, S.	27/5/18
7	41932	Pte.	Hirst, F.	15/12/18
8	235582	Pte.	Holt, A. E.	27/5/18
8	42563	Pte.	Hopper, L. C.	27/5/18
8	36611	Pte.	Howarth, B. H.	28/5/18
8	36558	Pte.	Hudson, L.	27/5/18
6	47282	Pte.	Hudson, J. L.	27/5/18
6	45600	Pte.	Hunter, J. F.	28/5/18

Battn.	Regtl. Number	Rank.	Name.	Date of Death.
7	47546	Cpl.	Ingram, S. J.	27/5/18
7	36279	L./Cpl.	Jackson, C., M.M.	27/5/18
7	41933	Pte.	Kendrew, S. G.	27/5/18
7	42033	Pte.	King, G. T.	23/5/18
6	30150	Pte.	Kirby, J. T.	28/5/18
7	28784	L./Cpl.	Knowles, G. H.	27/5/18
7	42086	Pte.	Lay, A H.	27/5/18
7	41836	Pte.	Leatham, H.	27/5/18
7	11404	L./Cpl.	Lister, J.	27/5/18
7	41061	Pte.	Littlewood, D. A.	27/5/18
8	42535	Pte.	Lovatt, D.	27/5/18
7	41867	Sergt.	McFarlane, J.	27/5/18
6	46982	Pte.	Mack, T., M.M.	27/5/18
6	42334	Pte.	McNaughton, A.	27/5/18
8	14725	Sergt.	Major, C. H.	27/5/18
8	235365	Cpl.	Manley, H.	27/5/18
8	42543	Pte.	Marshall, N. E.	27/5/18
8	45694	Pte.	Millbam, S. W.	27/5/18
7	41941	Pte.	Minor, V. G.	27/5/18
8	39960	Pte.	Moody, W.	27/5/18
8	202086	Cpl.	Moore, A. B.	27/5/18
8	21575	L./Cpl.	Morley, J. E.	27/5/18
8	13504	Cpl.	Morris, W. H.	27/5/18
8	—	2/Lieut.	Moss, F. W.	28/5/18
8	10443	L./Cpl.	Mott, J. W.	27/5/18
6	235490	Pte.	Newton, A.	27/5/18
8	42544	Pte.	Nield, R. T.	27/5/18
7	13056	L./Cpl.	Oakes, J. H., D.C.M.	7/6/18
7	41637	Pte.	Parkinson, T.	27/5/18
8	41664	Pte.	Peppercorn, F.	27/5/18
7	13057	Pte.	Pollard, H.	27/5/18
7	42087	Pte.	Rant, A. J.	27/5/18
6	47204	Pte.	Rhodes, F.	27/5/18
7	41957	Pte.	Roome, J. M.	27/5/18
7	33079	Pte.	Rowson, W. C.	11/1/19
9	—	Capt.	Scott, F., M.C.	27/5/18
6	10217	C.S.M.	Sellars, W.	27/5/18
8	47221	Pte.	Silk, J.	27/5/18
1	—	2/Lieut.	Simmons, F. W.	27/5/18
6	36049	Pte.	Simpkin, B. G.	28/5/18
8	40283	Pte.	Smith, P.	27/5/18
8	40228	L./Cpl.	Spouge, H. R.	27/5/18
7	41601	Pte.	Spurgeon, H. A.	27/5/18
7	41890	Pte.	Stead, N.	27/5/18
8	42170	Pte.	Sullivan, D.	27/5/18
4	—	2/Lieut.	Tasker, W.	27/5/18
7	41974	Pte.	Taylor, M.	27/5/18
8	203539	Pte.	Tivey, F. J.	27/5/18
7	37748	Pte.	Tomlin, G. F.	27/5/18
6	41988	Pte.	Trigg, H.	25/5/18
7	28365	L./Cpl.	Turner, W. E.	27/5/18
7	41981	Pte.	Vickers, A.	27/5/18
6	235424	Pte.	Wainwright, W.	29/5/18
7	46250	Pte.	Walker, R.	27/5/18
7	41988	Pte.	Walker, W. H.	28/5/18
7	47309	Pte.	Webster, H.	27/5/18
7	47242	Pte.	Webster, J.	27/5/18
8	11018	Pte.	Weston, H.	27/5/18
7	15263	Sergt.	Weston, H.	28/5/18
8	41697	Pte.	White, W. H.	27/5/18
7	41624	Pte.	Willatt, C.	27/5/18
6	42207	Pte.	Wilson, J. O.	27/5/18
8	46190	Pte.	Wood, C.	27/5/18

officers killed, wounded or captured, and thirteen hundred other ranks likewise. It had effectively done for the 8th Battalion, which had to all intents and purposes ceased to exist as an organised unit after the start of the battle, and which in June would go the same way as the 9th Battalion. The 8th was to be replaced in the 110th Brigade by the 1st Battalion Wiltshire Regiment, and so technically it would no longer be a purely Leicestershire Brigade.

For those captured in the fighting of the previous days, their first challenge would be to survive the journey out of the battle area, during which time they were extremely vulnerable to the fire of their own guns. One of the men captured at Cormicy was Private G. E. Buckingham, ex-9th Battalion, now 8th Battalion. He left an account of his experiences, part of which reads:

British prisoners of war, in German hands, following the fighting near Rheims, May 1918. They have retained their gas-masks and steel helmets, as shellfire and poison gas claimed the lives of many prisoners, both Allied and German, before they had left the battle area.
M.Bier, Liddle Collection

After being passed on to the rear of the German lines, we were conducted to a dressing station and after being there two hours had to carry a wounded German to the Regimental Aid Post which was about 2 miles further back.

After resting about 15 minutes the RAMC orderly called for the four who were with him to return to fetch more wounded.

He was rather windy and as the English were shelling the way we came down, went by a circuitous route to get back. Half way on the road, we had to pass a quarry which contained reserve troops, and it was being heavily shelled by our 6 inch guns. We went into a trench,

A collection point for PoWs at Amifontaine, following the German breakthrough on the Aisne. The majority of this group is British, with a few French visible. M.Bier, Liddle Collection

and soon the Germans moved farther up as the firing was good so we were left to occupy our position ourselves. After ten minutes or so, my steel helmet was hit by a small fragment of shell and I considered it was time to move, so I asked the other three if they would slope with me, as it was impossible to get through the lines owing to the numbers of troops in front of us, and I was not going to carry their wounded back, and stand a good chance of being knocked out by our own shells. They agreed, so we picked the stretcher up and carried it across the quarry as if we were following someone; on reaching the bend, we dumped it, and ran 300 yards to another turn we reach [sic] BOUGOGNE in three minutes and was stopped by a German who was one of the party for conducting prisoners to a cage at Brienne. We reached it at 7pm and outside had some particulars taken by an officer who told us that if we were found with knives or razors on us the next day we should be punished, so we had better give them up. So we did. Slept on the grass all night.[16]

The experiences of those taken as prisoners of war varied dramatically during the First World War. To begin with, officers were held at different camps from NCOs and men. Officers were, under the Hague Convention, not expected to perform manual labour for their captors, whilst enlisted men were. Additionally, during the Great War, prisoners captured by the Germans were not subject to any central administration. Instead, they 'belonged' to the Army Corps which had captured them, and would in theory be sent to camps in that Corps' home area of Germany.

Buckingham, as a non-commissioned officer, was also separated from the remainder of the rank and file, but it is unlikely that he received better treatment as a result:

'The next day [28 May] the NCOs were fell in separate, and we marched away under a Uhlan escort to RETHEL, a distance of 30 kilos and only had one rest. We stopped there in the civil prison one night and the next day went by train to MONTMEILLANT ST JEAN but before entering were given our first meal. It consisted of carrot and parsnip peelings, and rotten apple cores [which was] all boiled together for half an hour. We were not clamped down to that yet, so threw it away; also one slice of black bread for the 24 hrs train journey.[17]

The worst conditions were undoubtedly those experienced in the early months of 1918 by the influx of thousands of PoWs captured in the spring offensives. Many of these men were not even taken to Germany, but were kept behind the lines for road building and labouring duties. Fed on scraps and given no proper shelter, many were half-starved and clad in rags by the end of the war.

George Buckingham was not transferred to a camp in Germany until the October of 1918, and only then in the face of an Allied offensive which forced the Germans back. He noted:

32225 Pte Percy Beck, 7th Battalion, with his wife and son. He was captured on the Aisne and died as a prisoner of war in Belgium, on 6 November 1918. The Germans held numbers of British PoWs just behind their own lines (rather than transporting them to Germany) for the purposes of road building and other labouring work. Many died from dysentery and influenza resulting from ill treatment, and others were killed by the shells of their own side.
Mrs M.Preston

> *While at the French camp I flogged the only thing I had to a German – my puttees for ¹/₂ loaf of black bread. From the French [prisoners] my cap badge fetched 1 slice bread, watch fetched ten biscuits. I was offered half-crown for two biscuits immediately but refused to sell. There was simply a barbed wire square when we arrived, and we had a week sleeping on the grass, but had to go out working all day and had mangel soup when we came in.*[18]

By September he and his fellow prisoners were clearing supply dumps in readiness for abandoning them to the advancing French Army:

> *We have had a hard days work no Sunday off, clearing all material away, and it is nearly finished bar rails on track. The weather has been rotten, very rainy, windy and raw, and we have had to work out in it all and as we have no top coats, our khaki all worn out, and thin, we have suffered. I was able yesterday to hide an empty cement sack, and have slit one side, a hole in the bottom and today it has made a cardigan jacket for me. (Roll on parcels). Owing to cold mornings, and turning out at 5.30am I have saved my chunk of bread for breakfast, as dinner is now 11.30 or 12 [I] go 18 hrs each day without any food, but it is the best way as work in the morning on an empty stomach is ruining several of the fellow's constitution, and it is easier to sleep on nothing than to work on the same.*[19]

In a camp, either in France or in one of the more established sites in Germany, the treatment that NCOs and men could expect varied enormously according to the nature of the camp commandant, and their individual circumstances. Some commandants were relatively enlightened in outlook, whilst others were virtual sadists who delighted in the exercise of power over others. In most camps however, men were expected to work, and often work hard, for little in the way of food. Some supplied labour for factories or for agriculture, but a good number were sent to work in coal

Güstrow ГЮСТРОВЪ 24/6/ 1918

Dear Mother

A letter head for PoWs to inform their Next of kin of their address. It is printed in English, French, Flemish, Russian, Portuguese and Italian, reflecting the varied nationalities the Germans held in their PoW camps. Mr Ken Holt

mines in place of the many miners who had been conscripted into the German Army. The Germans took careful note of the trades of the men that they had captured, and set them to work accordingly. In this way many of the Coalville and Ibstock miners of the Leicestershire Brigade who had been taken prisoner, found themselves separated from their fellows with whom they were captured, and put to work in German collieries.

Many thousands of Allied prisoners of war died in German hands as a result of overwork, and under-nourishment, as the British naval blockade of Germany bit hard. Influenza, dysentery and a host of other diseases linked to malnutrition took their toll. Buckingham records in October 1918 arriving at a camp on the German border, which was not yet finished, and the huts had no roofs. At night, the rain came through onto the huddled prisoners inside. In the daytime, they worked knee deep in water, with no fires to dry their clothes in the evening. Fever was rife, and he was hospitalised in a sick hut along with Russian and French prisoners. The bed in which he slept had been occupied by an Italian who had recently died of the fever. Food parcels, which Buckingham mentions in passing above, were an erratic affair. Many hundreds of women's groups and other societies made regular collections for local prisoners of war, and of course next-of-kin could send parcels to prisoners via the Red Cross. These parcels could contain foodstuffs, but the hardships being experienced by the German civil population by the end of the war made it uncertain that they would always arrive.

George Holt, captured at the same time as Buckingham, wrote to his parents in Snarestone asking for a range of goods to be sent out to him at his camp, Gustrow, in Mecklenburg:

don't forget to send me plenty of

A letter sent home to his parents by George Holt DCM, from Gustrow PoW camp, Mecklenburg, Germany. Mr Ken Holt

A group of Leicestershire Regiment officer PoWs at Schweidnitz, Germany, late in 1918. Two on the left are from a Territorial Battalion (probably the 2/4th or 2/5th) but the rest are mostly from the 110th Brigade. The photo was signed by 2nd Lieut H.Cardall, 8th Battalion (seated centre), who was captured in May 1918. C.Ward, Liddle Collection

> *quaker oats and a tin of golden syrup if they will allow you to send me them. Send plenty of tobacco & cigs as we cannot get any out here we are smoking dock leaves at the present time and anything we can get hold of...I very often think about the breakfast we used to have at home a bit of nice ham and an egg you might be able to send me over*

Schweidnitz officers' PoW camp (offiziergefangenlager), near Worms, Germany. C.Ward, Liddle Collection

an egg if you put it in the middle of a cake or loaf or something and a piece of bacon.[20]

At the end of the Great War, the German authorities could not even supply an accurate figure for the number of other ranks prisoners held in their camps, let alone one for those who had died. Such was the lack of proper record keeping. Many of the men who lived and whom the Germans released at the end of the war returned to Britain as broken men, their health permanently impaired. Physically ruined and unable to work properly, untold numbers died premature deaths as a result. They remained one of the most overlooked and shamefully treated groups in post war years.

Officers by contrast lived a life of comparative ease. Often the *Offiziergefangenlager* in which they were held was a converted castle in the countryside for example of Bavaria, and many like Pforzheim were relatively comfortable. Here the officers could read magazines, or play chess. Yet not being occupied with the constant daily battle to stay alive which faced the other ranks, it left the officers free to dwell upon their situation. During the First World War, being captured still carried some of the stigma and shame of surrender associated with this in former times. Indeed upon repatriation officers were required to submit an account of their conduct upon the occasion of their capture, and a Court of Enquiry was convened for each officer to establish that the circumstances were 'honourable'. Many officers were aware of this, whilst others simply had a burning desire to return to the war to help their comrades. A good number found the enforced leisure of captivity deeply frustrating and there were numerous attempts to escape, though relatively few were successful.

41317 Pte John Charles Crane, 6th Battalion, with his family after his return from a PoW camp. He had been wounded and captured at Epehy, and suffered great privation in enemy hands. The German guards stole the boots of Crane and his fellow prisoners, and in their place they issued wooden clogs. When he eventually reached York station on his way home in December 1918, he threw the clogs across the platform in disgust. 'Eee, they did make a clatter', he told his family, many years later. Mrs Dee Holt

With the end of the war on 11 November, the PoWs suddenly found themselves at liberty. However, the increasing civil strife and administrative chaos in Germany as she stumbled towards revolution at the end of October and beginning of November, meant that a number of men, like Lance Corporal George Holt, simply walked out of their camps and headed towards the Allied lines in Belgium. George Buckingham wrote as one of the final entries in his notes:

Nov 12th…The armistice has started and with it the guard of our camp have gone over to the revolutionists. They took the black, white and red buttons from their caps and tore down the Prussian eagle from over the gates, and put [the] *Socialist red flag up instead. A representative went from our camp to Berlin to confer with the Allied representatives there responsible for the cleaning of PoW camps and took a report from the English doctor condemning the camp as one of the worst in Germany as regards sanitation, so we are to be moved down the river on barges on the 27th November.*[21]

In fact, Buckingham's journey out of Germany was by train, to the port of Danzig, from where a liner took him back to England. It was some consolation for the ex-PoWs to be back home in time for Christmas 1918. Later on, each one received a scroll from HM King George V and Queen Mary, acknowledging the hardships that they had endured in the camps. However, as the PoW ships reached harbour, the first reception which many of the prisoners received was from the throng of anxious relatives who crowded the docks, brandishing photographs of loved ones. They mobbed the men as they descended the gang-planks, anxious for any news of a relative who was missing-believed-prisoner, or who might not have survived captivity.

BUCKINGHAM PALACE

1918.

The Queen joins me in welcoming you on your release from the miseries & hardships, which you have endured with so much patience & courage.

During these many months of trial, the early rescue of our gallant Officers & Men from the cruelties of their captivity has been uppermost in our thoughts.

We are thankful that this longed for day has arrived, & that back in the old Country you will be able once more to enjoy the happiness of a home & to see good days among those who anxiously look for your return.

George R.I.

Buckingham Palace letter sent to returning PoWs at the end of their captivity. This one was sent to George Holt, even though he had managed to escape from German hands before the end of hostilities. Mr Ken Holt

1 R.H.Kiernan, *Little Brother Goes Soldiering* (Constable & Co, 1930) p68
2 Kiernan, *op cit* pp68-69
3 Kiernan, *op cit* pp72-73
4 D.V.Kelly, *39 Months With the Tigers* (Ernest Benn, 1930) p123
5 A.C.Cave, unpublished typescript diary 27.5.18
6 Kiernan, *op cit* p77
7 Kiernan, *op cit* pp79-80
8 Kiernan, *op cit* pp80-81
9 Kiernan, *op cit* p81
10 Kiernan, *op cit* p88
11 Kelly, *op cit* p128
12 Kiernan, *op cit*t p90
13 Kiernan, *op cit* p91
14 Kiernan, *op cit* p92
15 War Diary, 6th bn Leicestershire Regt, LRO. 29.5.18
16 G.E.Buckingham, unpublished typescript account.
17 Buckingham, *op cit*
18 Buckingham, *op cit*
19 Buckingham, *op cit*
20 G.Holt. Original letter, undated
21 Buckingham, *op cit*

Chapter Eleven

The Final Advance

In June 1918 the 110th Brigade moved to the Normandy coast of France, to rest and recuperate. They were billeted in Dieppe, and here, as mentioned in Chapter Ten, on 28 June the 8th Battalion was 'reduced to Training Cadre'. Its few remaining personnel were distributed to the other two Leicestershire battalions, except for some officers and NCOs who would form the nucleus of a new battalion filled with men currently under training. It was transferred to the 25th Division at Boulogne, and then returned to England, and at Clacton on 7 July 1918, it was officially re-designated the 14th Battalion West Riding Regiment. It was replaced in the Leicestershire Brigade by the 1st Battalion Wiltshire Regiment, but for the purposes of this narrative, attention will focus solely on the doings of the two remaining Leicestershire battalions.

Whilst in Normandy, the 6th and 7th Battalions absorbed reinforcements, many of them from the now disbanded second line Leicestershire Territorial Force battalions, the 2/4th and 2/5th. About the middle of July the Brigade returned to the Somme country, pausing for a

To rebuild the battalions of the 110th Brigade in the summer of 1918, other battalions were broken up to provide reinforcements. 241062 CQMS Charles Hubbard (standing centre) and 241248 Sgt Edgar Culpin (standing right) both joined the 6th Battalion, from the recently disbanded 2/5th. Simon Jervis Photographic Archive

spell in the area of Raincheval. Here R. H. Kiernan was posted back to the Brigade, after being hospitalised through the inhalation of gas at the end of the Aisne battle. With his 8th Battalion no longer in existence, he was now posted to the 6th Battalion. However, he found that much of the old spirit of the Leicestershire Brigade, which had still persisted even at the time he originally joined, had now gone.

I rejoined the battalion near Eu. I don't know any of them, except Ben. He's still here. But I am in a different platoon and not on the machine guns. Most of the men seem to have been in a division that was disbanded after the '21st of March', and they have been 'out' since then, and have now been drafted to us. They are an awful lot of merde, as selfish as Hell; they seem to be watching the main chance down to the prettiest detail.[1]

At the end of July 1918 the Brigade moved south, and occupied trenches on the old Somme battlefield:

[we] took over trenches running along the river Ancre, facing the battle-scarred hill of Thiepval. Here, exactly two years before, had raged one of the bloodiest sections of the Somme attacks, and during one year the whole place had been a forgotten corner of our back areas. It seemed odd and a little discouraging to be back again in the old trenches where the Ulstermen had fought in 1916, as though so much blood and effort had been wasted.[2]

A private soldier of the 7th Battalion, identifiable by the faintly visible yellow horizontal bar, at the top of his sleeve, photographed in 1918.

The line now after two years of war in this sector ran roughly parallel with the Ancre. The village of Hamel lay in No Man's Land, whilst Aveluy Wood, which in 1916 had been a British possession, was now shared between British and Germans, and Thiepval Wood, from which the Ulster Division had made its attack in July 1916, was entirely in German hands. Kiernan recorded his experiences of moving up to the trenches around this time:

We filed on, and by dark we lay down in trenches - the front line. It is Thiepval Ridge that we can see opposite, like a great, black hump ...We have been in here some days. The trenches are very shallow and open, stony and falling away, as though the earth were too tired to stick together any longer. All night and especially at 'stand to' Jerry puts over a whizz bang strafe. There is hardly any warning - there is a 'zip', then a burst and a shower of stones. It is 'jumpy' and nerve-racking, because you never know when Jerry will start again ...Down in front of our trenches there is a railway line, all torn and mangled, at the foot of a slope; there is the Ancre River too, with a bridge flush with the water. Nowhere is there any solid ground, but shell holes, shell-holes, bits of aeroplane and old iron. There are no trees. In front is the brow of Thiepval, brown and yellow, scarred with trenches.[3]

After a few days the front line troops moved back and took over the reserve line trenches at Englebelmer. Here, in this village which had been used for billeting in 1915 and 1916, houses and orchards were still intact, and the

Ruined farm labourers' cottages – latterly used as pig sties – in the village of Englebelmer. These buildings, dating from the 18th Century and built in the traditional Picardy style, were used as billets during the First World War, and graffiti has been carved into the soft chalk brickwork by soldiers. These houses probably sheltered Leicestershire Brigade men in 1918.

men could move about relatively freely, collecting apples. Only the odd shell at night caused them to take cover in trenches. Whilst here they also formed carrying parties for the front line garrison, bringing up boxes of bombs and small arms ammunition.

Around this time, some way away to the north, one of the saddest personal sagas in the history of the 110th Brigade was coming to a finale. 11682 Private John James Nisbet was an original member of the 8th Battalion, having enlisted in September 1914. He was born at South Shields, the son of an unmarried mother (a fact which carried considerable stigma at the time). It seems that from the very first moment, Nisbet was in trouble. He was before his battalion commander on 7 August 1915, eight days after arriving in France, charged with leaving the ranks to ask for water during a route march. For this he received one month Field Punishment No 1 (reduced to 21 days by the brigade commander). He was one of those men who were to be seen fastened to the wheels of wagons at Eecke (see Chapter Four) as a consequence. On 26 March 1916, he was awarded 28 days FP No 1, again by Lieutenant-Colonel Mignon, for disobeying the command of his superior officer, and then two days later on 28 March he was awarded three years penal servitude for a similar offence. The sentence was later commuted to Field Punishment No 1 by the Army Commander. On 10 April 1916, Nisbet was again before a Court Martial, this time charged with two offences:

1. *When on active service without urgent necessity quitting the ranks.*
2. *Disobeying a lawful command.*

249

For this he was awarded the one years' imprisonment which had previously been suspended. Finally, on 11 May 1916, he was tried on two further charges of

> *When on active service disobeying in such a manner as to show wilful defiance of authority a lawful command given personally by a superior officer in the execution of his office.*[4]

For these offences he was sentenced to death but the punishment was suspended and commuted to ten years penal servitude. Whilst in a Military Prison at Maidstone in December 1916, Nisbet attempted to strike the governor whilst he was in the act of sentencing him for another minor misdemeanour, and as a result four more years were added to his sentence but were suspended. Whether prison had reformed Nisbet's character or whether the acute shortage of manpower on the western front was the more significant factor is not clear, but on 12 April 1918, he was released from Maidstone Prison.

However, instead of a posting back to his old 8th Battalion, Nisbet was instructed to report to the 1st Battalion Leicestershire Regiment. Perhaps there was a feeling that the stronger sense of discipline and 'spit and polish' in a regular battalion might be better for him than that to be found in his old Kitchener's Army Battalion. If so, such ideas must have been short-lived. He was quickly in trouble with his new battalion commander, receiving a sentence of Field Punishment not long after his arrival. Then, on 15 July 1918, his platoon was ordered to parade for the trenches. As witnesses would later testify, Nisbet was not seen again after this until he was apprehended in a dugout behind the Medical Base Depot at Beaumarais without rifle or equipment. Now things were taken more seriously. He was charged with Desertion, and at this Court Martial his past offences seemed to have counted heavily against him. Nisbet in his defence argued that he been feeling ill at the time of his disappearance, but this was not enough to convince the Court, and he was sentenced to death by firing-squad. This time the sentence was not commuted, and the brigade commander in his notes confirming it commented that Nisbet had had several chances to redeem his character and had not taken them. He also stated that in his opinion he was a bad influence on any other soldiers who came into contact with him. The battalion commander also noted in effect that Nisbet had been nothing but trouble since he arrived at the battalion. The sentence was carried out at Hilhoek, Belgium at 5am on 23 August 1918. His age was recorded as twenty-six and a half, and he was shown as the son of Jessie Ann Nisbet, of 39 Westoe Street, South Shields. Today his grave can be found in Nine Elms British Cemetery, Poperinghe, Belgium.

Returning once more to events on the Somme, during this month of August, 1918, the Germans gradually evacuated their positions in Aveluy Wood, and withdrew from positions around Hamel. They had suffered a severe blow on 8 August, at the Battle of Amiens (which the German commander Ludendorf described as 'The Black Day of The German Army').

15089 Sgt George Simpson MM, ex-9th Battalion, photographed in 1918. Simpson was from Wigston, and before the war worked at the Two Steeples factory there.
Duncan Lucas

13671 Pte Ernest Walter Dakin. He was from Chesterfield, and was the son of an Inspector on the London Midland & Scottish Railway. He enlisted on 28 August 1914, aged 21, and served with the 7th Battalion. By 1918, he was with the 110th Brigade Trench Mortar Battery, which drew its members from the battalions in the brigade.

Mrs Ruth Pearson

Shortly afterwards came the 110th Brigade's attempt to force what they perhaps assumed to be a rather demoralised enemy off the Thiepval Ridge. However the German infantry showed that they were still able to put up considerable resistance when challenged. On 20 August, Second-Lieutenant Ralph Alcock of the 6th Battalion carried out a daring reconnaissance of the enemy positions across the River Ancre in broad daylight and in full view of the Germans. He brought back valuable information as to their dispositions there, prior to the offensive which was planned for the following day.

On 21 August 1918, four companies (two each) of the 6th and 7th battalions Leicestershire Regiment crossed the Ancre under cover of early morning fog, but could not maintain their positions once the fog lifted. Exposed to heavy German fire, they were driven back again. Kiernan described the terrific weight of fire encountered as they crossed the river:

> *I have been 'over the top' for the first time. We lay out all night near the railway, and just before dawn our machine guns put up a barrage over our heads. It is a terrifying sound - like a thousand winds all whistling at once, carrying the sound of a million little threatening hammers, striking a thousand strokes a minute. At dawn we rushed over the bridge, and three German machine guns fired down and across it, and shells yelled down the ridge and sent up high fountains of water. The air was singing with bullets, and fellows were dropping and lying still, all spread out. A hand-grenade burst on a man's helmet twenty yards in front, but only cut him slightly on the neck. We took cover in a shell crater, and along the sides of the bridge near the water, which is dirty green, and filled with iron and wheels, and helmets and rifles and boots.*
>
> *The firing stopped. But when we moved it started again. We crawled back as best we could.*[5]

The 6th Battalion War Diary records that the companies which returned to the west bank of the Ancre had been badly shaken by their experience. Undoubtedly for a significant proportion it would have been their first taste of action of any description. Kiernan at least had been under fire before. That same night, under cover of darkness, the 6th Battalion pushed some patrols back across the river. The following morning two companies of the 6th Battalion crossed the Ancre north of the village of St Pierre Divion. By bombing along the trenches there, they made contact with the 12th/13th Battalion Northumberland Fusiliers, and remained in position until relieved by the 6th Battalion Dorset Regiment that night.

Now with a toe-hold on the other side of the Ancre, the 21st Division quickly pushed its forces across. On 23 August the 110th Brigade followed up the attack of the 64th Brigade,

> *We went forward along a very deep sunken road which ended in a cross-roads. The sky was dotted with shrapnel high above it, looking beautiful with its white puff against the deep blue sky. Men were hit on all sides, and leaned against the banks of the road with grey faces.*

We halted a moment and crouched near the side of the bank. A man lay beside me on his side, with a clean cut triangle taken of the rim of his tin hat. There was the exact triangle on his temple, bright red, and wet. The splinter had driven the bit of tin hat into his head. He was warm but dead. From the sunken road we filed out on to the open fields left and right on each side of the road. The bullets were sending up little spouts of dirt everywhere on the ground. It was a miracle, but no one was hit then. We lay down and an officer said 'Over there, near the telegraph poles, half-right, 300 yards, rapid fire'. I fired like blazes, but could see no one'[6],

recorded Kiernan.

On the early morning of 24 August the brigade concentrated in Battery Valley (between Thiepval and Grandcourt). At 7.45am it moved off once more in support of the 64th Brigade, encountering opposition from German stragglers in the valleys leading up from the Ancre.

we chased a lot of Jerries along a trench, just as it was getting light, we on the top and they on the inside. We threw bombs at them and they put their hands up. They were in a greenish uniform and were all very young and small, fair and round-headed. There were about eighty, and they sang and danced when they had to form fours and march back as prisoners.

That afternoon a cavalry patrol came up to where we were resting. We said eagerly 'Are you going through? Is he breaking up?' They seemed to get very irritated at this, and said, 'Going nothing. You've got to finish this bloody war'. They had some fine food which they ate by the roadside. Seeing them all shiny and clean, with their beautiful horses, it was like the pictures in the books of the old fashioned wars. They ate and then rode away. Someone said their job is to round up stragglers.'[7]

Pte Frederick James Petcher, of Market Street Lutterworth, 7th Battalion. A Saddler by trade, he served in the Leicestershire Yeomanry initially but in 1918 was transferred to the Leicestershire Regiment.

John Taylor/Alan Petcher

Towards the end of the war, younger and younger German boys were captured.

Near Courcelette, Captain H.R.Horne of the 7th Battalion ran into unexpected opposition from parties of Germans armed with machine-guns. The village lay in a slight depression in the ground, and had been overlooked as columns of troops advanced on either side, leaving it still occupied by the enemy. Horne was decorated with a bar to his Military Cross for his actions, the official statement of which read:

> His company and another became detached from the rest of the battalion, but in spite of this he was instrumental in rounding up four machine guns and strong points, with the result that seventy-eight prisoners were captured. He showed great skill and courage through out operations.[8]

Late in the afternoon, supported by artillery fire, the 6th Battalion began to advance eastwards on Le Sars. Over shell-torn ground, and in the gathering gloom, the battalion lost direction, but still managed to advance as far as Pys by morning. All around the 110th Brigade positions the ground was held by enemy troops. The Germans were particularly strongly entrenched in Destremont Farm, just south of Le Sars. It was an advanced and exposed position, but during the night, friendly troops of another brigade came up to take position on the left.

On the following day (25 August) the plan devised by the commander of the 21st Division, Major-General Campbell, was for his three brigades, including the 110th, to 'leap-frog' over each other in a series of advances to begin at 6am. The 62nd brigade passed through the line held by the Leicestershire battalions, and after encountering stiff resistance from German machine-gunners, captured the village of Le Sars, and the Butte de Warlencourt. This was a huge prehistoric burial mound near the village of Warlencourt, offering commanding views of the countryside around in all directions. It had presented a great deal of resistance to the troops fighting in this area in 1916, but now fell relatively easily, with a large party of Germans on it who were made prisoners. The Butte had been at one time covered in grass and an undergrowth of scrub and bushes (and this is the condition in which it may be observed today, just off the Albert-Bapaume road). However by 1918 it was an eerie sight with nearly all vegetation blasted off by shellfire, revealing the white chalk underneath across much of the surface. Near the top a number of wooden crosses, erected when the Butte was in British hands in 1917, stood as memorials to the battalions which had fought there.

The 62nd Brigade had suffered heavily, and was now too weak to link up with its neighbouring formation. A gap of about a thousand yards had opened up in the British front, opposite Eaucourt l'Abbaye, by about mid-day. The Germans had observed this, and were initiating a counter-attack through the breach when, at about 2pm, the 6th Battalion was rushed up to check them and plug the gap.

> This afternoon our Company went over at the Butte de Warlencourt. The Butte is a sort of big hillock, entirely covered with

The Butte de Warlencourt as it appeared after the war. The crosses placed on the top are memorials, in the main left by the battalions which fought in the area and took part in the capture of the Butte in 1916.

> *graves. It stands near a big route nationale, and there is a plain and some thin woods or trees in the left distance beyond it, at about 1,500 yards.*
>
> *As soon as we moved out past the Butte the shells began to fall around, and the machine guns to whip up the ground round our feet. I waited for the bullet that was for me, or the close crash of a shell...*
>
> *A runner came up. His thumb had been smashed by a bit of shell, and he was bloody and shaking. We were not to attack; we were the only company attacking, it is a mistake; we are to crawl out lest he puts a box barrage round us. We went back on hands and knees, or running and crouching, using all the cover,*[9]

remembered Kiernan, who was with the battalion.

However, the Commanding Officer of the 6th Battalion, Lieutenant-Colonel M.C. Martyn (attached from the Nottinghamshire and Derbyshire Regiment) was taken prisoner of war. The exact circumstances under which this occurred are by no means clear. The Battalion War Diary is silent on the subject, recording only that Martyn was listed as 'missing', and that Major J.C. Burdett had assumed command. Possibly he was wounded, and being unable to resist was carried away by a party of Germans. In any event, the enemy counter-attack was broken up and driven off, and the Leicestershire Brigade remained in position for the remainder of the day in front of Eaucourt. On the next day, 26 August, Second-Lieutenant Robert Miles Jalland, also of the 6th Battalion, was killed in action. Today he lies buried in Warlencourt British Cemetery (VIII-K-29).

The advance was now rapid, in comparison with those in 1916, and the new Brigade positions were east of the Le Barque-Eaucourt road. On 1 September 1918 the Leicestershire battalions took part in the Battle of Bapaume. This involved the capture of the village of Beaulencourt by the 110th Brigade, in a model attack which incorporated all the lessons which had been learned in the previous two years. Instead of a head-on assault on the well defended western edge of the village, in which scattered riflemen and machine-gunners were emplaced, in a night-time manoeuvre the

Major J.C. 'Jimmy' Burdett, who took over command of the 6th Battalion in place of Colonel Martyn in August 1918. Burdett was to remain in command until the battalion was finally demobilised in 1919. Margaret Nobb

254

British soldiers digging a shallow trench through a field of corn, summer 1918. French War Office official photo

northern edge of the village was assaulted. The 6th Battalion were again in the front line, assisted by the Wiltshires, with the 7th Battalion in reserve.

> *Under cover of complete darkness the village was rushed and the defences taken in the rear, the whole affair being a complete surprise. One hundred and thirty three unwounded prisoners, two field guns and nine anti tank guns (enormous rifles mounted on stands), and no less than thirty-six machine guns were taken, besides a well equipped hospital with a hundred and one beds.*[10]

Kiernan in the 6th Battalion was one of those taking part in the assault. Prior to attacking the village that night, he and his comrades moved into position several hours earlier:

> *It is afternoon and warm and sunny. Last night we lay out in front of a village called, somebody said, Beaulencourt. [The Germans] knew we were there, and lashed the ground with machine guns, and sent up all sorts of lights, white, yellow, red and green. A fellow lying next to me rolled over me, and kicked a lot before he died. We rushed through some huts outside the village. I fired at a Jerry three times point-blank and missed him, and he was firing back with a revolver at me. It was all in the dark, and redly lit up by the shell flashes all over the huts ....*[11]

They paused again briefly, before undertaking the second stage of the attack and clearing Beaulencourt:

> 'While we were lying out again before going through the village, there was a red flash and a roar right above me, and a thud on the man lying next to me. He did not move. He was dead. He had been telling me that he was a tram driver in civil life, and that he had three children, a boy and two girls. He had been staring along the ground into the darkness, anxious and excited. When the lights went up I could see the sweat still trickling on his face. We went through the village before dawn, and the Germans came up out of the cellars and surrendered. But the village is on fire now. We have been shelled and swept by machine guns in the little trenches we dug, but all is quiet now. They say the worst fighting was at a sugar refinery.*[12]

The 7th Battalion as already noted was the reserve battalion for this attack, and moved in to clear up any isolated pockets of German opposition overlooked by the leading battalions. One officer of the 7th who gained distinction for his part in this action, near Le Transloy, was Temporary

255

Second-Lieutenant George Waite Beesley. His citation for the Military Cross, dated 2 September 1918, stated:

> For conspicuous gallantry and devotion to duty. During an attack on a sugar factory he skilfully organised and controlled mopping-up parties. When he saw some of the enemy making for some trench mortars, which were out in front of the line, he dashed out and drove them back single-handed. He showed marked ability and leadership.[13]

Another Military Cross was awarded to Second-Lieutenant Ralph Alcock, 6th Battalion, for a combination of his actions in going forward with the front line infantry and maintaining vital communications with Brigade HQ, and his daring work earlier, on 20 August. The attack may have been conducted with textbook precision, but there were still casualties among the 6th Battalion and in the 7th Battalion. Even though the Germans were still able to inflict losses, and one or two determined enemy defenders armed with a machine-gun could certainly wreak havoc until checked by Lewis gun or Stokes mortar fire, casualties were nowhere near the scale of those in 1916. This was an indication that now at last the run of events was going the way of the Allies.

The Germans retired for several miles now before deciding to stand and fight, and it was not until 10 September that the Leicestershire Brigade was in action again. They were now once more entering the countryside which had first been abandoned by the Germans in their withdrawal to the Hindenburg Line in February 1917. On the dark and rainy night of 9/10 September, they took over positions north west of the village of Epehy, which had been the home of the 6th and 7th Battalions throughout the winter of 1917/18. Here they held trenches which had been at one time the reserve lines of the formations on their left flank.

Although they were in the front line, there was little enemy activity to speak of, except for shellfire:

> We have been in the line near a big railway cutting. One line of the railway runs toward Jerry and joins a main line running

To be pasted in A.B. 439 and A.B. 64.

KEEP YOUR MOUTH SHUT!

The success of any operation we carry out depends chiefly on surprise.

DO NOT TALK.—When you know that your Unit is making preparations for an attack, don't talk about them to men in other Units or to strangers, and keep your mouth shut, especially in public places.

Do not be inquisitive about what other Units re doing; if you hear or see anything, keep it to yourself.

If you hear anyone else talking about operations, stop him at once.

The success of the operations and the lives of your comrades depend upon your SILENCE.

If you ever should have the misfortune to be taken prisoner, don't give the enemy any information beyond your rank and name. In answer to all other questions you need only say, "I cannot answer."

He cannot compel you to give any other information. He may use threats. He will respect you if your courage, patriotism, and self-control do not fail. Every word you say may cause the death of one of your comrades.

Either after or before you are openly examined, Germans, disguised as British Officers or men, will be sent among you or will await you in the cages or quarters or hospital to which you are taken.

Germans will be placed where they can over-hear what you say without being seen by you.

DO NOT BE TAKEN IN BY ANY OF THESE TRICKS.

Ptd. in France by A.P. & S.S.   Press C. X515. 250000. 7/18.

'Keep Your Mouth Shut!' – instructions to be pasted into the soldier's paybook (AB64), August 1918. This incorporated intelligence information gathered in the latter part of the war, in particular that the Germans placed their own English-speaking intelligence officers among newly captured PoWs to gain information. This had on occasions led to details about forthcoming attacks being given away.

A British Mk IV tank, in use in September 1918. Tanks became an increasingly common element in the assaults of the final months of the war.

256

*north and south. We have been shelled a good deal and have lost a lot
of men. As we went up in the night, Ben was wounded. I had not seen
him for a long time, as he had been sent to another company. We had
to pass some of our field guns, and Jerry was searching for them. Their
shells burst near the ground with a dull red flash. I heard him cry out.
I shouted, 'Is it you Ben, are you hit?' There was no answer. We were
moving at top speed, and I could not fall out to see. I have seen his
team, and they say he was hit in the shoulder by a bit of shell. They
did not even know that his name was Ben.* [14]

On the night of 15/16 September, the Leicestershire Brigade was relieved,
prior to taking part in an offensive scheduled for 17 September. Much of the
camaraderie which had characterised the battalions during their early days
had, inevitably by now, seeped away as if into the mud like rainwater. The
battalions had been made up to strength again and again by reinforcement
draft after reinforcement draft. Most of the men did not know each others'
names, nor did they bother to try to find them out as all too often they
would be replaced by an entirely new set of comrades within a few weeks.
Likewise the officers changed too often for the men to learn their names, or
for the officers to get to know the men in their platoons properly. This had
certainly not been the case in the early days, when officers had usually even
known which of the men in their platoon were married and which were not.
Falling out after leaving the line on the night of 15 September, Kiernan
noted the absence of a spirit of sharing and 'mucking in together' which had

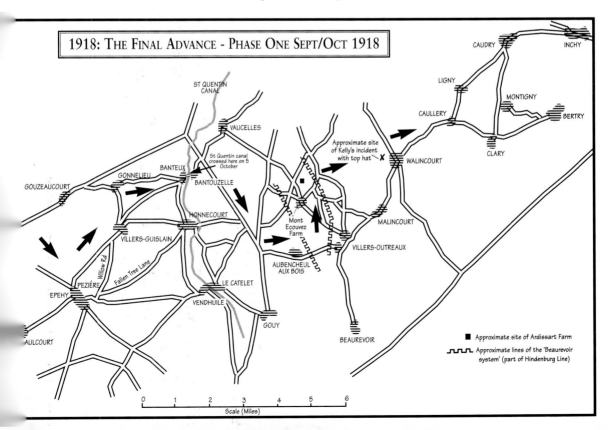

characterised the early volunteers:

> The men in the Company are a strange lot. Most of them are not [Leicestershire] men. When we go to a new place and are halted, say in the middle of a field, their eyes sweep round to find bits of shell-hole or covered trench or bivvy where they can be comfortable. As soon as 'dismiss', they rush to the places they've spotted, and hold them against all comers - just like miners at a Californian gold rush on the pictures. I lie down where I am, and let it rain.[15]

The forthcoming attack was intended to clear the Germans from what had been the old British positions prior to the 21 March battle, and from their own old front line positions. By 1918 Allied gunnery tactics had been refined and modified, but the crash and roar of an artillery barrage was just as much of an awe-inspiring spectacle, and going over the top was still an experience the prospect of which left the stomach in knots and the palate dry. R.H. Kiernan, as yet not eighteen, wrote of this battle for Epehy:

Pte W.Roome of Harrogate, 6th Battalion. Wounded for the fourth time in 1918.

> We have come up and are 'lying out' to 'go over'. The air is alive and shaking with fire. It is hardly dawn yet, just grey and black. Along the railway line our barrage is down, a great wall of grey smoke covered with yellow flashes. It is the first time I have seen a barrage from behind. It is raining and very cold.
>
> Everything is banging and roaring, and there is the steely shriek of hundreds of shells, and that great wind overhead. There's the big whistle and 'shee-ing' and hammering of the machine guns, firing over us from the railway embankment.[16]

The battle saw the conclusion of Kiernan's short but eventful period of service in France. Wounded in the attack, he was to spend the remainder of the war recovering in hospital in Britain. Meanwhile, David Kelly recalled:

203745 Pte Reuben Dolby, 7th Battalion. A Painter by trade, he arrived in France as a reinforcement following the March 1918 offensive, and was killed on 18 September.

> The progress of the attack brought our troops back into parts of our old front line east of Epehy, and the 1st Wilts established their headquarters in the road called 14 Willows, and close to the trees from which the name was derived. It was thrilling to encounter our old trench notice-boards, 'Poplar Trench', etcetera, still in position ...We had taken four hundred and twenty six prisoners, including no less than twenty officers, and eight field guns.[17]

Earlier on in the day Kelly's headquarters had taken over an abandoned dug-out in a road just north of Pezieres-Epehy, which had prior to the March offensive been the headquarters of a battalion of the 62nd Brigade. Lying on a shelf they found a regimental cheque-book and other papers relating to that battalion, undisturbed under six months' worth of dust.

The next major action came on 25 September, as the Brigade took over trenches from the 17th Division, facing Gonnelieu. An attack launched on 29 September was only partially successful, but the Germans retired anyway on 30 September. Their new position was the Honnecourt-Banteux canal, and the Leicestershire battalions followed them up, taking over what had been the old British front line here in 1917, facing the canal. For some days

42263 Pte Hedley Goodwin, 6th Battalion, of Horton-in-Ribblesdale, Yorkshire. Killed in action on 8 October 1918.

36346 Pte Harry Wileman, 6th Battalion, killed in action on 8 October 1918. On his last leave home, Harry had become convinced that once he returned to France he would be killed. He had already been hospitalised and returned to duty twice, and it is likely that he was suffering from some form of shell shock or war neurosis.
Norman Hastings

the line was static, and patrols each night attempted to find a suitable crossing point on the canal.

The foremost posts, occupied by the 7th Battalion, here lay among the ruined houses of Banteux itself. On 5 October, the Germans retired voluntarily once again, and the 110th Brigade crossed the canal by means of the battered bridges still across it, and took up position in the old Hindenburg Line opposite. They now faced the Germans in what was known as the Beaurevoir system, and an attack on this network of trenches was planned for 8 October 1918. The scheme was a complicated one, but one which illustrated the improvements in tactics and the handling of bodies of troops since 1916. The 1st Battalion Wiltshire Regiment was to attack in an easterly direction, and capture a road and trenches east of Montecouvez Farm. From here an attack would be launched in a northerly direction by the 6th and 7th Battalions Leicestershire Regiment, from a line marked on maps inside the area to be captured by the Wiltshires. It was a complicated scheme requiring first for the Wiltshire Regiment's attack to go ahead successfully, then for the Leicesters to arrive in position on time, and then also for their attack not to be attended by excessive misfortune.

David Kelly, after examining prisoners captured in the first phase of the assault between 3am and 4.30am, then hurried to check that the two Leicestershire battalions were in place ready for zero hour, which was scheduled for them at 5am:

The German batteries must have been well behind the line, for they were now very active, and as I entered Montecouvez Farm – in reality a small village – falling shells and a shower of bombs from a low-flying aeroplane combined to produce a terrifying uproar. Houses were crashing and bricks flying in every direction, always a specially unpleasant sound in the darkness, and I ran hard through the village and on along a road which brought me to the positions just taken by the Wiltshires. From the spot where the trenches they had captured crossed this road, there was another road running north to the assembly positions of the other two battalions, and following this, visiting the Company commanders on the way, I found the attacking waves of the two battalions already moving towards Ardissart Farm.[18]

The citation for the Military Cross awarded to Lieutenant M.C. MacLaren, 7th Battalion, in October 1918. M.C.MacLaren, Liddle Collection

```
            Awarded the Military Cross.
            ----------------------------

     T/Lieutenant Malcolm Colquhoun McLAREN,
          7th Battalion Leicester Regt.

--------------------------------------------

        For conspicuous gallantry and devotion to duty
during the attack on the Masnieres-Beaurevoir line West of
Walincourt on the night of the 7th-8th October, 1918. When
the Battalion was approaching the assembly position, and had
to file through one gap in the wire under fire from three
enemy machine guns, he did fine work in directing the
Companies to their positions. His coolness at a critical
moment contributed to the ultimate success of the operations.
```

The day was a complete success, with four field guns, over sixty machine guns and some six hundred prisoners taken. As darkness was falling, Kelly recalled,

'our enthusiasm was dampened by an astonishing order to make a fresh attack the same evening, but vehement protests from the Brigadier-who was always ready to risk unpopularity in high quarters when he felt his duty to his subordinates

German large calibre howitzers, abandoned behind a line of trees by their retreating crews, October 1918. C.E.Townley, Liddle Collection

demanded it – led to this order being cancelled.[19]

After this battle, the Germans again retired a considerable distance, relinquishing another large swathe of territory. Now for the first time in the war, the Leicestershire men were coming across villages which had been abandoned not merely intact, but also full of civilians who had been living under German rule since 1914. Kelly remembered:

> *The effects on the spirits of the troops of seeing civilians and feeling that the enemy was at last beginning to break was instantaneous, and I remember the delight of a column of troops marching along a road when I galloped back over the fields from the village of Walincourt wearing a battered top hat I had picked up.*[20]

41383 Pte Wilfred Smith, of Earby, Yorkshire, 6th Battalion. He died on 31 October 1918, possibly of influenza.

However, as D.A.Bacon recalled, there were also dangers involved with taking over billets in the civilian-occupied villages previously controlled by the Germans:

> *Units of the 110th Brigade moved from their respective positions about 10am, and marching via Walincourt, obtained billets in Caullery. The latter was a fair sized village captured that morning from the enemy, and contained almost a full compliment of civilians. Prior to this retreat, the enemy had mined all cross-roads and large buildings – the huge craters at the crossings greatly impeding the passage of Transports and Guns; as a result of this propensity, all houses and buildings in the village were examined by Tunnelling Companies RE, before occupation as billets, and in some instances as much as 1000 lbs of dynamite were found in cellars, with fuses set. Long after our arrival, many houses, cross roads and portions of the railway, blew up. [Meanwhile] the food distribution and administration was entrusted to the French gendarmerie (several of whom had followed closely our*

A railway bridge destroyed by the retreating German army, as they sought to impede their pursuers, in October 1918.

A German propaganda leaflet, left behind by the retreating Germans in October 1918. This and several other similar types were intended to demoralise British soldiers.

advance) in conjunction with the British Military authorities.'[21]

The battalions remained at rest until 22 October, when they moved to the vicinity of Neuvilly, a small town to the north of Le Cateau (which was famous for the stand made here by General Sir Horace Smith-Dorien's II Corps in August 1914). On this day an attack was scheduled for the early hours of the following morning from one of the roads running north-south between Neuvilly and the German held-village of Ovillers. The Wiltshires and the 7th Battalion were to lead the attack, with the 6th Battalion in reserve. Kelly takes up the story:

'Some instinct led the enemy to lay a violent barrage on this very road just before that hour [2am], and Maclaren the Adjutant of the 7th Battalion was killed by a shell at the corner of a little orchard. Never the less the Battalions cleared the area, the 6th Leicesters assisting on the line east of Ovillers, and the latter battalion continued the advance towards Vendegies at 7.15am. One company worked round the wood which lay in front of Vendegies Chateau and took it in flank, capturing the German regimental commander. The latter said he had gone below to avoid a crash of shells, and that 'When I came out again, Tommy was in the garden'.[22]

In fact Lieutenant Malcolm Maclaren was the last officer of the 7th battalion to be killed in the Great War, and his grave can be seen in

---

The National Bank of India, Limited.

No. 95 Staff Circular Letter. No. 95

LONDON, 14th November, 1918.

Captain M. C. MACLAREN. Leicestershire Regiment. Killed in action 23rd October, 1918.

As the War entered its final stages, it was with a more intense anxiety that we watched the welfare of our men. To fall with victory achieved is a bitter fate. It is that of our gallant colleague and splendid soldier—MacLaren. He was instantaneously killed by a [she]ll on 23rd October when his Battalion was forming up for attack. We print a letter from [his] Commanding Officer to his father, than which no finer tribute can be paid. For some time [he] had been acting as Adjutant and had been recommended for the Military Cross for gallant [con]duct on 8th October. He entered the Bank's service in 1911, and was high on the list for [ap]pointment to the East when War broke out. Then, in August 1914, he was among the first to [enl]ist in the famous 10th Battalion, Royal Fusiliers. Within a few weeks, and two high on the years' [ser]vice, two of the survivors of the courageous band that joined the Battalion together from the Office [—]Sharpe and MacLaren—have been killed. In the summer of 1915 he was in France as a [La]nce-Corporal and shortly after was promoted to Quartermaster-Sergeant. He received his com[mis]sion in the Leicestershire Regt. in the autumn of 1916, and since then has served with them to their [ben]efit and his own honour. His loss is deeply deplored in the Bank, and will be keenly felt by many contemporaries who are with the Forces, among whom are those who had been in close [tou]ch with him in work in the office and in play upon the football field. In the sorrow that we [feel], we realise the distress that his parents suffer in the death of their son, when the fulfilment of [thei]r longing to have him home again seemed soon to be granted. He was buried at Neuvilly on [25t]h October aged 27 years. Thirty-five of our men, the flower of the manhood of the Bank, [hav]e lost their lives. Shall we forget?

"They shall not grow old, as we that are left grow old :
Age shall not weary them, nor the years condemn,
At the going down of the sun and in the morning
We will remember them."

In Memoriam : Private T. Laing, London Scottish. Died 1st November 1914.

Our older men on service will learn with deep regret that Mr. John Black, our [ma]nager in Madras, died on 18th October, the result of septic poisoning in the foot.

[Li]eutenant MacLaren's death in action, reported in the [s]taff newsletter of the National Bank of India, for which [h]e worked prior to the war. M.C.MacLaren, Liddle Collection

[A] letter received [b]y MacLaren's [f]ather from [Li]eutenant [C]olonel Dwyer, [c]ommanding the [7t]h Battalion, [in]forming him of [th]e circumstances [o]f his son's death.

Letter from Mr. JOHN MacLAREN re the late Carptain M. C. MacLAREN. 1st November.

"It is my painful duty to inform you that my son Captain M. C. MacLaren was killed in action on the 23rd October. The following is an extract from a letter received yesterday from his Commanding Officer Lieut. Col. Dwyer :— 'On that night the Battalion was forming up for the attack and he and I went up together to the forward companies. When we reached the line I told him to go to the left while I went to the right. Just after he left the enemy opened a heavy bombardment. He was killed by a shell which fell close to him and death must have been instantaneous. He was buried in the Military Cemetery at Neuvilly on the 24th, and the Battalion Drums attended the funeral. He had been acting as my adjutant for some time and in consequence I had every opportunity of realising what a splendid fellow he was. He had been promoted to acting rank of Captain only two days before for his gallant action on 8th October, he had been recommended for the M.C. I feel that in 'old Mac' as we called him I have lost a very great friend.' We were expecting him home on leave this week and we cannot yet realize that we shall never see him again."

Neuvilly Communal Cemetery and Extension (B-37).

The advance was continued by other formations, and the 110th Brigade was relieved on 26 October, returning to Ovillers for a rest. This was a short-lived affair, however, and the brigade took over from the 52nd Brigade at Poix du Nord on the night of 29 October. There was little enemy activity apart from shelling, and on 4 November the advance was on again. Much of the difficulty now as far as the Allies were concerned stemmed from the fact that they were no longer fighting in a deserted wilderness populated only by the soldiers of the two sides. In this part of the country, towns and villages were still full of civilians. Gas shells had already fallen on Poix du Nord, and as the soldiers donned their gas masks, they realised that the civilians cowering in cellars had none. A lorry load of gas masks arrived presently from the French Army, but not before a number of civilians had been gassed. There is some evidence to suggest that the retreating Germans deliberately fired gas shells into towns they had evacuated, as a means of hindering the Allies who had to deal with the casualties. The tactic worked the other way also, and for much of the remainder of November up to the end of hostilities, the Allies had to plan each new step without the aid of their now-customary bombardment, for fear of hitting civilians. There was also the emotional factor – David Kelly, who had seen countless dead men in the previous three years and had become hardened to it, wrote of being shocked at the sight of a young girl's body, mangled by a shell, lying by the roadside between Futoy and Pont-a-Vache on 4 November.

The Leicestershire Brigade was now to attack alongside the 17th Division, through the Foret de Mormal. This heavily wooded area had been the obstacle in the path of the retreating BEF in 1914, and Haig's I Corps

10269 Pte Albert Henry Locke, 6th Battalion. He died of wounds one day prior to the Armistice.

Leicestershire Record Office

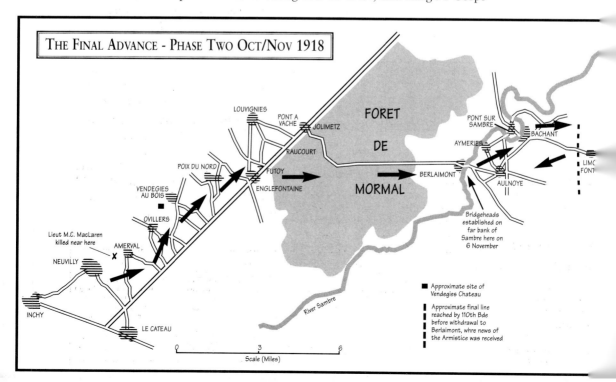

THE FINAL ADVANCE - PHASE TWO OCT/NOV 1918

LOUVIGNIES
PONT A VACHE
JOLIMETZ
FORET
DE
MORMAL
RAUCOURT
POIX DU NORD
FUTOY
ENGLEFONTAINE
BERLAIMONT
PONT SUR SAMBRE
AYMERIES
BACHANT
LIMC FONT
AULNOYE
VENDEGIES AU BOIS
OVILLERS
Lieut M.C. MacLaren killed near here
AMERVAL
NEUVILLY
INCHY
LE CATEAU
River Sambre

Bridgeheads established on far bank of Sambre here on 6 November

■ Approximate site of Vendegies Chateau

▮ Approximate final line reached by 110th Bde before withdrawal to Berlaimont, whre news of the Armistice was received

Scale (Miles)
0   3   6

A Special Order issued by 21st Division to its component units (including the 110th Brigade) announcing the signing of the Armistice, on 11 November 1918.

A Field Postcard or 'quickfirer', sent home to his father by Pte Herbert Sutton, of the 6th Battalion. He has signed it 'Bert', and added the date and time – 11am, 11 November 1918. A clear indication that he had survived. Mrs J.Moreton

had retreated around the eastern edge, whilst Smith Dorrien's II Corps had withdrawn around the roads to the west. All of this of course had occurred whilst the Leicestershire Brigade was still in civvies at Wigston Barracks. The incident has some relevance to the events of November 1918, however,

A 7th Battalion group, photographed around the time of the Armistice. Front row, third from left, RQMS Arthur Cave. Front row second from right, Charles Cattell, now serving as a Company Sergeant Major. Mr R.J.Cattell

Second Lieutenant L.A. Foxon, (right) with his brothers at the end of the war. He still wears the yellow square insignia of the 8th Battalion, even though he ended the war as a staff officer.
Eric Kellaway

as when they arrived in this area, many Leicestershire Regiment officers heard stories from the locals of how, seven or eight months after the Retreat from Mons, the Germans began to fell trees in the wood, and discovered two companies of British infantry who had been cut off in there and were being fed by the local population. There were many other variations of this story, concerning either individuals or groups, British or French who had been cut off here for several years.

Although heavy opposition was expected, the Foret de Mormal was cleared by 11.30am that day (4 November). Kelly commented,

> *This unopposed passage through the forest, which even a few machine guns could have converted into a formidable obstacle, was a welcome surprise and confirmed the tales we now began to hear from civilians of the growing discouragement and disorder in the ranks of the retreating army.*[23]

For some, the end came too late: 41326 Pte Stanley Duffill, 6th Battalion, who died in hospital in Germany on 13 November 1918. Shortages of food and medicines, as well as neglect and overwork in some German camps contributed to the deaths of many British PoWs in 1918.

The next obstacle was the Sambre River, and this the Germans seemed more willing to fight for. Attempts by the 62nd Brigade to cross the bridges in the town of Berlaimont had met with fierce opposition, but on the night of 5 November they managed to establish bridgeheads on the far bank. The following day the leading battalions of the 110th Brigade (6th Battalion Leicestershire Regiment, and Wiltshires) crossed by means of a captured bridge and by planks laid across a damaged lock, to continue the advance, until 7 November.

They then withdrew to rest back at Berlaimont. Three days later, whilst still out on rest, came the news that hostilities would cease at 11am on 11 November.

> *Despite all the portents we had had of an impending collapse,* wrote Kelly,

14066 A/Sgt Charles Cyril Beaver, formerly 8th Battalion, photographed with his family at the end of the war. He was wounded twice, as his two wound stripes testify. The first occasion was on 14 July 1916, and the second time possibly on 3 May 1917. He was born at Oakham.

Mr S.Beaver

we had grown so accustomed to the routine of war that the news did not excite the emotion it would have done in earlier years, and I can still remember the polite smile with which our serjeant-clerk read the order.[24]

Whatever the reaction to the news on the Home Front, among the soldiers in France, feelings were muted. Everyone was tired after the relentless advancing and fighting of the previous hundred days, and all too often, the thoughts of servicemen turned to the friends, brothers, and other relations who would not be celebrating and who would not return. Kelly wrote:

This mood, and the atmosphere of a large French village, made impossible any counterpart to the delirious scenes which, as we heard later, took place in London. The officers of one of our battalions which I visited in the evening celebrated the event with a convivial, though not unduly riotous, gathering, except perhaps for certain destruction caused by a horse which some of us led through a chemist's shop to visit a major who had, we thought, gone to bed too early.[25]

For Bacon, the news of the Armistice was not unexpected, but what was more surprising to him was the simple pleasure to be gained from being able to spend a night in peace. He was able at last to enjoy a good night's sleep, for virtually the first time since the beginning of that year at least, free from the fear of enemy bombs or shells which might fall on his billet. Another soldier in the ranks, Corporal John Little of the 6th Battalion, wrote home to his wife in Market Harborough on 13 November. For him, the relief to be found in safety and comfort of warm billets, was tempered by the memory of the exhilaration of the fighting of the previous four months:

What do you think to the splendid events which have happened lately, to think that at this time last week we were in the midst of fighting, and could hardly hear one another speak for the roar of the Guns and now everything quiet and peaceful, I can hardly realise it, but still it was bound to come to an end sometime.

I am very thankful I have been spared to come through it all and hope I may soon be at home with you the home I love so much.

I am full of joy and thankfulness, I and one or two more are the only ones left in the company who started with us on August 21st; when we crossed the Ancre, and Thiepval Ridge, we have had new drafts nearly every fortnight and they all got wounded or killed and dwindled away.

te E T Watson
th Battalion,
otographed on
s return home
om a German
isoner of war
mp, December
18.

265

I don't think the war will start again, so we can say we have peace or as good as peace.

We saw some thrilling scenes when we advanced through the French Villages, the civilian people who had been under the Germans for four years were full of joy to be released again, the women ran and put their arms around the Soldiers necks and kissed them, never been kissed so much before in all our lives, they had been robbed of everything and have had a terrible life under the huns for the last four years...

Well I hope the day is near when I shall be coming home, I am in Group 1 for demobilisation, I made that all right as I put my occupation down as farm hand.

There is one thing now we have a roof over our heads now every night which is a great thing now that winter is coming on and the cold nights and rain make it terrible to stand out in all night.[26]

So ended the Great War, for the battalions of the Leicestershire Brigade. Three years and three months of continuous service in France and Belgium had left a formation which had arrived in France with four strong battalions nearly all the members of which hailed from Leicestershire or its neighbours, and which had ample reserves behind it reduced to three battalions, which were badly under strength. Only two of these could claim to have a Leicestershire connection, but this was by now largely in name only, for constant drafts of reinforcements, drawn from across the country as a whole, had left it with few members who were actually from the county. There were fewer still who had served with it from its formation until the end, as Kelly or Bacon had. Yet, all who had served could draw pride from the fact that they had been associated with a brigade which had played a part in nearly every major action on the Western Front.

Arthur Cave, 7th Battalion. By the end of the Great War, he had reached the rank of Regimental Quarter Master Sergeant, as denoted by the insignia on his sleeves, a crown within a laurel spray. Col Terry Cave

1 R.H.Kiernan, 'Little Brother Goes Soldiering' (Constable & Co, 1930) p101
2 D.V.Kelly, '39 Months With the Tigers' (Ernest Benn, 1930) p134
3 Kiernan, *op cit* p109
4 J.J.Nisbet, Court Martial papers. Public Record Office, Kew.
5 Kiernan, *op cit* p113
6 Kiernan, *op cit* pp114-115
7 Kiernan, *op cit* p116
8 Captain H.R.Horne, Military Cross citation, London Gazette
9 Kiernan, *op cit* pp116-117
10 Kelly, *op cit* p138
11 Kiernan, *op cit* p121
12 Kiernan, *op cit* pp121-122
13 Second-Lieut. G.W.Beesley, Military Cross citation, London Gazette
14 Kiernan, *op cit* p128
15 Kiernan, *op cit* p129
16 Kiernan, *op cit* p135
17 Kelly, *op cit* 143-144
18 Kelly, *op cit* pp146-147
19 Kelly, *op cit* p147
20 Kelly, *op cit* p148
21 D.A.Bacon. Unpublished typescript memoir, LRO p135
22 Kelly, *op cit* pp150-151
23 Kelly, *op cit* p155
24 Kelly, *op cit* p158
25 Kelly, *op cit* p158
26 Original letter from 200686 Cpl John Little, 6th bn Leic Regt. 13.11.18. Barry Summers collection.

Chapter Twelve

A Land Fit For Heroes

After the Armistice was announced, the Leicestershire Brigade continued to march eastwards for several more days, reaching Beaufort. Here their orders to join the Army of Occupation on the Rhine were cancelled, much to the disgust of many, including Arthur Cave, now RQMS of the 7th Battalion. D.A.Bacon recalled that:

> Though the war was now virtually over, training was carried out during the mornings and the afternoons were devoted to sports or free for the men. Nothing exciting, that is, of a warlike nature, happened during this period, with the single exception of the continued explosions of enemy mines, which frequently blew up in unexpected places. By far the greatest comfort obtained by the conclusion of hostilities was that of a good night's rest, which was more or less certain, though as an actual fact one had become so used to being on the 'qui vie' for enemy planes and bombs that the unnatural quietness was not appreciated for some time. [1]

George Griffin Ward Sleath in 1919. He wears the ribbons of the Military Cross and 1914/15 Star.
Courtesy of Leicestershire Record Office/Jean B.Sleath

Arthur Cave in particular now had to consider his future carefully, for the Army was seeking to retain Warrant Officers like him in order to form the backbone of the new post-war army. He was offered a generous gratuity and three months leave in exchange for a further three years enlistment. After some deliberation he eschewed his former life in the hosiery trade in Leicester, and opted to become part of the Regular Army. Cave had been with the 7th Battalion since its inception, but few of the 'originals' were still with the Brigade in 1918. As well as those who had been wounded or killed, a high proportion of the recruits of September 1914 had been selected for officer training at a later date, a clear indication of their calibre. Dick Read was one such, being commissioned in 1917, as was George Sleath, who had been wounded at Gueudecourt. He was commissioned in 1918, and served with the East Surrey Regiment, winning a Military Cross shortly before the end of the war. Dick Read meanwhile opted to serve with the Royal Sussex Regiment. It was with them that he saw out the end of hostilities, a period in the Army of Occupation, and ultimately a return to civilian life. He was to have a successful career in Leicester for many years after the war, designing and manufacturing machinery for making boots and shoes.

In December 1918, the 6th and 7th Battalions marched to Ferrieres near Amiens. The rigorous discipline which had been necessary in wartime was now relaxed somewhat, and the men at least felt that there should be more informality, now that they were all soon to be civilians once again. Corporal Charles Monk of the 7th Battalion recalled one occasion after the war had finished:

Corporal Charles Monk in 1919.
onny Monk

267

'I happened to say - and my officer [the Quartermaster] heard me, I said to Charlie Partridge, 'Oh Charlie, will you do so and so' and the officer heard me, he said 'Come here Corporal', I said 'Yes, Sir'. He said 'Don't let me hear you ask privates to do things, while you've got those stripes on your arm, you order them.' He said, 'You'll never make a good soldier as long as you've a hole in your arse.' I said, 'Thank you Sir - my mother would be ashamed of me if I went home what you call a good soldier'.[2]

The officer in question here was Lieutenant Clay, an ex-Regular soldier, Boer War veteran and formerly RQMS of the 6th Battalion. It was not just the strength of the language that he used which betrayed Clay's regular army background - accustomed as he was to the harshness of pre-1914 peacetime soldiering; to his mind, discipline was not to be slackened simply because hostilities had ceased.

Another indicator of the changed circumstances in which the men now found themselves was the snap election of December 1918, called by the Prime Minister David Lloyd-George, who was seeking endorsement for his coalition government. Reform of the franchise was introduced prior to the election, and as well as women over 30 who were admitted to the ballot for the first time, more men were entitled to vote than ever before – a tacit acknowledgement of the part that both women and the working classes had played in winning the war. Everyone recognised that the as yet un-demobilised soldiers would be major power brokers, their votes would be crucial to the outcome, and there was much speculation as to how far the soldiery had been 'radicalised' by the events in Russia and by Bolshevik propaganda now coming out of Germany. Charles Monk again recalled:

We had what they call a Khaki General Election...they sent out literature [to the troops in France] pertaining to your own area and my two pals and I, we had one for the Harborough Division...I'd been in the Labour movement before I went in the Army, and I hung beside my bed a photo of the Labour candidate...the officer said, 'Oh, we've got a Labour man here', and I said, 'Yes, Sir'. But you wouldn't have dreamt of doing that while the War was on. There was

Above: A hand-tinted 'parlour portrait' of Pte Frank Wileman and his mother, commissioned by the family to mark his safe return home. Below: Frank's Demobilisation Account. He received £24 War Gratuity, in addition to his normal pay, for his four years and three months of service. Mrs Eileen Springthorpe

SOLDIER'S DEMOBILIZATION ACCOUNT.

Regtl. No. 15493 Rank Pte Name Wileman. F.R.

Corps or Regiment Leicestershire

SOLDIER'S EARNINGS.	£	s.	d.	Date.	STOPPAGES AND PAYMENTS.	£
Balance due to soldier on the date of arrival at Dispersal Station	2	13	11		Balance due from soldier up to the date of arrival at Dispersal Station ...	
28 days' furlough at ... 1/4 (net rate)	1	17	4		Clothing, equipment, &c., deficient on dispersal ...	
28 days' ration allowance at 2/1	2	18	4		Advance at Dispersal Station ...	2
Allowance for plain clothes ...					Deposited in Post Office Savings Bank ...	24
Family allowance, including ration allowance ...					Paid by demobilization postal draft—	
* Pay Warrant gratuity, or gratuity under Army Order 285 of 1914 ...					Date...20/1/...	1
Balance of bounty under Army Order 209 of 1916, or Army Order 222 of 1918 ...					Date...27/1/...	2
* War gratuity ...	24	—			Date...8/19...	
Total ... £	31	9	7		Total ... £	31

* Less £1 payable on return of the military great-coat (see Army Book 472).

To the Soldier.—You will receive in a few days a communication from the Controller, Savings forming you at what office your Savings Bank Book is ready for issue to you. If you should change your before receipt of the notification you should immediately inform the Controller, Post Office Savings London, W.14, of your new address, and take any necessary action to secure that the notification despatched reaches you.

Section Officer's Stamp.

(2913.) Wt. W8039/G1626. 1,200,000. 12/18. P.P.Ltd. E. 4277.

no question of your political affiliation. You were all wanting to get the job done and get home. But he [the Labour candidate] *didn't get in. Lloyd George gave his supporters all a coupon, and nearly everyone who got Lloyd George's coupon won.*[3]

Here at Ferrieres, in December 1918 and January 1919, demobilisation began in earnest. Men were divided into classes, according to their civilian employment. Those trades which were considered to be crucial to the restarting of the national economy were demobilised first, the theory being that they would create employment for the men coming afterwards. However, it was possible to jump the queue if a soldier had a letter from an employer stating that there was a job waiting for him. This of course favoured those soldiers who had been in the army the shortest time - as they were most likely to have retained links with their old employers - at the expense of those men who had been out in France the longest. The system was also wide open to abuse, with some men arranging for letters to be sent to them on employers' note paper when no job existed, simply to get out of the army faster. One who did just that was Charles Monk, who persuaded a builder in Kibworth falsely to state that he had a job available. After much protest, and some demonstrations by soldiers, later in 1919 the system was revised.

D.A.Bacon described the procedure for demobilisation:

Every man was dispatched from his unit in a good serviceable uniform and boots, and fully equipped with the exception of Arms and Ammunition. All were warned that this was very important as any deficiencies on arrival in England would have to be made good. On arrival at the base port, the men were marched to a camp for the night. The following day was spent in handing in certain articles of clothing, authorised for the Armies in France only and not for the Army in general – having a bath and getting ones clothes fumigated. After the latter operations the men were marched to a 'clean' camp to wait their turn for the boat; sometimes but a day was involved in the waiting, though more often two or three.[4]

Occasionally there was congestion at the ports, usually caused by bad weather which prevented the boats from sailing for one or two days, but given the enormous scale of the undertaking, the demobilisation of the British armies in France was undertaken with remarkable efficiency and speed. Once in England, the soldier was processed out of the army at a dispersal camp: his paperwork completed, he was given an insurance policy to provide for him if he was out of work for any

To mark the official signing of the Peace Treaty between Germany and the Allied Powers in July 1919, a day of thanksgiving was held in Market Harborough and other towns and cities across the country. The Harborough celebrations included the presentation of decorations to veterans, and here Sergeant S.Bale formerly of the 8th Battalion Leicestershire Regiment receives the Distinguished Conduct Medal.

Barry Summers

length of time, and given a cash gratuity. His uniform was handed in, but he could also either retain his army greatcoat or exchange it for a further gratuity.

Those who were in poor physical condition and who should never really have been called up at all were it not for the general shortage of manpower towards the end of the war were given complete discharges from the army, but the vast majority of those still serving with the Colours in 1918 were upon demobilisation transferred to the Class Z Army Reserve and sent home. Unlike the old Class A and Class B Army Reserves of pre-1914 days, this class carried no gratuity or payment. It was simply a pool of trained soldiers who were liable to be recalled should hostilities with Germany erupt again, and the Class Z men by virtue of their previous military experience remained liable for call-up for the rest of their lives.

Immediately after the Christmas of 1918 education classes had been started up in France for the benefit of the men. No expense was spared. Nissen huts were put up, special Education Pay was found for those men appointed as instructors, in addition to their basic pay, while books, pamphlets, writing materials and so on were provided by the tonne. Some observers, like Bacon, whilst marvelling at the efforts the army had gone to in order to try to prepare the men for civilian life, were saddened by the fact that speedy demobilization robbed most soldiers of the chance to benefit from this:

> With regard to Education, this from the start was conceived and put on a broad basis, and well handled. All the existing military schools of instruction were employed for the purpose, and from Bombing, Lewis-Gun, Sniping etc schools were transformed into Schools of Agriculture, Chemistry, Mathematics etc. Applications were circulated for Teachers in every and any subjects, from all units, those selected being appointed at the various schools, and officers, NCOs and men were sent from all units for courses varying from one to six weeks...Every opportunity was offered, in fact, to Officers, NCOs and men, to improve their education and learn a trade.[5]

Both the officers and the non-commissioned men would need as much help as they could get however, as employment opportunities for many ex-soldiers of the Leicestershire Brigade were to be severely limited in the depressed economic climate of the post-war years. Albert Smith, late of the 7th Battalion and with four years' army service behind him, was typical of the many miners from north-west Leicestershire who could find no work at the pits when they returned home. Unable to find a job in any pit near Newbold, he was eventually taken on at a colliery at Measham, eight miles away. Of the other soldiers who came back from the war to find themselves unemployed, a number decided to go to Russia, where the war of intervention against the Bolsheviks was still raging. The Inter-Allied force based at Archangel had gone into action on the side of the Tsarist White armies as Russia descended into civil war in August 1918, before the First World War had ended. The troops sent by Britain had been enlisted in the main for the duration only, and believed they would be fighting the

Germans; many were conscripts, and were dismayed to find themselves shipped to the wilderness of North Russia. Generally speaking, there was little enthusiasm for the campaign among the troops, especially as casualties began to mount. Accordingly in 1919 the Royal Fusiliers began to raise new battalions in London specifically for service in Russia, ostensibly to relieve the pressure on the troops fighting on the River Dvina and bring them home (although their brief was in reality to hit the Red Army harder). This North Russian Relief Force was recruited almost exclusively from unemployed ex-soldiers.

Jack Horner, who had served with the 6th and 8th battalions, had been discharged from the Army in 1918, before the end of the war. His arm though healed was of little use, and although he returned at first to heavy engineering, his former employers (British United Shoe Machinery Ltd.) having given him a job as a Fitter, he was not able to do the work, and had to leave. He took a variety of odd jobs, but was forced eventually to sign on the dole:

The Labour Exchange had moved from its two huts in Albion Street to the Market Place in anticipation of an increase of the men on the Dole. How right they were, for by mid-March [1919], the queues were three deep and four or five hundred yards long, and it took a long time before you could sign on, and that didn't leave much time to go looking for a job, and always, on Signing-on Days, there was a posse of Policemen, waiting in a back street, in case of trouble, whenever it came.[6]

The Roll of Honour board of St Charles' Roman Catholic church, Measham. One of those listed among the survivors (at the bottom) is Frank Wileman, of the 6th Battalion. Among the killed is another 6th Battalion man, Pte John Cullaghan who fell at Bazentin, and Frank's brother John who was killed while serving with the Machine Gun Corps. Mrs Eileen Springthorpe

South Wigston Ex-Servicemens' Association Committee. *A photo taken at the time of the unveiling of the War Memorial, in 1923.* Mrs Nobbs

The ex-soldiers were proud men, who wanted only to work:

'These men, like myself, did not take kindly to signing on the Dole. If there was no work to be had, then [the authorities] would create it. The excavations on the Roman Site of the Jewry Wall was done by spade and shovel by quite a large number of men. I don't know how it was paid for, possibly by the Dole money, with extra relief from a Block Grant, to give them a comparable and equal wage called relief work...The Castle Gardens, once a council dump, was cleared, and the gardens created. This was done by Relief Work. Saffron Lane in those days was a lane, with a level crossing to allow coal trains to get to the Gas Works nearby. [It] was made by hand labour, pick and shovel and a wheel barrow.

A hillock, which today would be removed in three or four hours, by a power-driven shovel biting in three or four tons a bite, was reduced by a gang of men, working in tiers, with pick-axe, shovel and wheel barrows, loading on to a horse drawn truck, then unloading into a disused clay pit, which is now the Saffron Lane Sports Arena. This was called Relief Work, and employed many men on good wages who would otherwise be drawing the soul-destroying dole-money. Likewise the Abbey Park Lakes were cleared and cleaned, as was the area round the waterfall, near the island. All these and many more schemes kept men off the Dole, as more and more men were demobilised.'[7]

Captain J.T.S. Nobbs, at a Leicestershire Regiment dinner in the 1930s. In a remarkable career he had gone from a boy soldier who enlisted in the 1890s against his stepfather's wishes, had been bought out at once and almost immediately re-enlisted, to become one of the most respected officers to serve with the 6th Battalion or indeed the 110th Brigade. Below: John Nobbs' pub, the Swan Inn at Sherington, near Newport Pagnell, Buckinghamshire.
Margaret Nobbs

Horner eventually found work in the tiny premises of a man who had set up a firm manufacturing shoe accessories, in a yard off a back street in Leicester. This was not however, before he had (as he put it) debased himself, by wearing his war medals in order to gain sympathy whilst hawking goods on the Market to try to earn money. Ashamed of himself, he vowed never to wear them for this purpose again. None the less, Horner's luck had now changed for the better, and a short while after gaining this job, he was offered another by his old foreman, who had now gone into business on his own account and had set up his own light engineering firm. Jack Horner married his girlfriend Sally on 30 July 1919.

The post-war officer corps, in a much reduced peace-time army was necessarily going to be much smaller than its wartime counterpart. The War Office in its wisdom had foreseen this, and not wishing to have large numbers of officers holding Regular Commissions on its hands had appointed most of the wartime officers to temporary commissions. At the beginning of 1919 most of these were rescinded, and the officers themselves were expected to announce in the London Gazette that they had renounced their commissions. As with the men from the ranks, with so many officers often with fine fighting records and decorations released onto the labour market at once, a Military Cross was no guarantee of work. It was not unusual to see ex-officers advertising for employment in the small ads columns.

John Nobbs, the Adjutant of the 6th Battalion and a life-long soldier, had no former occupation to return to. He had been with the Colours since the 1890's, enlisting as a Boy Soldier, against the wishes of his family. Bought out of the Army by an angry step-father, he at once ran away and re-enlisted, this time for good. His service had taken him to exotic stations in India and Burma, but upon his final demobilisation he took a pub in Sherington, Buckinghamshire. The Great War had had a curious effect upon Nobbs - in India he had been a staunch teetotaller and a leading light in the 2nd Battalion Leicestershire Regiment branch of the Royal Army Temperance Association. Something - it was said to be the rum ration issued in the early morning prior to an attack - changed his mind during his time in France and in later life he was a drinker, albeit a moderate one. He remained a senior figure in the Leicestershire Regiment Association through out the 1930s and 1940s.

Some felt so shaken by their experiences that they could not return to their old jobs. George Sleath could not settle back into the confines of the classroom, in his former role as a schoolmaster. Eventually he took a post as a school attendance officer, which allowed him the freedom to be out of doors for most of the day as he sought out truants. Others were hampered in their quest for work by debilitating wounds. Figures are not available for those from the Leicestershire Brigade who suffered permanent disabilities as a result of their war service, through loss of a limb or loss of sight, but there must have been many. So numerous were the cases of blindness across the army as a whole however that a new home, St Dunstan's, was founded to care for these men, as it still does today. It would not be unreasonable to assume that more than one blinded ex-Tiger was accommodated by St Dunstan's. Some injuries plagued men, and made their lives unbearable. The American actor and dancer Wallace McCutcheon, formerly of the 8th Battalion, had a silver plate fitted to his skull after suffering serious head injuries in action. His unsteady mental state and the fits that he was prone to suffer were cited as grounds in his divorce from the film star Pearl White

The Great War left a legacy of thousands of women widowed across Leicestershire, and countless children without a father. Here, in 1938, Percy Beck's widow and son visit his grave in Belgium. Right: Pte Percy Beck of the 7th Battalion, during the war. Mrs M.Preston

Limbless ex-servicemen attending the Limb Centre at Chapel Allerton hospital in Leeds, around 1938. Seated in the chair is Walter Malkin of Leicester, a double amputee. W. Malkin

Facing the future: blinded soldiers at St.Dunstan's. Liddle Collection

in 1919. McCutcheon spent some time in mental institutions in the 1920s, until 1928 when he took his own life at his home in Hollywood by putting a gun to his head.

Former-Second-Lieutenant L.A. Foxon, of Leicester, was troubled for the remainder of his days by a chest complaint, which he attributed to the effects of inhaling poison gas during a German attack. He went as far as to seek specialist medical advice in an effort to increase his pension award. Even a wound that did not leave the casualty maimed for life could be a major obstacle on the road back to normal life. Jack Holyoak, wounded in the chest at Ypres in 1917 whilst with the 9th Battalion was discharged from the

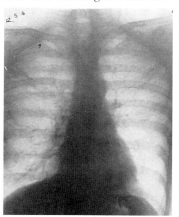

Ex-Lieutenant L.A. Foxon's attempts to secure a pension for the after-effects of inhaling poison gas, led him to seek specialist medical advice in the 1940s. Eric Kellaway

Case of Mr. L.A. Foxon.

On screening one thought that the right half of the chest did not light up quite so well as the left half, but the difference in shade observed in the film is trifling and almost negligeable. Movement of the diaphragmatic zones was very fair but Apical movement was poor though there was no disparity between the sides.

No gross opacity was seen either on screening or in the films in any part of the Lung Field, and the only shadow which is at all suspicious of infiltration is situated in the Right Upper Zone and coincides with the shadow of the First Rib so that it is difficult to be certain it is actually in the Lung Fields, and from its density if it is due to infiltration the latter would appear to have healed (or nearly so).

Apart from appearances consistent with Bronchitis, no other abnormality is detected.

Conclusions. The appearances seen in the Right Upper Zone make one suspicious of an earlier infection at this site with subsequent healing.

There is no sign of gross active disease but the slight difference in shading between the two sides may be due to a residual thickening of the Pleura of the Right Lung following the earlier infection.

There is evidence of a certain amount of Bronchitic change but no sign of Pneumonic consolidation.

3, Stanley Road,
Leicester. 6. 2. 41.

Army the following year as 'No Longer Physically Fit For War Service'. A piece of metal was lodged so close to his heart that doctors considered it unsafe to try to remove it. For many months he was too weak to work, but in those times there was no welfare state to provide a safety net. Holyoak received only a few shillings a week disability pension. Encouraged by a sympathetic employer, he returned to his old job in the hosiery trade for a few hours a week until he felt strong enough to work full time. A proud man, he had vowed that he would not marry his fiancée until he could earn enough money to support her. He managed this after a year or so, but nevertheless, it was this old injury which contributed to his early death in the 1950s.

One officer who did find a successful post war career was David Kelly. Prior to 1914 he had been destined for the Diplomatic Corps and in March 1919, upon demobilisation he was summoned by Theo Russell, then Private Secretary in the Foreign Office. He was offered a posting either to Copenhagen, where he would be involved in operations in Russia, or to Buenos Aires. Having, in his own words,

Sir David Kelley, photographed around 1950. After serving with the Tigers he was to have a distinguished career as a diplomat. Steve Law

> *an instinctive desire to get as far away as possible from Europe and everything connected with the war*[8],

he opted for Argentina. It was to be the start of a long and distinguished diplomatic career, which led Kelly to the rank of Ambassador to the Soviet Union in the 1940s and to a Knighthood. R.H.Kiernan, author of *Little Brother Goes Soldiering*, also found success. He went on to become a writer, and published a biography of T.E.Lawrence.

The City of Leicester Corporation, like many others across the country, tried to help disabled ex-servicemen as best it could, by setting them up in

Like a number of other corporations, the City of Leicester made some efforts to ensure that those citizens crippled in the war or unable to return to their previous occupation were provided with a livelihood. As part of that scheme Walter Malkin, a double amputee, was provided with this sweet shop, on Tudor Road, which he ran for a number of years in the 1920s. W.Malkin

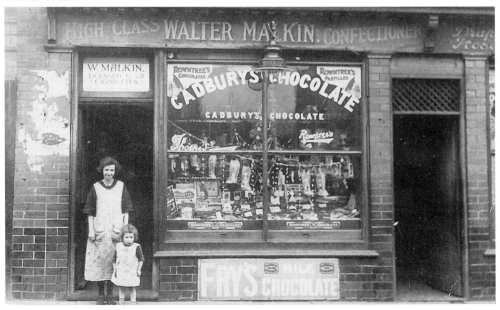

HRH the Duke of York, (later HM King George VI) visits Countesthorpe in November 1921 to unveil the village war memorial. As a proportion of the total number who served, Countesthorpe lost more of its young men than any other village in the country during the Great War.

their own businesses, but by and large, the City of Leicester and the county decided to move on, and to put the war behind them. The War Memorial on Victoria Park in Leicester is dedicated both to those men from Leicester who lost their lives, and to those of the Leicestershire Regiment. It was designed by Sir Edwin Lutyens, the architect who planned the great monument to the missing at Thiepval. Loughborough has its Carillon Tower, and many other towns and villages have their memorials, but only Rutland in the 1920s followed the pattern set in some other parts of the country, and produced a beautifully bound volume containing biographies and photographs of those who had lain down their lives. As the years pass, and one reads the obituaries and looks at the long dead faces which stare out from the plate sections, one is left with a peculiar sense of closeness with the events of the past. It must be admitted, that this has proved to be a far more evocative and moving method of ensuring that the memory of the dead lives on long after their grieving mothers, sisters and in some cases children, have passed on themselves. Far more so indeed, than simply carving the names in stone or casting them in bronze relief.

The ex-Tigers themselves tried hard to ensure that their dead comrades

Veterans of the Leicestershire Regiment at a reunion at De Montfort Hall, possibly in 1938. The man marked with a cross is William Voss, who served in France in 1918. Peter Voss

were not forgotten. There were a number of reunions in Leicester in the 1930s, both for the former members of the Leicestershire Regiment in general, and also specifically for the ex-soldiers of the 110th Brigade. The menus from these reunions make interesting reading. Far from eschewing the horrors of the war, they would seem to indicate that the veterans positively revelled in it! At first glance, names like Bazentin Soup make one wonder about the sense of humour of those who drew up these menus, but in recalling the horrors, they recalled the comradeship that had made it bearable, and the friends who were lost. Their one overriding aim was to ensure that the brotherhood which had existed in the trenches persisted, and part of this process was recalling the black jokes and at times almost schoolboyish sense of humour which had brought them through. There were also many informal reunions, often sparked off when one happened to meet a long lost comrade by chance on the street. Jack Horner met his former platoon sergeant in Leicester whilst on his way to a job interview, and they arranged to go for a drink later:

I did so at a pub on Archdeacon Lane, long since demolished, on a Sunday morning. He was a very proud man when he told his friends, 'this is Jack Horner – one of my lads, who was with me all the while, in the trenches or out, for many long months, in fair weather or foul, till we went into the attack on the Somme'

[I said] 'You know, Sarge, you were a bit of a bugger at times, weren't you ?'. He said, 'Yes, but I had to be, with a mob like you lot, otherwise I couldn't have got any discipline out of you.' He told me that Woody had his leg smashed, and that it was amputated later …After a lot more talk and another beer, we shook hands and said 'So long', and I never saw him again, although I did meet many more officers and men who, like me, were thrown onto the scrap heap by a grateful Government.[9]

During the Second World War, the reunions ceased out of necessity as the

Leicestershire Regiment veterans in 1955, including 'Charlie' Meekings, ex-7th Battalion.
Mrs R.M.Snart

nation found itself once again in a titanic life-or-death struggle. Indeed, many former members of the Leicestershire Brigade quickly rejoined the armed forces in order to offer their services wherever they were needed. Most, like Dick Read, served in the Home Guard. Arthur Cave however had joined the Regular Army. He had served in India with the 1st Battalion Leicestershire Regiment, reaching the rank of Lieutenant and Quartermaster. In 1938 he was posted to the 2nd Battalion in Palestine as Quartermaster, and served with them and saw active service again in the Western Desert between 1940 and 1942, before returning home to serve as Depot QM at Glen Parva. After the Second World War he retired from the army, and for a spell he was Editor of The Green Tiger, journal of the Royal Tigers Association. He died in November 1961.

In the brave new world of the 1950s the First World War was largely forgotten. The Second World War veterans had their stories to tell, and it was these that were made into Hollywood movies and Pinewood classics, not the tales of the Great War soldiers. There were no more grand reunions of First World War veterans at De Montfort Hall, as there had been in the 1930s. This was partly because the more senior members of the old Brigade, the colonels and majors, and the old soldiers who had also been in the Boer War, had either passed away or were of advanced years. However, the 50th anniversary of the end of the First World War in 1968 brought renewed interest in the subject, and many of the remaining veterans got together for probably the last time.

Whatever hardships post-armistice life threw at them, and when in the 1950s and 60s, British society largely forgot about them, the surviving members of the 110th Brigade carried with them indelible memories. Many of these had been seared into place by the ferocity, sheer terror or even exhilaration of battle. Who of the men who had lived through it could forget that hot, dry summer's day in 1916 which lasted over fourteen hours, the shells which rent the air, the crashing trees, the smell of cordite mixed with tree sap, the dust and smoke which streaked and blackened the face? There were other memories too: the wilderness of mud at Polygon Wood; the peaceful times; the Candle factory at Arras; the friendships forged on carrying parties, whilst sharing a billet in a barn, or sharing a meal; the faces of those friends who did not reappear again after a particular attack. These were the memories that made the ex-members still feel part of their old battalions, something that could never leave them, for the rest of their lives. Dick Read articulated his memories of that powerful comradeship within his own circle of pals, when he wrote the draft of his book *Of Those We Loved* in 1967. They must have been the same feelings felt by many another Leicestershire Brigade survivor, when they reflected upon the comrades that they had left behind on the battlefields of France:

> *After all these years, how can I put on paper the jovial features of the over six-foot, fourteen-and a half stone Horace Phillips, 'Phillipe Auguste', as he sits there by the stove, replenishing his pipe with Bruno from an india rubber pouch. The frail chair looks though it can scarce*

Arthur Cave as Lieutenant and Quartermaster of the 1st Battalion Leicestershire Regiment in 1930.
Col Terry Cave

Dick Read, photographed in the 1960s.
Chester Read

278

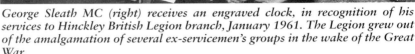

George Sleath MC (right) receives an engraved clock, in recognition of his services to Hinckley British Legion branch, January 1961. The Legion grew out of the amalgamation of several ex-servicemen's groups in the wake of the Great War.

The reverse of the 1914/15 star earned by 20632 Pte Thomas Crawfoot, of Thurmaston, Leicester. It was sent to his next of kin, as Crawfoot himself was killed at Bazentin with the 7th Battalion. Today, no one of this surname lives in Leicestershire, and it seems likely that Crawfoot was the last of his line.

support his weight, and creaks every time he laughs, which is often. See his huge red hands as he presses the tobacco home; yet they are capable hands, for he had been a market gardener in happier days... He sings often, in a clear if not strong, tenor voice. Snatches of a ballad, very sweet and somehow haunting, so that at odd moments we find ourselves humming the same tune and repeating what we could remember of the words, a song of a minstrel – a great lady, and a knight who wooed her...Laughingly Phillips begs a match; as he turns in the chair, it creaks again. See his great knees and countryman's legs. His size eleven service boots at an angle of more like ninety than forty-five degrees; his blue eyes as he looks at the now drawing pipe bowl, the glint of the flickering matchlight on his fair curly hair. Horace Philips...Phillippe Auguste...Yeoman of Uppingham, England.

Then there was Ted Lineker – 'Lin', we called him – training as a lithographic artist with a nationally known firm of colour printers in Leicester when he enlisted. Standing just on six foot in his socks and well proportioned, he was in no danger of being rejected for bad teeth either; his seemed about perfect, and when he laughed he was good to see. His eyes were grey, his brows finely arched and pencilled, almost like a woman's; his nose, and particularly his upper lip, had what I believe novelists describe as a 'chiselled' appearance, but he had cultivated of recent weeks a fair, clipped military moustache which made him look somewhat older than twenty. He smoked a Dunhill pipe which his mother had sent him and John Cotton tobacco. He carried her photograph in his wallet, and very little else. She looked to us extraordinarily youthful and we thought, at the time, beautiful.

1982 – George Holt DCM, the oldest exhibitor at the Packington Horticultural Show (left) shows his prize winning shallots to the president of the show committee.
Mr Ken Holt

Of a very different type was our third comrade. Try to picture Freddy Smith as he sits in the chimney corner, turning away at the coffee mill in his lap. A shorter, stockily built lad with swarthy features, crisp black hair inclined to curl and an equally black 'Charlie Chaplin' on his upper lip. He needed to shave twice daily to look presentable in the evening. His father had the grocery business in the North Leicestershire shoemaking and sock-knitting village of Shepshed. In 1914 he was following in his father's footsteps in the shop, and the training had alerted and sharpened his senses in many ways. Now watch him. As Phillips asks for a match, see him instantly pickup a spent one and place it in the outstretched hand; listen to his merry laugh at the latter's disgust – the green eyes twinkling under bushy black brows – the white teeth...such was Private Smith, F., the perfect campaigner – our champion scrounger. If we wanted anything, 'leave it to Freddy' we would say, and in due course he would turn up with the twinkle bespeaking success.

Of such stuff then were my comrades of the autumn, winter and spring of 1915-16; companions alike in moments of danger and of pleasant relaxation... [10]

Charles Monk in 1986.
Oadby & Wigston News

It was this sense of comradeship which motivated Read, each year on the anniversary of 14 July 1916, to place in the classified pages of the Leicester Mercury a small notice, 'in memory of those we loved', until his death in 1971. The last members of the 110th Brigade hung on until the 1980s and 1990s. Jack Horner died in 1989. Charles Monk reached the age of 100, in 1995. He was a lifelong Labour Party member and for many years was active in local politics. Perhaps the very last survivor was Bill Wilson, like Monk formerly of the 7th Battalion. He had been one of the first to enlist at the Magazine in 1914 and indeed one of the youngest, having lied about his age. He died in 1998, aged 102.

Jack Horner in the mid-1980s.

1 D.A.Bacon. Unpublished typescript memoir, LRO p142
2 Charles J.Monk. Interview with author 1989.
3 Charles J.Monk. Interview with author 1989.
4 Bacon, *op cit* p144
5 Bacon, *op cit* p143
6 J.W.Horner. Unpublished typescript memoir, author's collection.
7 Horner, *op cit*
8 D.V.Kelly, 'The Ruling Few' (Hollis & Carter, 1952) p109
9 Horner, *op cit*
10 I.L.Read, 'Of Those We Loved' (Pentland Press, 1994) pp58-59

The last survivor of the 110th Brigade? An original member, ex-Pte Bill Wilson, 7th Battalion, died in 1998 aged 102. Leicester Mercury

Bibliography and Sources

Undoubtedly the finest personal memoir published in recent years in connection with the Leicestershire Brigade is I.L. Read's *Of Those We Loved* (Pentland Press, 1994). Read served with the 8th Battalion as a Sergeant, before being commissioned into the Royal Sussex Regiment in 1917. His account strikes the reader with gripping immediacy, and his ability to draw his audience into the events as they unfold, together with his extraordinary eye for detail, make him a master of the chronicler's art. An added bonus are Read's sketches and watercolours, which even though reproduced in monochrome help enormously when one tries to visualise the events which he describes.

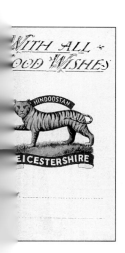

Prior to this, one has to go back as far as the 1930s to find any other published first hand sources. David Kelly's *39 Months With The Tigers* was published by Ernest Benn Ltd in 1930. Kelly paints with a broader brush, covering the period from 1915 to 1918 in only 160 pages, but his ability to recount an anecdote, particularly an amusing one, is significant. A slightly altered version of his account forms part of his autobiography, *The Ruling Few*, published by Hollis & Carter in 1952.

R.H. Kiernan's autobiographical novel, *Little Brother Goes Soldiering* follows the events of the author's life in France with the 8th Battalion in France so closely that it may be considered a primary source. Kiernan calls the Leicesters the 'Huntshires', but this is apparently the only change the author has made. The account ends at the same point as the author was wounded, in September 1918. It was published by Constable & Co Ltd, also in 1930.

Leicester 1914-18, published by Edgar Backus in 1933, will prove a disappointment to the reader hoping for extensive coverage of the local Service battalions, which receive only around half a page's worth of coverage. Although there are a number of photographs in the book, none relates directly to any of the Leicestershire service battalions, and the coverage of the text is focused rather too heavily on the doings and various resolutions of the city council. More rewarding is the much more recent *Leicestershire at War* by Robin Jenkins, of Leicestershire Record Office. Largely a photo-history, this book covers most battalions and has some fine photographs of the 6th, 7th, 8th, and 9th battalions. It was published by Sutton Publishing Limited in 1998. More recently still, Nigel Cave's (grandson of Arthur Cave) book *Polygon Wood* (1999) in the Battleground Europe series examines in detail the part played by the 110th Brigade in this part of the Ypres Salient in 1917. His forthcoming work in the same series

'Bazentin' (due to be published in 2000) also promises to feature the Leicestershire Brigade to a high degree.

Of the unpublished sources, the two most complete personal accounts are those by D.A.Bacon (9th battalion) and Jack Horner (8th battalion & 6th battalion). Bacon's two hundred plus pages of closely typed narrative are held at the Leicestershire Record Office in Wigston. Like Read, Bacon has an eye for detail. Although his account is entitled *The History of the 110th Brigade* it is in fact for the most part chiefly concerned with the doings of Bacon's own battalion. The author mentions many individuals by name, especially officers, and this memoir which Bacon had probably hoped one day to publish makes for interesting reading. Copies of Horner's account, entitled *Diary of a Trench Rat* may be found in the Imperial War Museum Department of Documents, the Leicestershire Record Office, and the Liddle Collection, University of Leeds. Horner lacks the precision of some of his fellow chroniclers, particularly where dates are concerned, but his typescript has an 'authentic' feel, and the author describes his experiences with colour and flair. The Leicestershire Record Office also holds the account by Lieutenant E.G. Lane-Roberts of the 6th Battalion entitled 'How I was Captured' although this as the title suggests does not cover the whole of Lane-Roberts' war service, which is a great pity. It was however written in captivity, only a few months after the incidents in question occurred and so Lane-Roberts' ability to recall events in detail is correspondingly high. The diary of Quartermaster-Sergeant Arthur Cave is held privately, by his family, to whom any application to view it should be made. Whilst there is no doubt that Cave compiled the diary during the Great War, occasional comments about events which occurred later on suggest that he may have revised or added to it whilst writing it up. It is none the less an excellent firsthand account by an eye-witness to the doings of the 7th Battalion.

Other fragmentary sources, such as individual letters, are held by all three of the institutions mentioned above. Other personal accounts are held in the Liddle Collection, University of Leeds. These are all retrospective, and were in the main written in the 1970s. None is of great length, but include the work of ex-Privates Pothecary, A.D. Carpenter, and R.W .Taylor. The back copies of newspapers such as the *Leicester Daily Mercury* and *Leicester Evening Mail* are held by the Leicestershire Record Office, as are the War Diaries of the four battalions in question with copies at the Public Record Office, Kew. The newspapers make for particularly interesting reading and shed much light on social attitudes and values at the time of the First World War. They may also be searched for the obituaries of soldiers who had been killed, often with a high chance of success. At Kew, the medal rolls for the Great War and the newly released service records may also be consulted, helping to flesh out much of the detail concerning a particular individual's army career.

From One of the
LEICESTERSHIRE REGIMEN

Appendix I

A Short History of the 10th Battalion Leicestershire Regiment

Whilst it was never part of the 110th Brigade, it would not be fitting to conclude this study without acknowledging the role of the 10th (Reserve) Battalion Leicestershire Regiment. Formed as a service battalion of the fourth New Army in October 1914, it was raised at Portsmouth, where the 3rd (Reserve) Battalion was stationed, and it seems likely that the first recruits for the 10th were administered by the 3rd Battalion until the proper infrastructure was in place. The 10th Battalion remained at Portsmouth with the 3rd Battalion as part of the port garrison, in case of an attempted German invasion. It was part of the 96th Brigade of the original 32nd Division, until the reorganisations of 1915 which created the 110th Brigade. This reorganisation brought together the four service battalions which had been raised first, into a single brigade, with the 10th left over, and the natural choice was to re-designate it as a reserve battalion to train and supply reinforcements for the other four.

So it was that it became a Second Reserve battalion (the First Reserve of course being the 3rd Battalion, which in the main supplied the 1st and 2nd battalions with reinforcements). In June 1915, with the threat of German invasion receding, it moved to Barnard Castle in the north-east of England, to continue to train recruits. The first drafts from the 10th Battalion joined the Leicestershire Brigade in France not long after it had arrived there, in July 1915.

Pte A. G. F. Meekings, a bandsman with the 10th Battalion in 1915.
Mrs R.M.Snart

In November of 1915 it moved again, to the collection of reinforcement and training camps at Rugeley, on Cannock Chase in Staffordshire. There on 1 September 1916 it lost its connection with the Leicestershire Regiment, being re-designated once again, this time as the anonymous 5th Training Reserve battalion. Many of the men who had served first with the 10th Battalion could be subsequently identified by the prefix '10' before their service number.

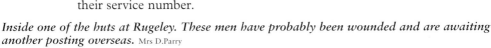

Inside one of the huts at Rugeley. These men have probably been wounded and are awaiting another posting overseas. Mrs D.Parry

Appendix II

A Nominal Roll of Officers known or believed to have served with the 6th 7th 8th or 9th Battalions, Leicester Regiment, together with additional information is available *(see below)*.

Appendix III

A Nominal Roll of Warrant Officers, NCOs and men of the 110th Brigade is also available *(see below)*.

The above two appendices are available either in hard copy or via e-mail. To order via e-mail contact: charles@pen-and-sword.demon.co.uk with your credit card details.

If you require hard-copy telephone 01226 734555 or write to Pen & Sword Books Ltd, 47 Church Street, Barnsley, South Yorkshire, S70 2AS enclosing a cheque for £10.00.

The author would be interested to receive any information regarding Leicestershire Regiment soldiers, and can be contacted via the publishers.

Selective Index

287